GENERATION ZERO

HEROSCAPE

FRED VAN LENTE | DIEGO BERNARD | JUAN CASTRO | ANDREW DALHOUSE

CONTENTS

Collection Cover Art: Juan José Ryp
with Ulises Arreola

Editor: Lauren Hitzhusen
Editor-in-Chief: Warren Simons

VALIANT.

Peter Cuneo
Chairman

Dinesh Shamdasani
CEO & Chief Creative Officer

Gavin Cuneo
Chief Operating Officer & CFO

Fred Pierce
Publisher

Warren Simons
Editor-in-Chief

Walter Black
VP Operations

Hunter Gorinson
VP Marketing & Communications

Atom! Freeman
Director of Sales

Andy Liegl
Alex Rae
Sales Managers

Annie Rosa
Sales Coordinator

Josh Johns
Director of Digital Media and Development

Travis Escarfullery
Jeff Walker
Production & Design Managers

Robert Meyers
Managing Editor

Peter Stern
Publishing & Operations Manager

Andrew Steinbeiser
Marketing & Communications Manager

Danny Khazem
Charlotte Greenbaum
Associate Editors

Benjamin Peterson
David Menchel
Editorial Assistants

Shanyce Lora
Digital Media Coordinator

Ivan Cohen
Collection Editor

Steve Blackwell
Collection Designer

Rian Hughes/Device
Original Trade Dress & Book Design

Russell Brown
President, Consumer Products,
Promotions and Ad Sales

Caritza Berlioz
Licensing Coodinator

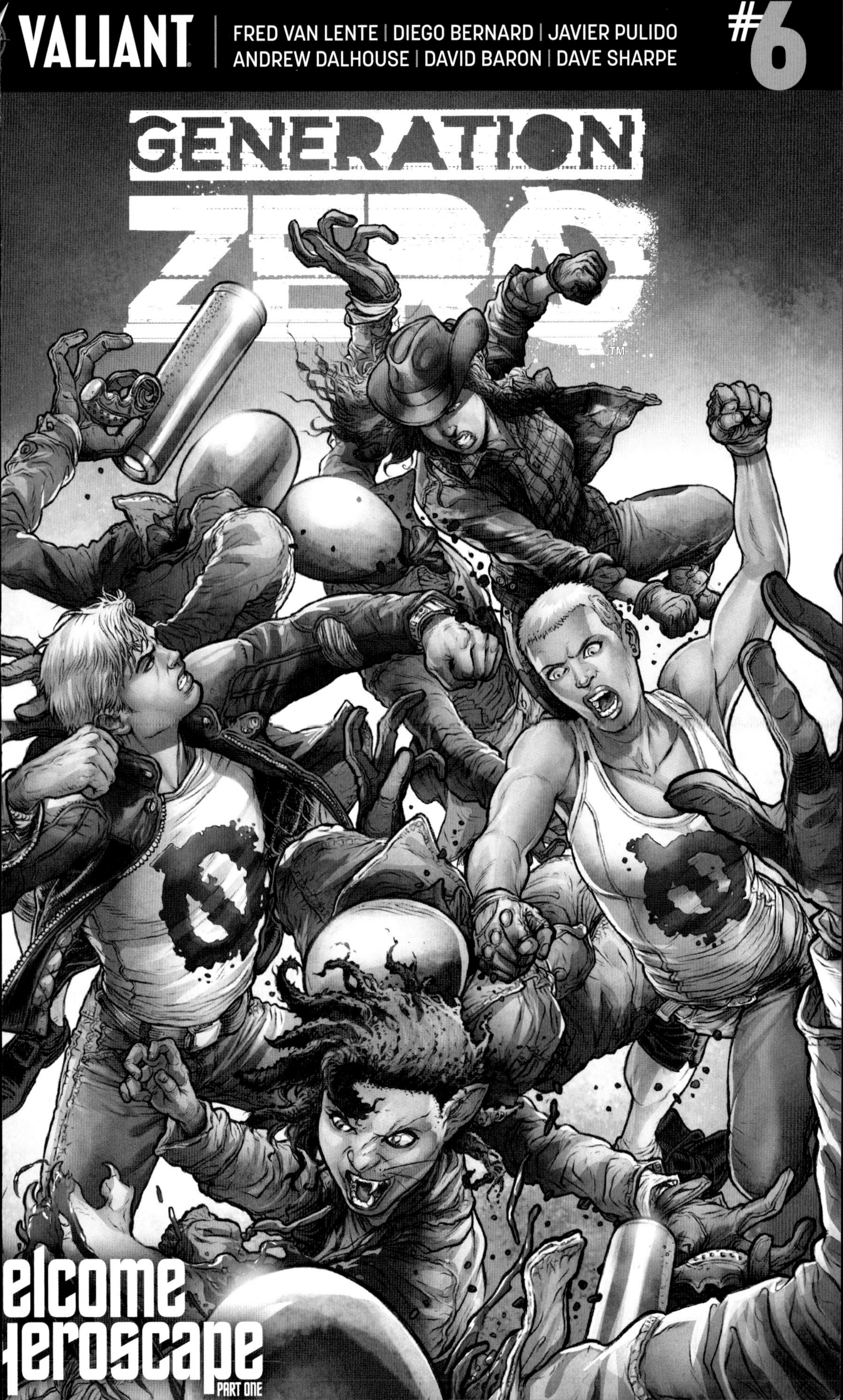
VALIANT
FRED VAN LENTE | DIEGO BERNARD | JAVIER PULIDO
ANDREW DALHOUSE | DAVID BARON | DAVE SHARPE
#6
GENERATION
ZERO
TM
elcome
eroscape
PART ONE

VALIANT

They are psiots - people born with the potential for incredible abilities of the mind. They were captured and trained by sinister corporate forces to become killing machines. They became one of the most lethal strike forces on the planet. They br free of their captors and, inspired by the heroism of their fellow psiots, struck out o their own to make the world a better place. They will help you - if your cause is just They are....

GENERATION ZERO™

The story so far...

Keisha Thomas, a high school student in Rook, Michigan -- a bankrupt midwest city that was saved by innovative technology and corporate interests -- called or Generation Zero to help her investigate the suspicious circumstances surroundin death of her boyfriend, Stephen. But she finds that there are even more mysterie Rook than she could've ever imagined.

Gen Zero and Keisha race to Rook High, where they discover that Momoo -- everyone's favorite drink -- is actually a mind-control beverage, designed to subdue the teens of Rook. Worse than that, the team runs into Keisha's dad, the sheriff, on the war path and armed to the teeth!

Keisha and Gen Zero fight against Rook's heavily armed sheriff's department barely escaping into the night. Meanwhile, in the distance, the mysterious Firewatch Tower has suddenly transformed into a frightening, floating building...

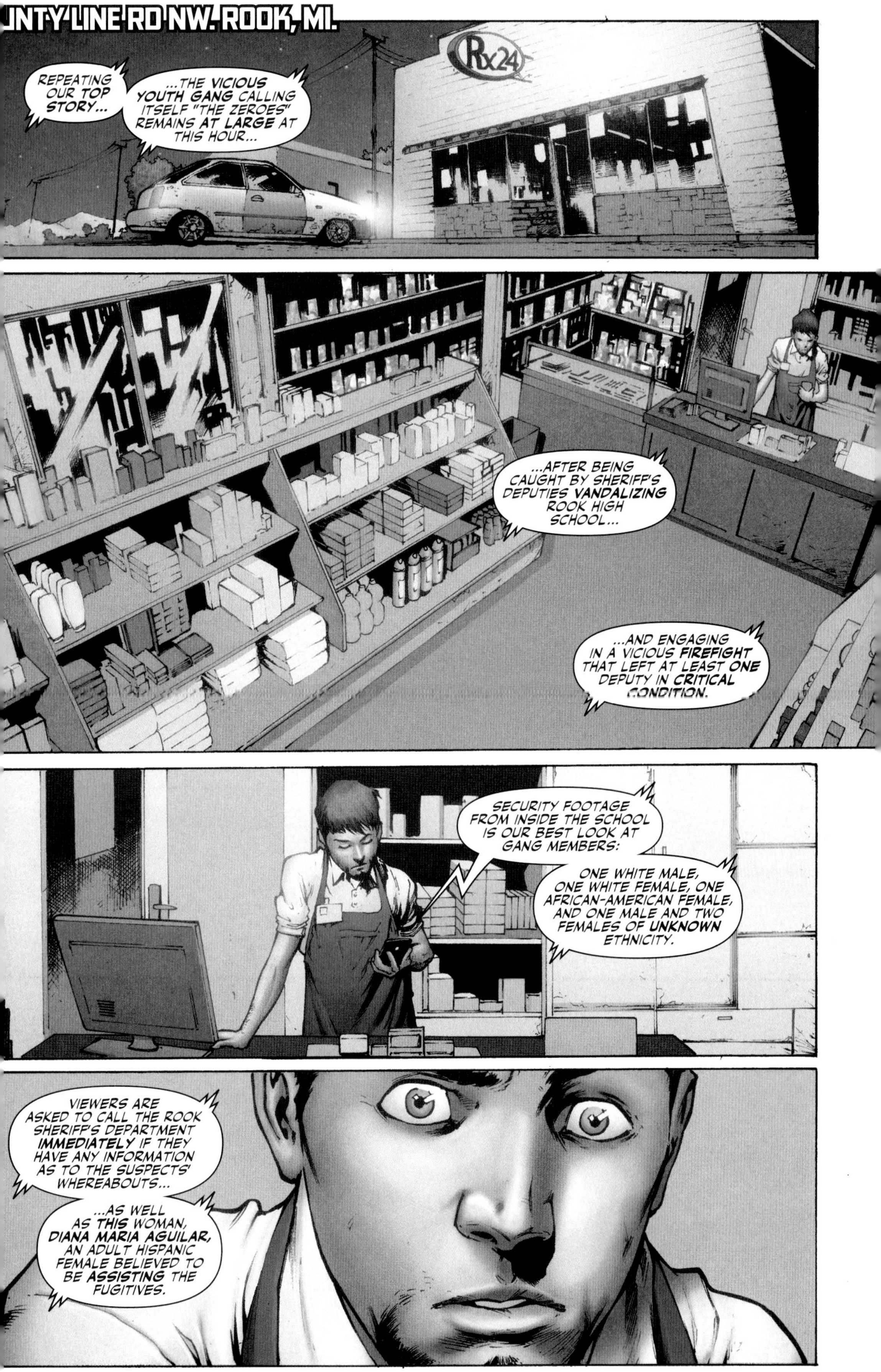
UNTY LINE RD NW. ROOK, MI.
RX24
REPEATING OUR TOP STORY...
...THE VICIOUS YOUTH GANG CALLING ITSELF "THE ZEROES" REMAINS AT LARGE AT THIS HOUR...
...AFTER BEING CAUGHT BY SHERIFF'S DEPUTIES VANDALIZING ROOK HIGH SCHOOL...
...AND ENGAGING IN A VICIOUS FIREFIGHT THAT LEFT AT LEAST ONE DEPUTY IN CRITICAL CONDITION.
SECURITY FOOTAGE FROM INSIDE THE SCHOOL IS OUR BEST LOOK AT GANG MEMBERS:
ONE WHITE MALE, ONE WHITE FEMALE, ONE AFRICAN-AMERICAN FEMALE, AND ONE MALE AND TWO FEMALES OF UNKNOWN ETHNICITY.
VIEWERS ARE ASKED TO CALL THE ROOK SHERIFF'S DEPARTMENT IMMEDIATELY IF THEY HAVE ANY INFORMATION AS TO THE SUSPECTS' WHEREABOUTS...
...AS WELL AS THIS WOMAN, DIANA MARIA AGUILAR, AN ADULT HISPANIC FEMALE BELIEVED TO BE ASSISTING THE FUGITIVES.

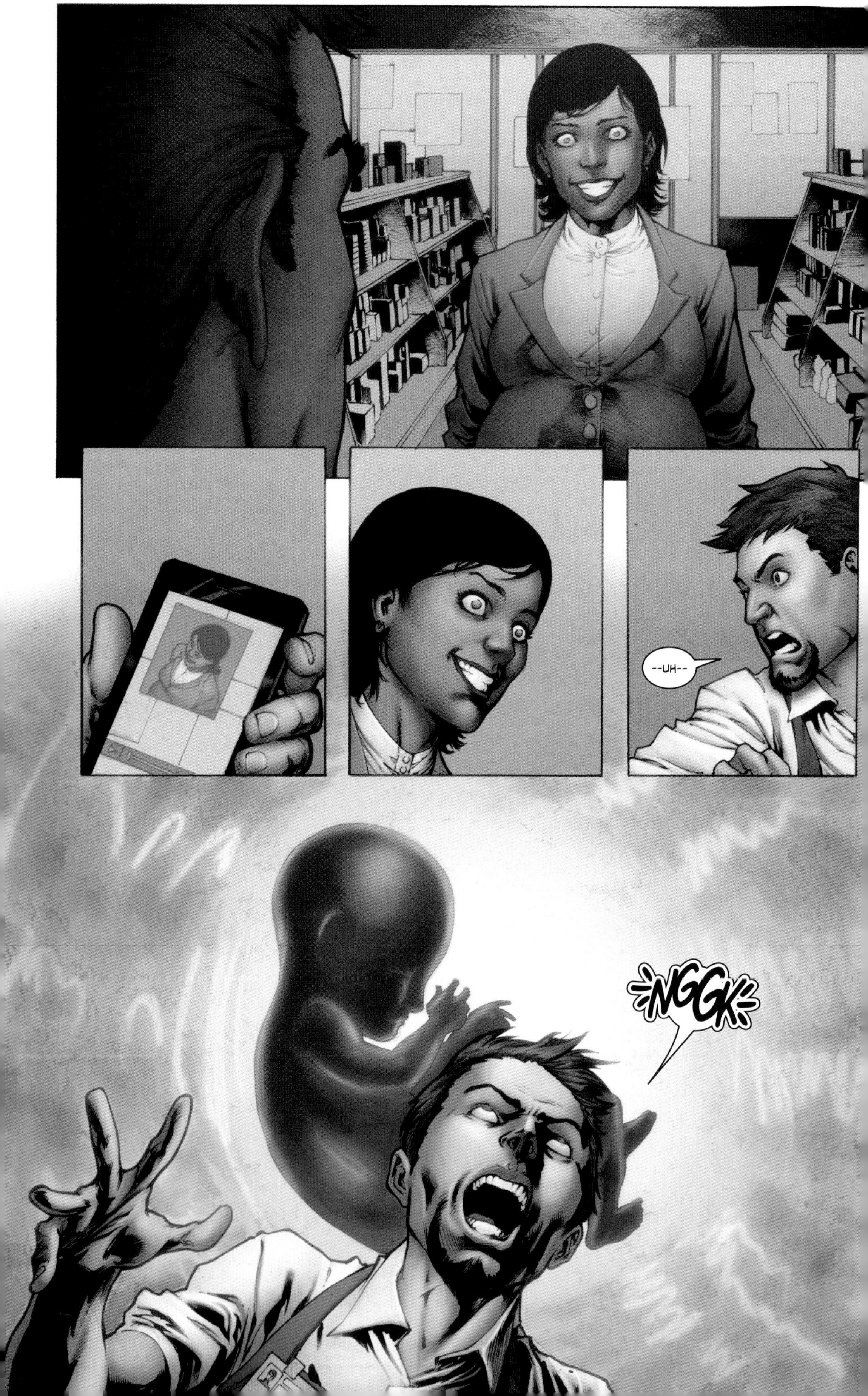
--UH--
NGGK

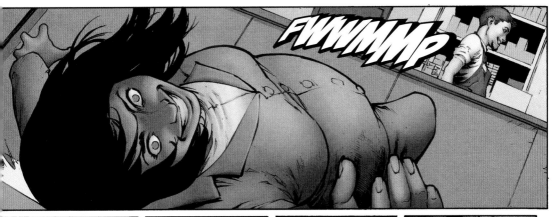

CITY MANAGER **JASON POOLE** HAS SCHEDULED A TWO-THIRTY A.M. PRESS CONFERENCE TO ADDRESS PUBLIC CONCERNS--

--BUT HE ASKS THAT EVERYONE LIVING INSIDE ROOK COUNTY REMAIN **INDOORS** AND DO NOT VENTURE INTO THE DOWN-TOWN AREA.

ALL ROOK DISTRICT SCHOOLS WILL REMAIN CLOSED INDEFINITELY AS THE CITY GOES INTO **FULL LOCKDOWN**...

YOU GOT IT ALL, GAMETE?

CLARO, KEISHA SHERMAN.

VAMANOS.

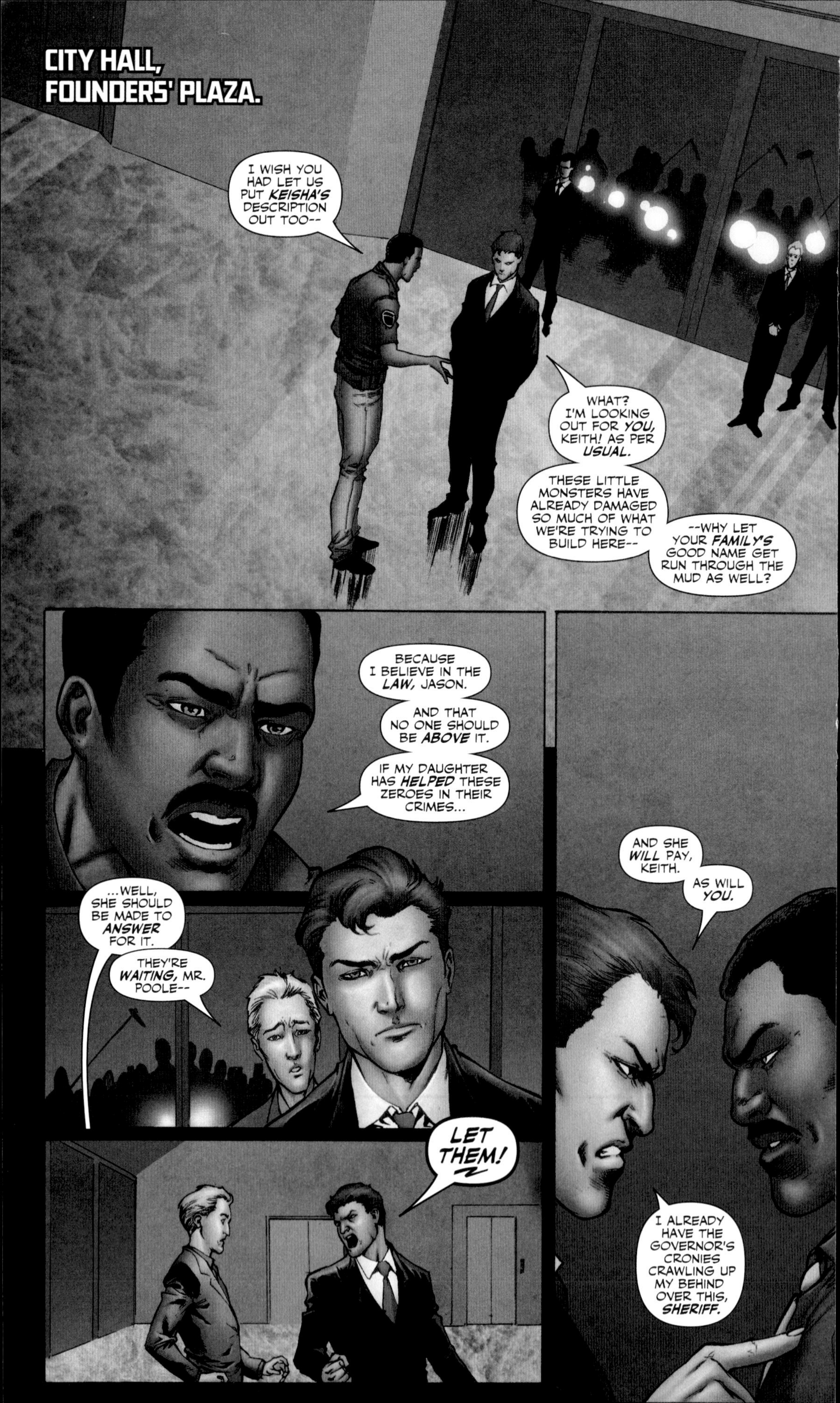
CITY HALL, FOUNDERS' PLAZA.
I WISH YOU HAD LET US PUT KEISHA'S DESCRIPTION OUT TOO--
WHAT? I'M LOOKING OUT FOR YOU, KEITH! AS PER USUAL.
THESE LITTLE MONSTERS HAVE ALREADY DAMAGED SO MUCH OF WHAT WE'RE TRYING TO BUILD HERE--
--WHY LET YOUR FAMILY'S GOOD NAME GET RUN THROUGH THE MUD AS WELL?
BECAUSE I BELIEVE IN THE LAW, JASON.
AND THAT NO ONE SHOULD BE ABOVE IT.
IF MY DAUGHTER HAS HELPED THESE ZEROES IN THEIR CRIMES...
...WELL, SHE SHOULD BE MADE TO ANSWER FOR IT.
THEY'RE WAITING, MR. POOLE--
LET THEM!
AND SHE WILL PAY, KEITH.
AS WILL YOU.
I ALREADY HAVE THE GOVERNOR'S CRONIES CRAWLING UP MY BEHIND OVER THIS, SHERIFF.

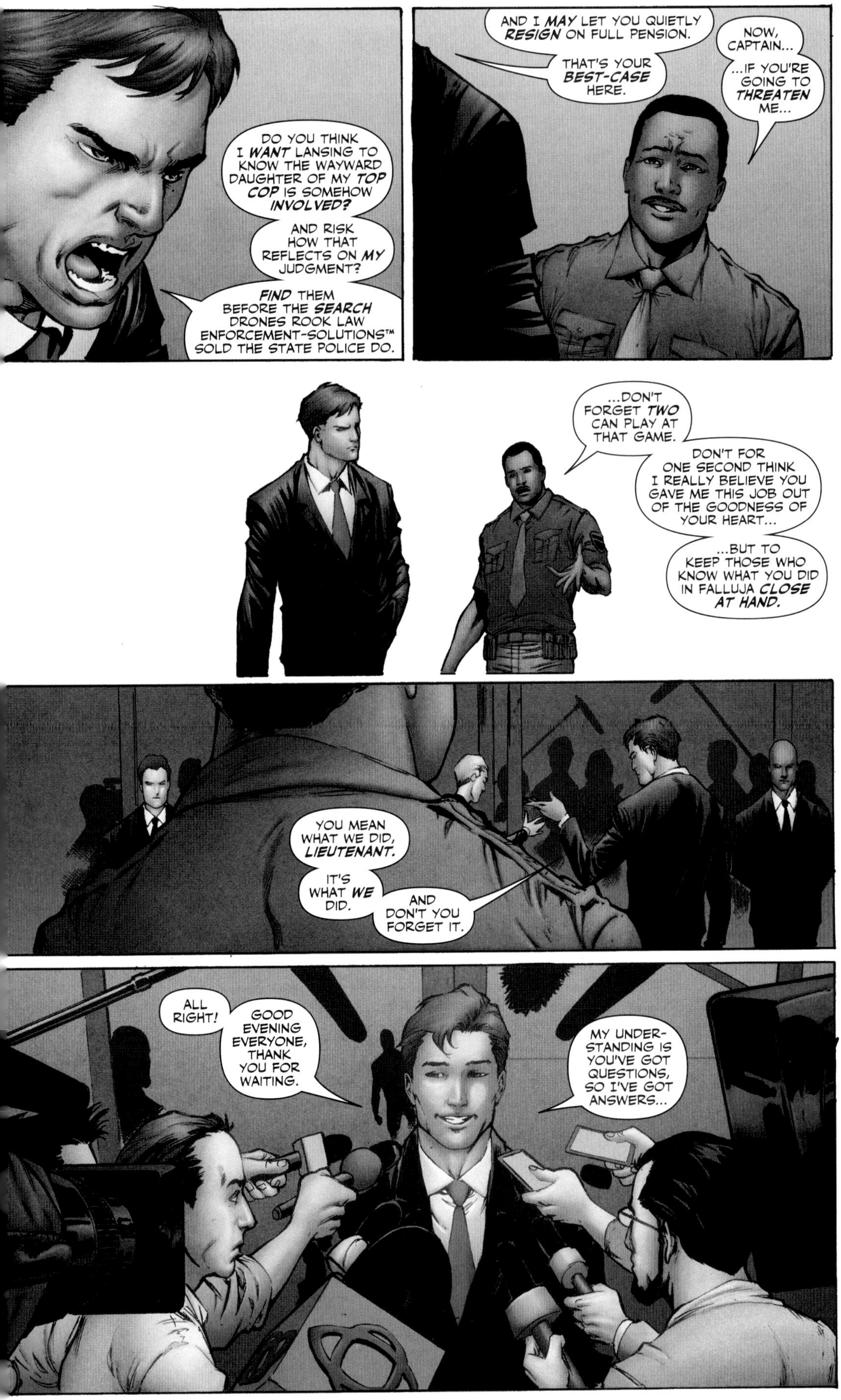
DO YOU THINK I *WANT* LANSING TO KNOW THE WAYWARD DAUGHTER OF MY *TOP COP* IS SOMEHOW *INVOLVED?*
AND RISK HOW THAT REFLECTS ON *MY* JUDGMENT?
FIND THEM BEFORE THE *SEARCH* DRONES ROOK LAW ENFORCEMENT-SOLUTIONS™ SOLD THE STATE POLICE DO.
AND I *MAY* LET YOU QUIETLY *RESIGN* ON FULL PENSION.
THAT'S YOUR *BEST-CASE* HERE.
NOW, CAPTAIN...
...IF YOU'RE GOING TO *THREATEN* ME...
...DON'T FORGET *TWO* CAN PLAY AT THAT GAME.
DON'T FOR ONE SECOND THINK I REALLY BELIEVE YOU GAVE ME THIS JOB OUT OF THE GOODNESS OF YOUR HEART...
...BUT TO KEEP THOSE WHO KNOW WHAT YOU DID IN FALLUJA *CLOSE AT HAND.*
YOU MEAN WHAT WE DID, *LIEUTENANT.*
IT'S WHAT *WE* DID.
AND DON'T YOU FORGET IT.
ALL RIGHT!
GOOD EVENING EVERYONE, THANK YOU FOR WAITING.
MY UNDER-STANDING IS YOU'VE GOT QUESTIONS, SO I'VE GOT ANSWERS...

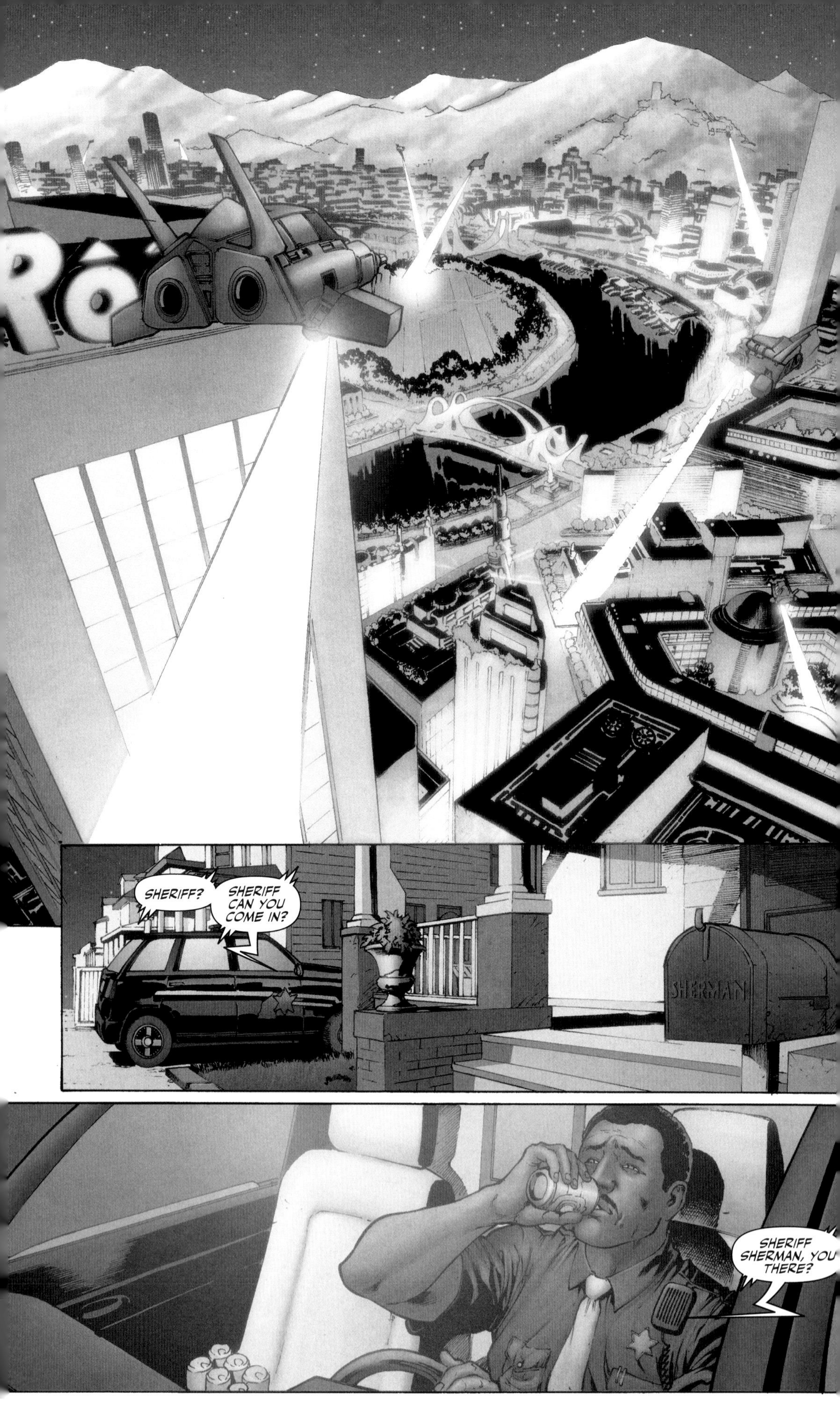
SHERIFF?
SHERIFF CAN YOU COME IN?
SHERMAN
SHERIFF SHERMAN, YOU THERE?

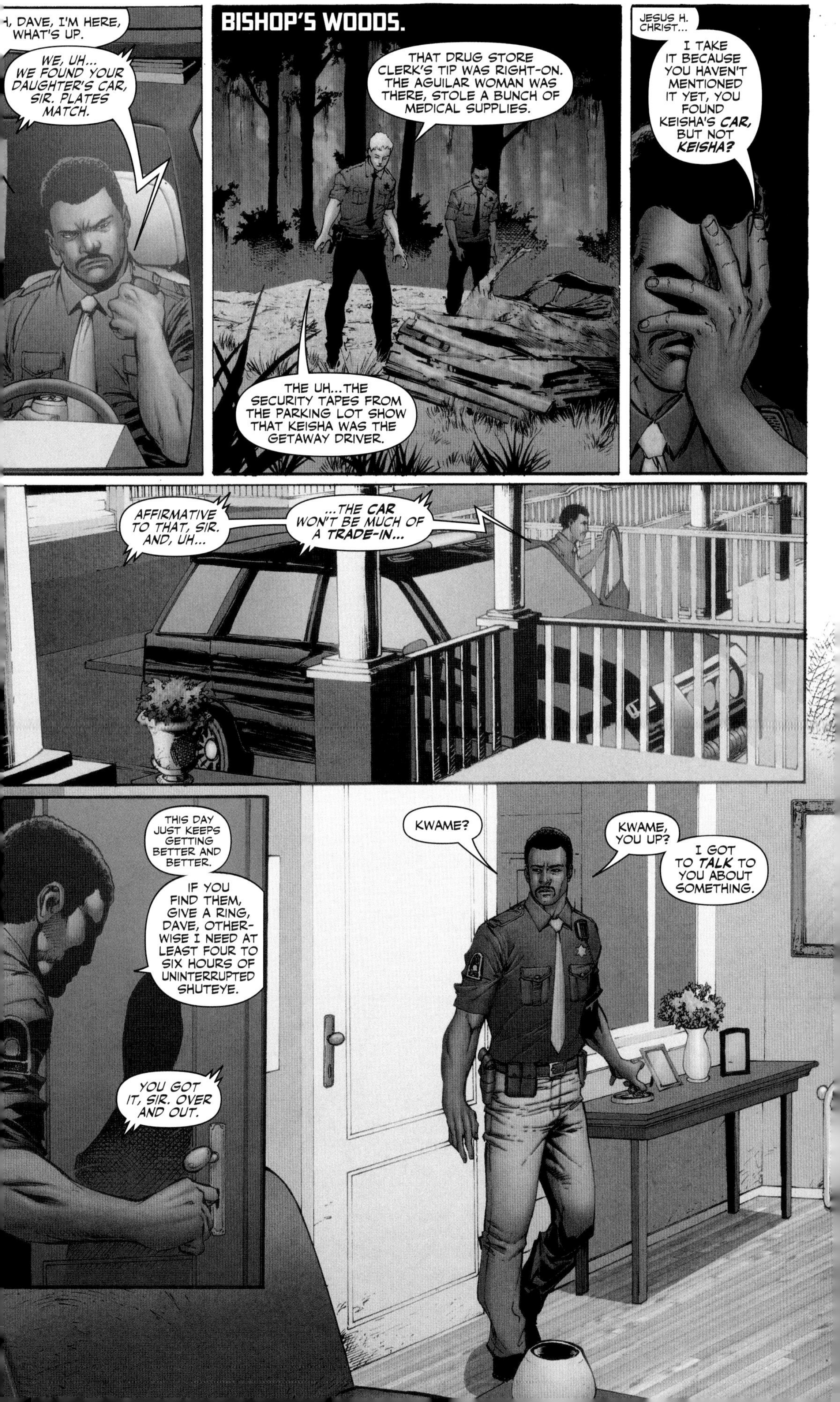

-I, DAVE, I'M HERE, WHAT'S UP.
WE, UH... WE FOUND YOUR DAUGHTER'S CAR, SIR. PLATES MATCH.
BISHOP'S WOODS.
THAT DRUG STORE CLERK'S TIP WAS RIGHT-ON. THE AGUILAR WOMAN WAS THERE, STOLE A BUNCH OF MEDICAL SUPPLIES.
THE UH...THE SECURITY TAPES FROM THE PARKING LOT SHOW THAT KEISHA WAS THE GETAWAY DRIVER.
JESUS H. CHRIST...
I TAKE IT BECAUSE YOU HAVEN'T MENTIONED IT YET, YOU FOUND KEISHA'S CAR, BUT NOT KEISHA?
AFFIRMATIVE TO THAT, SIR. AND, UH...
...THE CAR WON'T BE MUCH OF A TRADE-IN...
THIS DAY JUST KEEPS GETTING BETTER AND BETTER.
IF YOU FIND THEM, GIVE A RING, DAVE, OTHER-WISE I NEED AT LEAST FOUR TO SIX HOURS OF UNINTERRUPTED SHUTEYE.
YOU GOT IT, SIR. OVER AND OUT.
KWAME?
KWAME, YOU UP?
I GOT TO TALK TO YOU ABOUT SOMETHING.

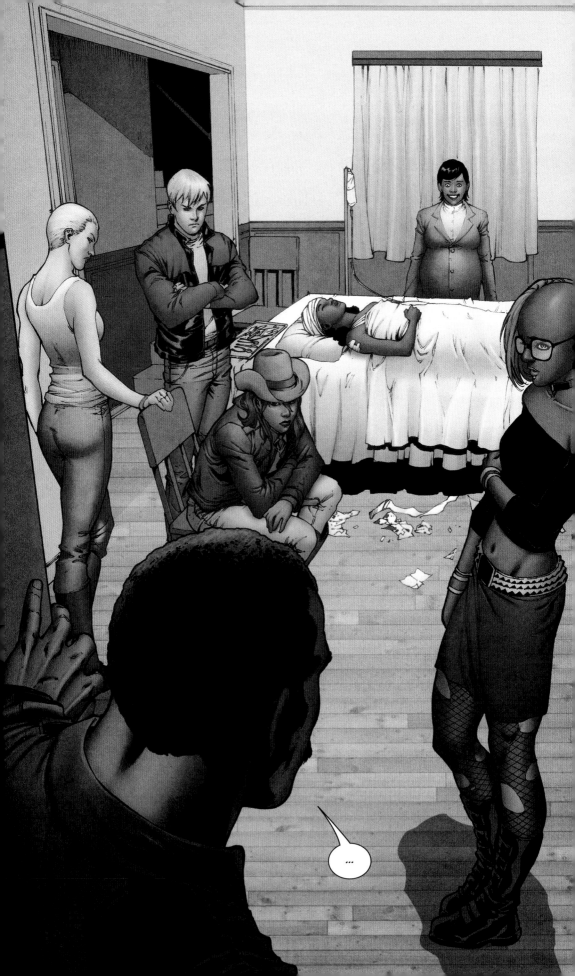

...

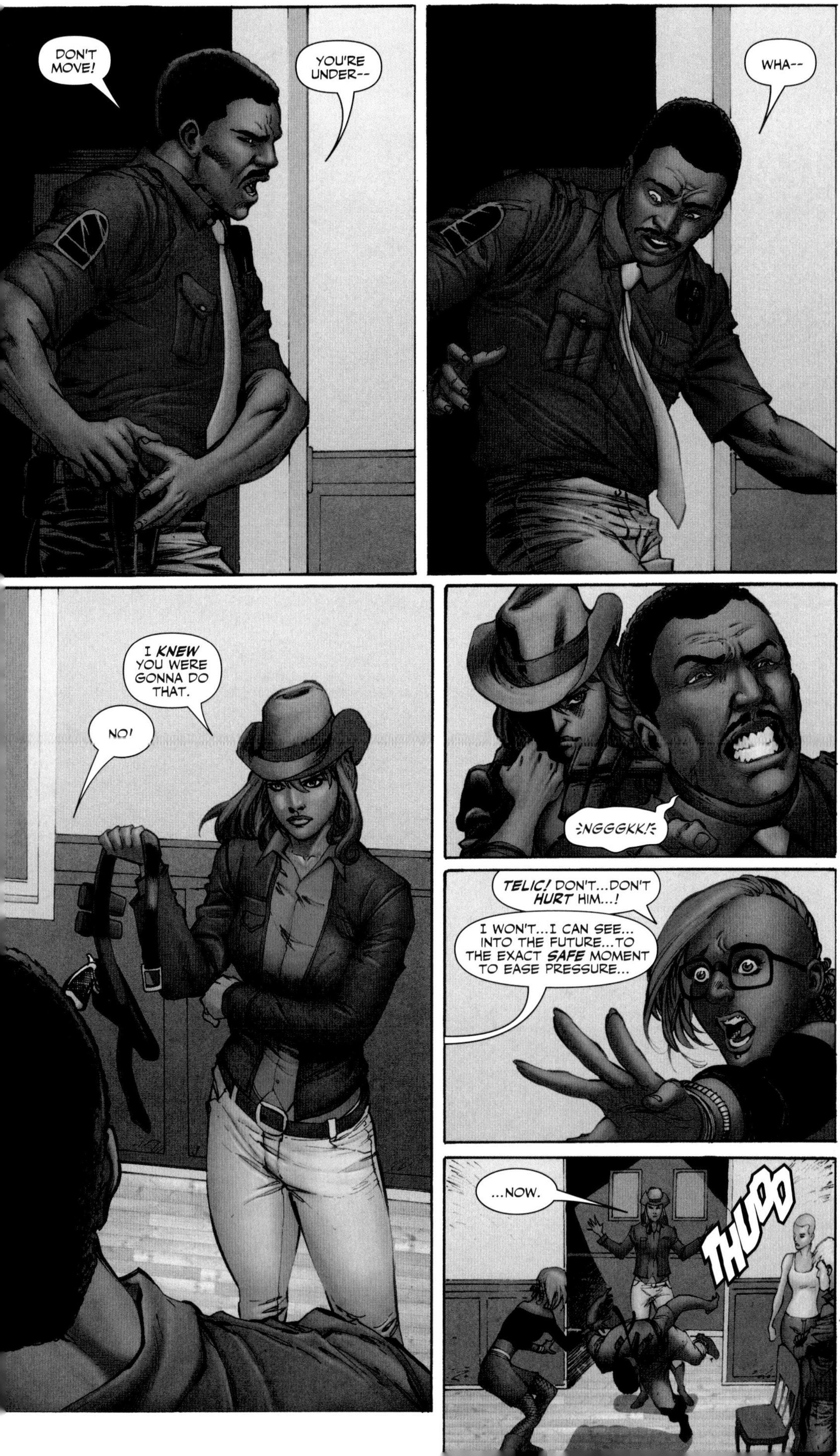
DON'T MOVE!
YOU'RE UNDER--
WHA--
I KNEW YOU WERE GONNA DO THAT.
NO!
NGGGKK!
TELIC! DON'T...DON'T HURT HIM...!
I WON'T...I CAN SEE... INTO THE FUTURE...TO THE EXACT SAFE MOMENT TO EASE PRESSURE...
...NOW.
THUDD

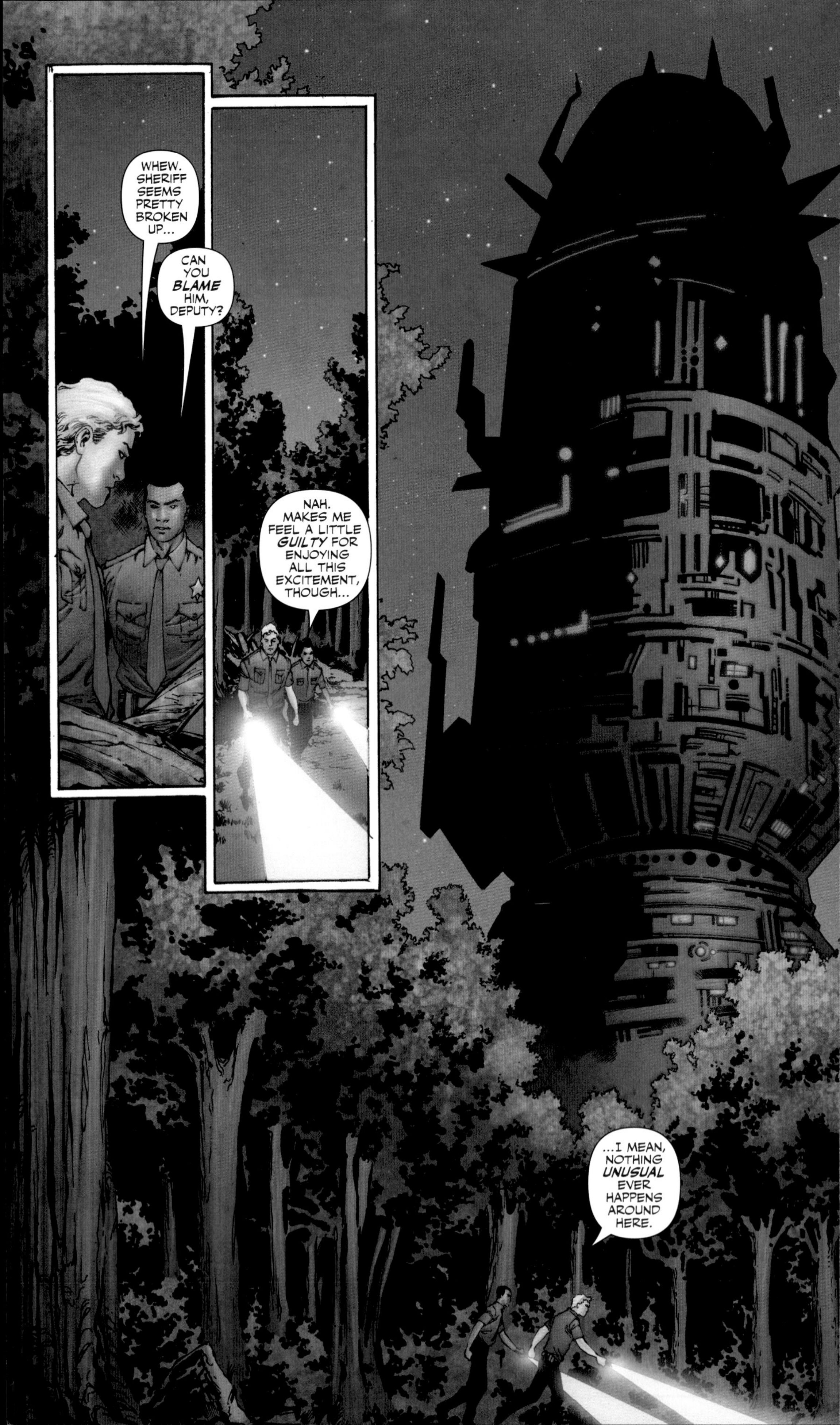
WHEW. SHERIFF SEEMS PRETTY BROKEN UP...
CAN YOU *BLAME* HIM, DEPUTY?
NAH. MAKES ME FEEL A LITTLE *GUILTY* FOR ENJOYING ALL THIS EXCITEMENT, THOUGH...
...I MEAN, NOTHING *UNUSUAL* EVER HAPPENS AROUND HERE.

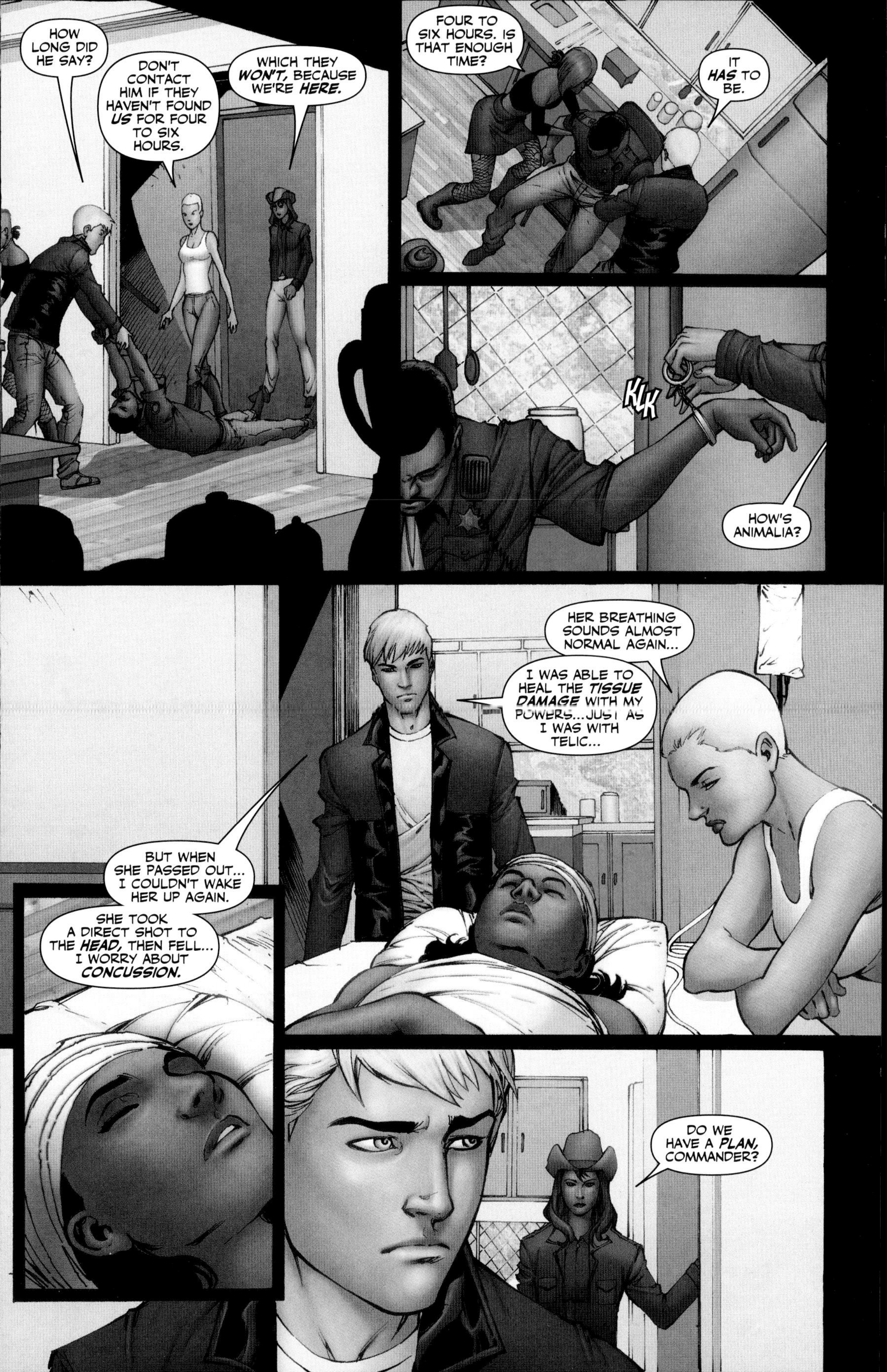
HOW LONG DID HE SAY?
DON'T CONTACT HIM IF THEY HAVEN'T FOUND *US* FOR FOUR TO SIX HOURS.
WHICH THEY *WON'T,* BECAUSE WE'RE *HERE.*
FOUR TO SIX HOURS. IS THAT ENOUGH TIME?
IT *HAS* TO BE.
KLK
HOW'S ANIMALIA?
HER BREATHING SOUNDS ALMOST NORMAL AGAIN...
I WAS ABLE TO HEAL THE *TISSUE DAMAGE* WITH MY POWERS...JUST AS I WAS WITH TELIC...
BUT WHEN SHE PASSED OUT... I COULDN'T WAKE HER UP AGAIN.
SHE TOOK A DIRECT SHOT TO THE *HEAD,* THEN FELL... I WORRY ABOUT *CONCUSSION.*
DO WE HAVE A *PLAN,* COMMANDER?

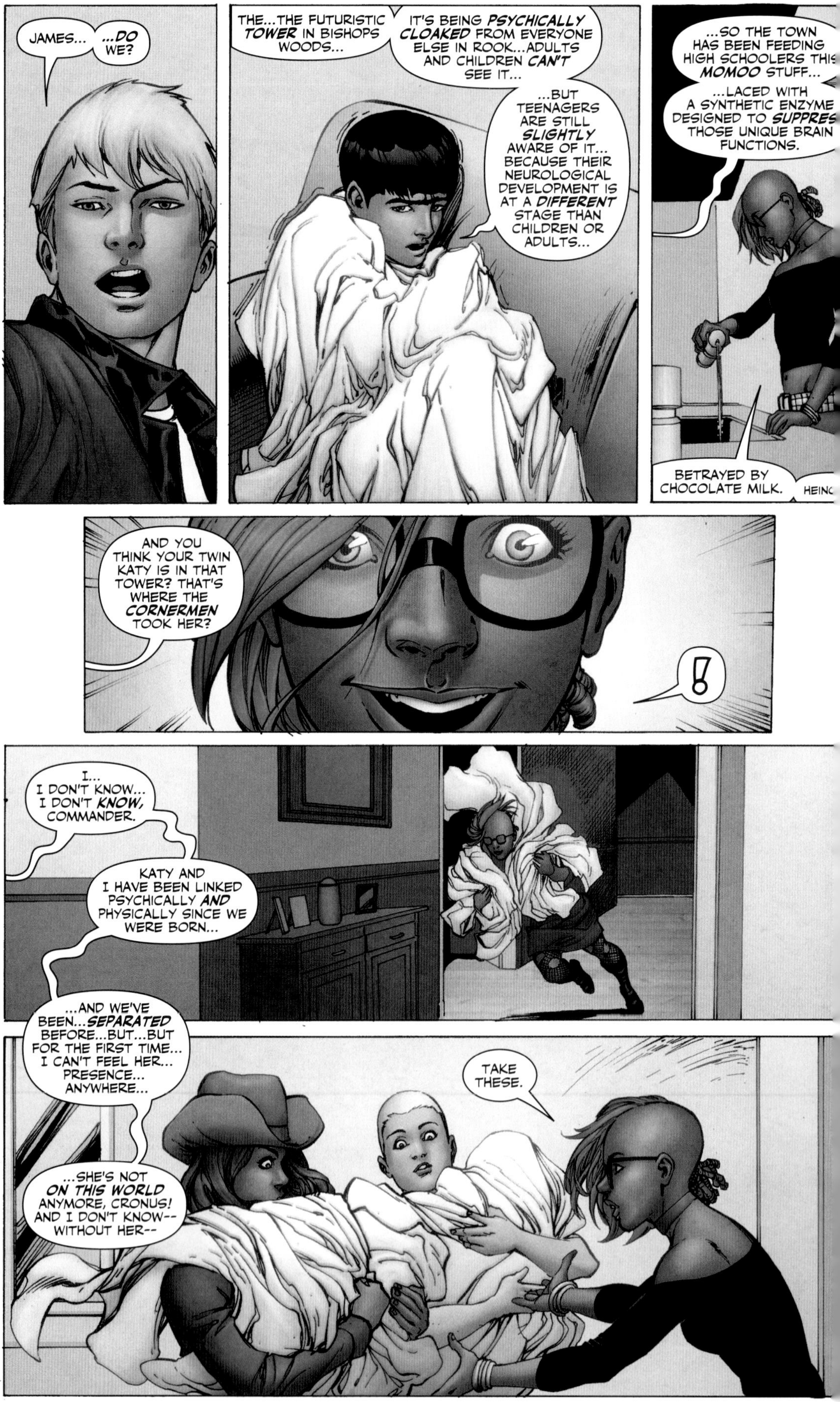
JAMES...
...DO WE?
THE...THE FUTURISTIC TOWER IN BISHOPS WOODS...
IT'S BEING PSYCHICALLY CLOAKED FROM EVERYONE ELSE IN ROOK...ADULTS AND CHILDREN CAN'T SEE IT...
...BUT TEENAGERS ARE STILL SLIGHTLY AWARE OF IT... BECAUSE THEIR NEUROLOGICAL DEVELOPMENT IS AT A DIFFERENT STAGE THAN CHILDREN OR ADULTS...
...SO THE TOWN HAS BEEN FEEDING HIGH SCHOOLERS THIS MOMOO STUFF...
...LACED WITH A SYNTHETIC ENZYME DESIGNED TO SUPPRES THOSE UNIQUE BRAIN FUNCTIONS.
BETRAYED BY CHOCOLATE MILK.
HEINC
AND YOU THINK YOUR TWIN KATY IS IN THAT TOWER? THAT'S WHERE THE CORNERMEN TOOK HER?
!
I... I DON'T KNOW... I DON'T KNOW, COMMANDER.
KATY AND I HAVE BEEN LINKED PSYCHICALLY AND PHYSICALLY SINCE WE WERE BORN...
...AND WE'VE BEEN...SEPARATED BEFORE...BUT...BUT FOR THE FIRST TIME... I CAN'T FEEL HER... PRESENCE... ANYWHERE...
TAKE THESE.
...SHE'S NOT ON THIS WORLD ANYMORE, CRONUS! AND I DON'T KNOW-- WITHOUT HER--

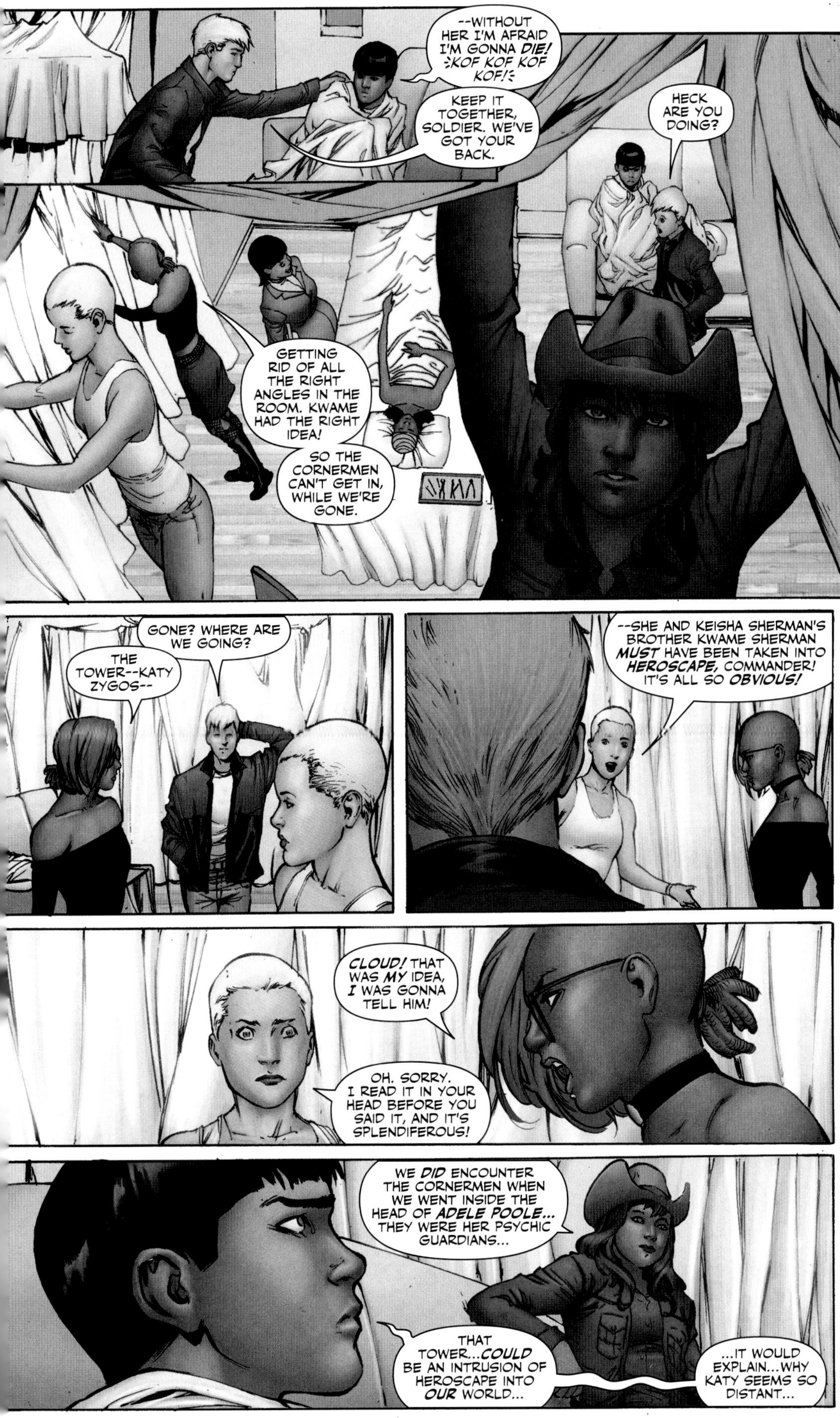
--WITHOUT HER I'M AFRAID I'M GONNA *DIE!* *KOF KOF KOF KOF!*
KEEP IT TOGETHER, SOLDIER. WE'VE GOT YOUR BACK.
HECK ARE YOU DOING?
GETTING RID OF ALL THE RIGHT ANGLES IN THE ROOM. KWAME HAD THE RIGHT IDEA!
SO THE CORNERMEN CAN'T GET IN, WHILE WE'RE GONE.
GONE? WHERE ARE WE GOING?
THE TOWER--KATY ZYGOS--
--SHE AND KEISHA SHERMAN'S BROTHER KWAME SHERMAN *MUST* HAVE BEEN TAKEN INTO *HEROSCAPE,* COMMANDER! IT'S ALL SO *OBVIOUS!*
CLOUD! THAT WAS *MY* IDEA, *I* WAS GONNA TELL HIM!
OH. SORRY. I READ IT IN YOUR HEAD BEFORE YOU SAID IT, AND IT'S SPLENDIFEROUS!
WE *DID* ENCOUNTER THE CORNERMEN WHEN WE WENT INSIDE THE HEAD OF *ADELE POOLE...* THEY WERE HER PSYCHIC GUARDIANS...
THAT TOWER...*COULD* BE AN INTRUSION OF HEROSCAPE INTO *OUR* WORLD...
...IT WOULD EXPLAIN...WHY KATY SEEMS SO DISTANT...

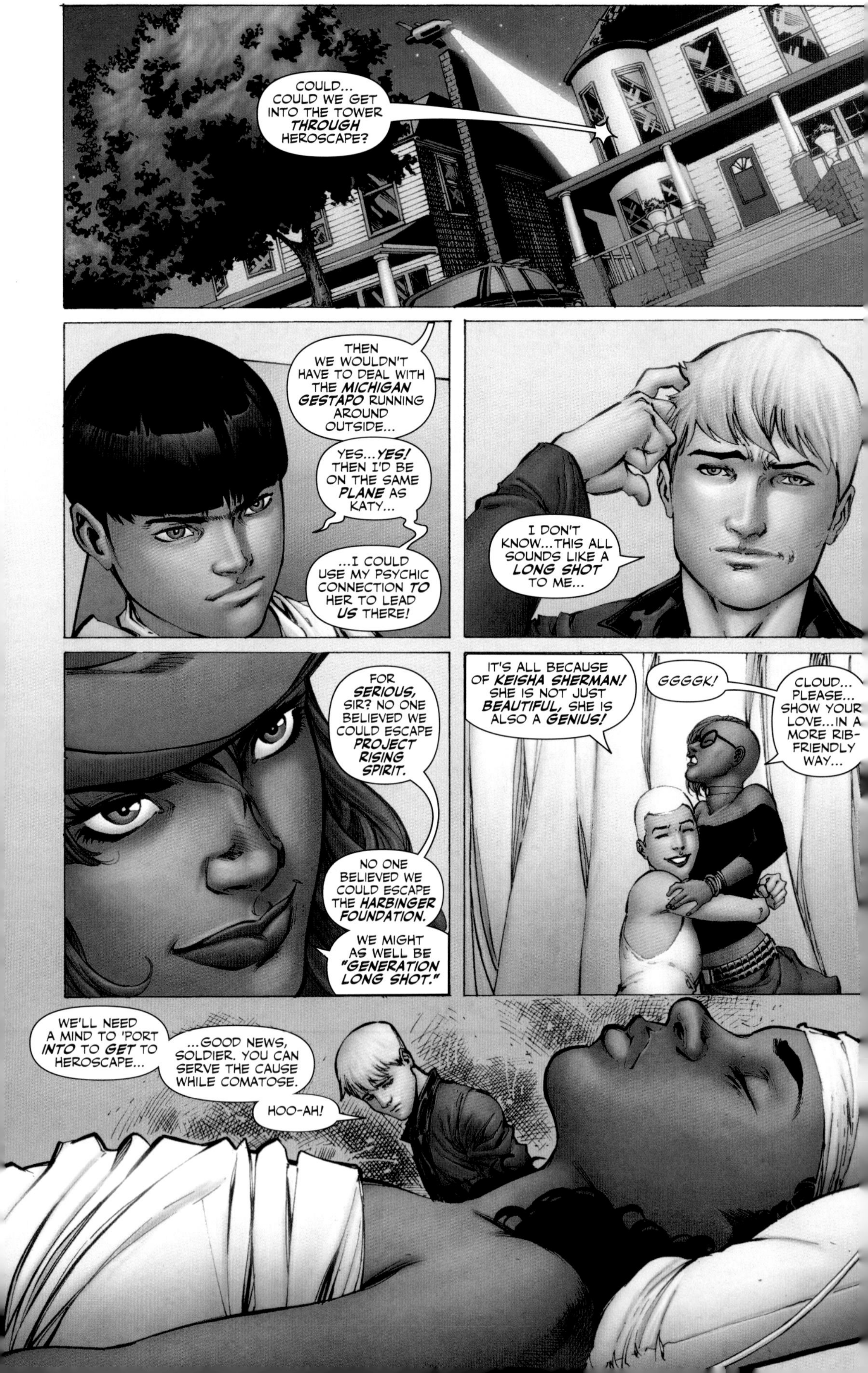
COULD... COULD WE GET INTO THE TOWER THROUGH HEROSCAPE?
THEN WE WOULDN'T HAVE TO DEAL WITH THE MICHIGAN GESTAPO RUNNING AROUND OUTSIDE...
YES...YES! THEN I'D BE ON THE SAME PLANE AS KATY...
...I COULD USE MY PSYCHIC CONNECTION TO HER TO LEAD US THERE!
I DON'T KNOW...THIS ALL SOUNDS LIKE A LONG SHOT TO ME...
FOR SERIOUS, SIR? NO ONE BELIEVED WE COULD ESCAPE PROJECT RISING SPIRIT.
NO ONE BELIEVED WE COULD ESCAPE THE HARBINGER FOUNDATION.
WE MIGHT AS WELL BE "GENERATION LONG SHOT."
IT'S ALL BECAUSE OF KEISHA SHERMAN! SHE IS NOT JUST BEAUTIFUL, SHE IS ALSO A GENIUS!
GGGGK!
CLOUD... PLEASE... SHOW YOUR LOVE...IN A MORE RIB-FRIENDLY WAY...
WE'LL NEED A MIND TO 'PORT INTO TO GET TO HEROSCAPE...
...GOOD NEWS, SOLDIER. YOU CAN SERVE THE CAUSE WHILE COMATOSE.
HOO-AH!

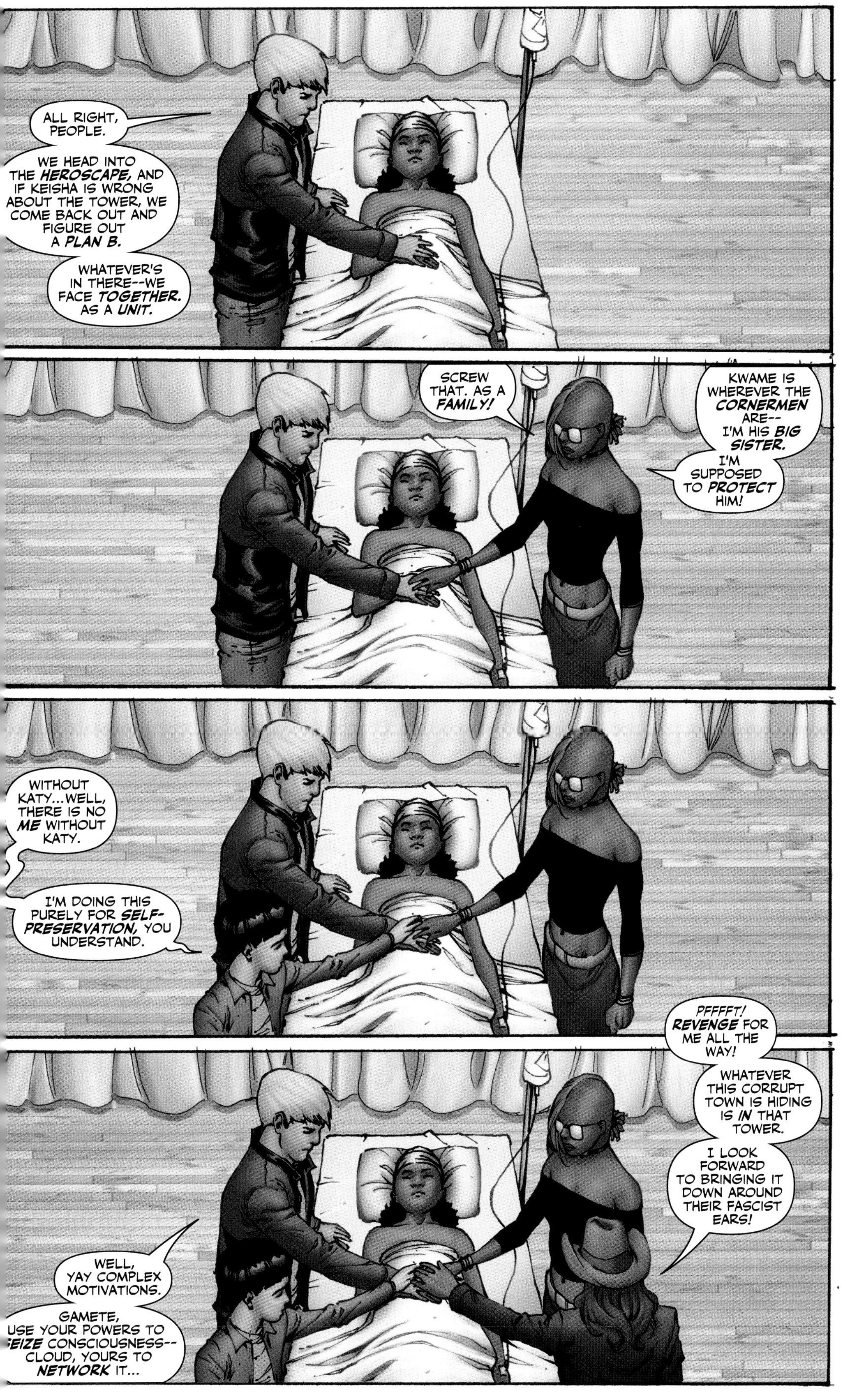
ALL RIGHT, PEOPLE.
WE HEAD INTO THE HEROSCAPE, AND IF KEISHA IS WRONG ABOUT THE TOWER, WE COME BACK OUT AND FIGURE OUT A PLAN B.
WHATEVER'S IN THERE--WE FACE TOGETHER. AS A UNIT.
SCREW THAT. AS A FAMILY!
KWAME IS WHEREVER THE CORNERMEN ARE-- I'M HIS BIG SISTER.
I'M SUPPOSED TO PROTECT HIM!
WITHOUT KATY...WELL, THERE IS NO ME WITHOUT KATY.
I'M DOING THIS PURELY FOR SELF-PRESERVATION, YOU UNDERSTAND.
PFFFFT! REVENGE FOR ME ALL THE WAY!
WHATEVER THIS CORRUPT TOWN IS HIDING IS IN THAT TOWER.
I LOOK FORWARD TO BRINGING IT DOWN AROUND THEIR FASCIST EARS!
WELL, YAY COMPLEX MOTIVATIONS.
GAMETE, USE YOUR POWERS TO SEIZE CONSCIOUSNESS-- CLOUD, YOURS TO NETWORK IT...

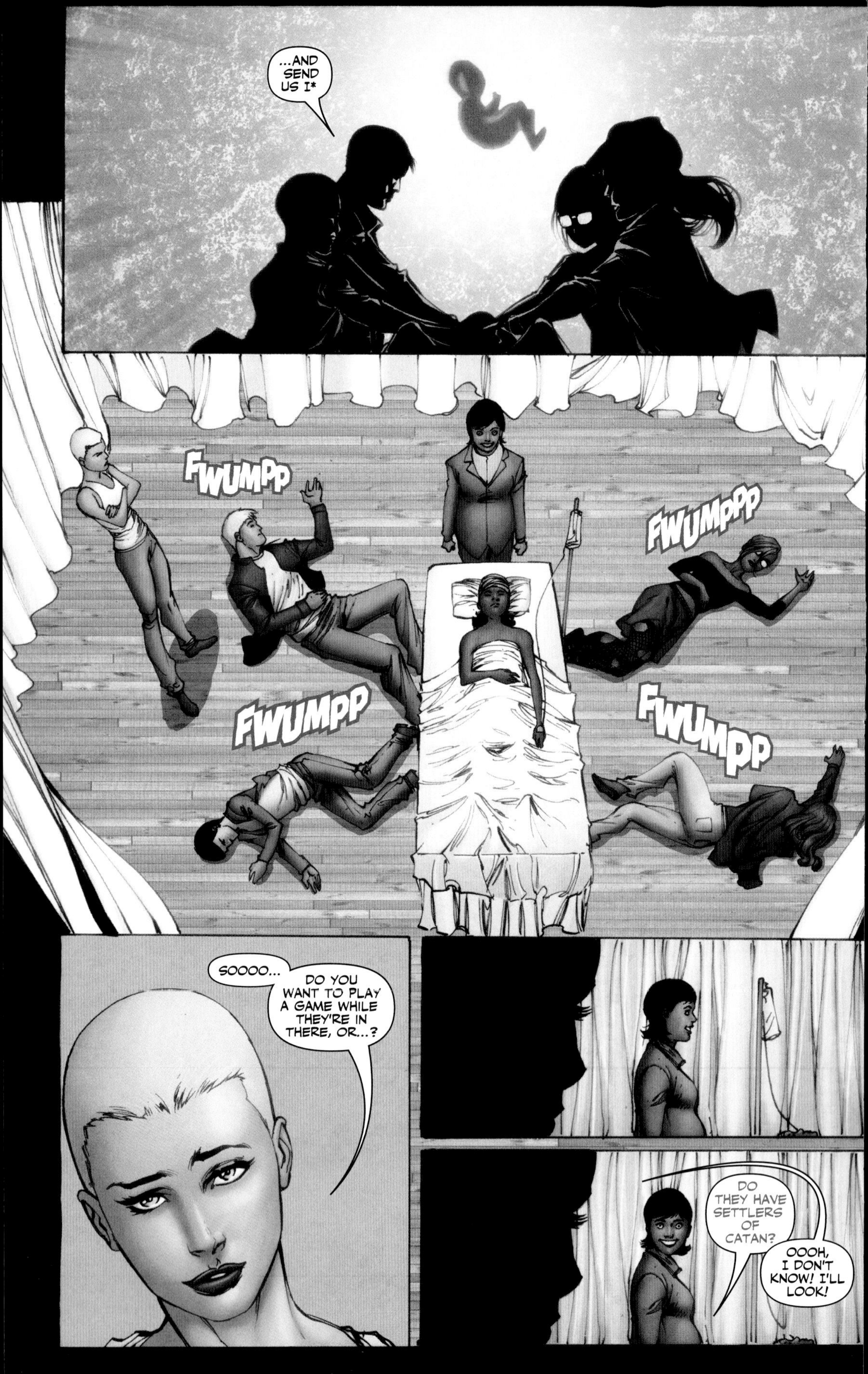
...AND SEND US I*
FWUMPP
FWUMPPP
FWUMPP
FWUMPP
SOOOO...
DO YOU WANT TO PLAY A GAME WHILE THEY'RE IN THERE, OR...?
DO THEY HAVE SETTLERS OF CATAN?
OOOH, I DON'T KNOW! I'LL LOOK!

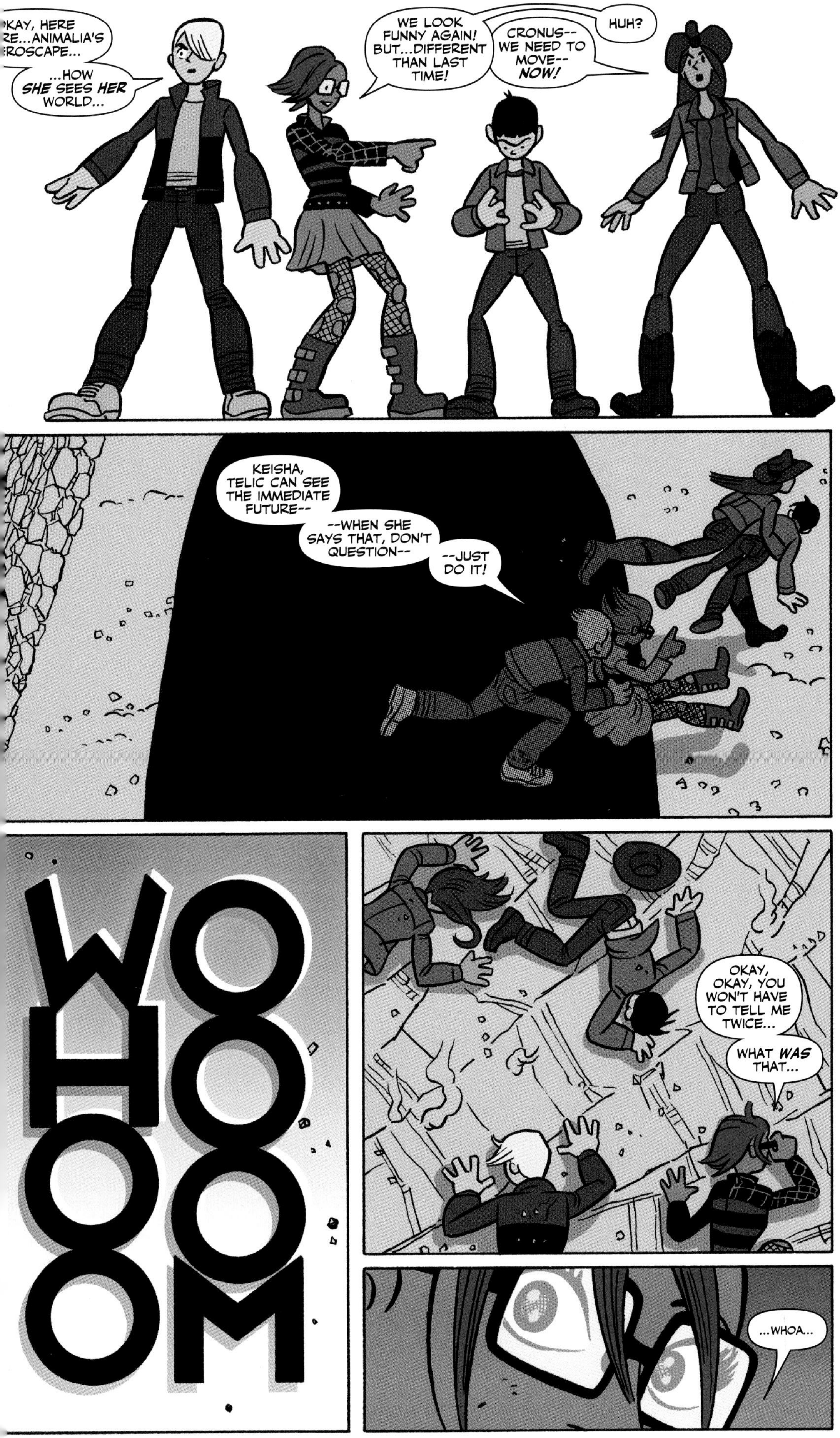
KAY, HERE
RE...ANIMALIA'S
EROSCAPE...
...HOW
SHE SEES HER
WORLD...
WE LOOK
FUNNY AGAIN!
BUT...DIFFERENT
THAN LAST
TIME!
HUH?
CRONUS--
WE NEED TO
MOVE--
NOW!
KEISHA,
TELIC CAN SEE
THE IMMEDIATE
FUTURE--
--WHEN SHE
SAYS THAT, DON'T
QUESTION--
--JUST
DO IT!
WHOOOOOOOM
OKAY,
OKAY, YOU
WON'T HAVE
TO TELL ME
TWICE...
WHAT WAS
THAT...
...WHOA...

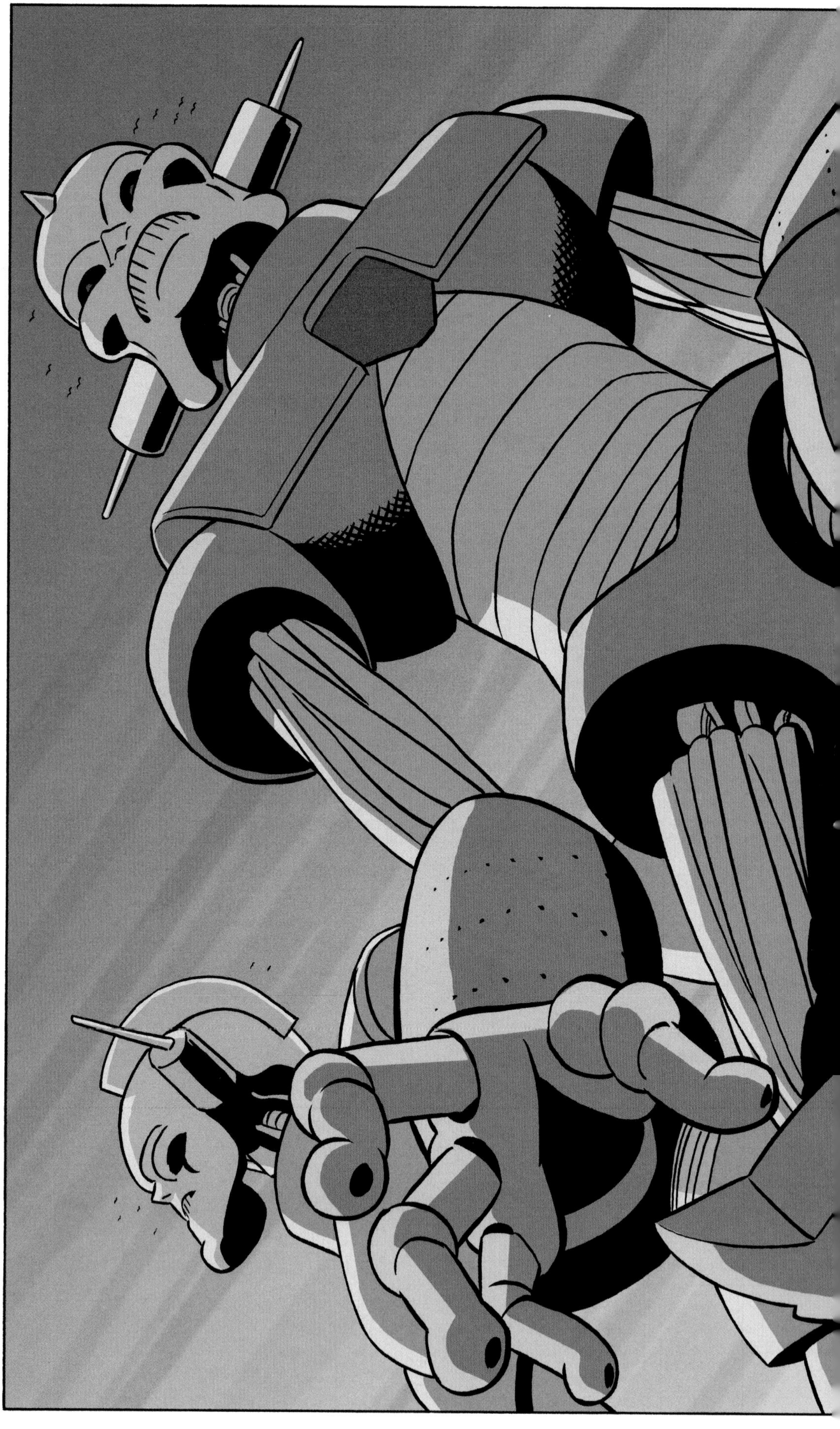

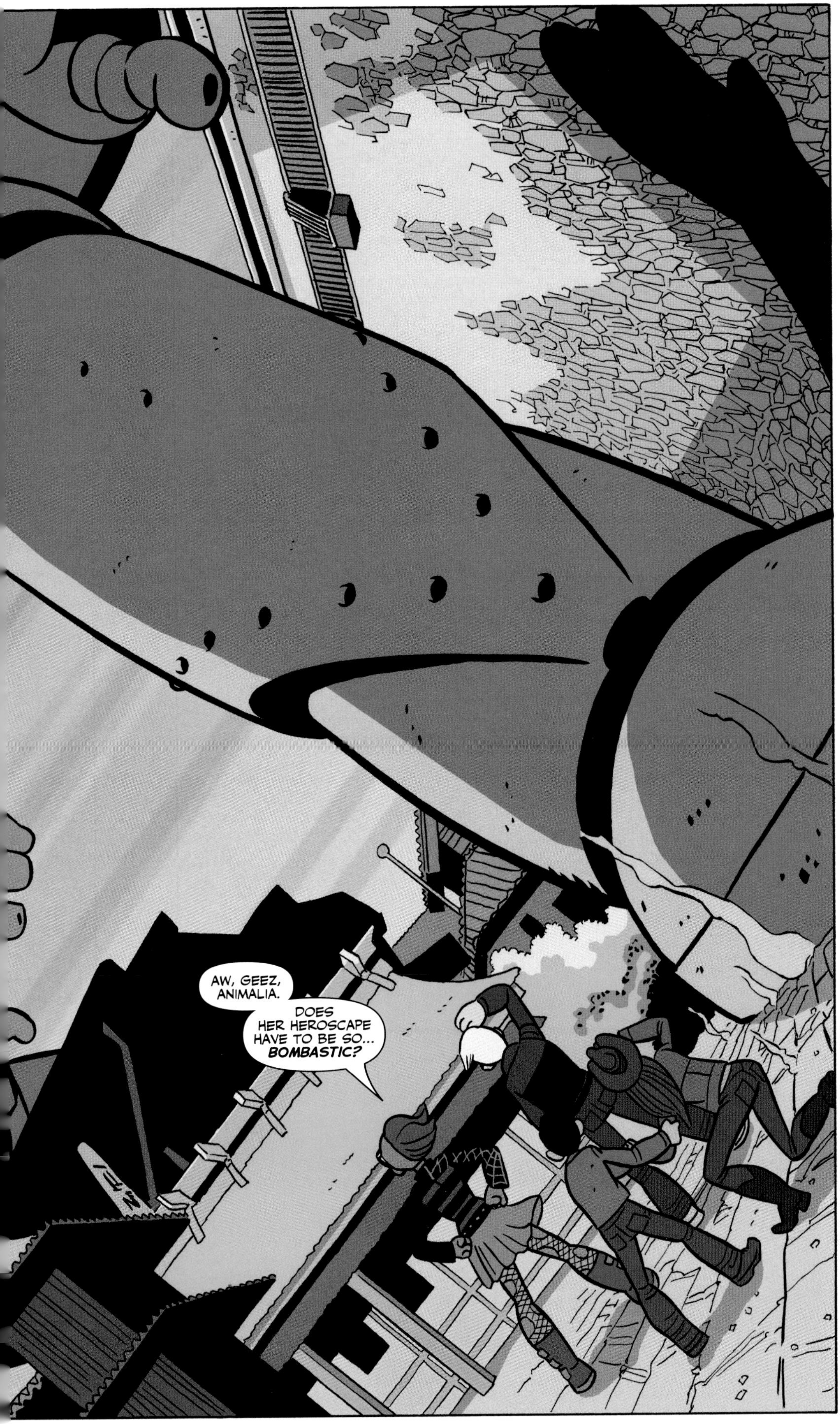
AW, GEEZ, ANIMALIA.
DOES HER HEROSCAPE HAVE TO BE SO... ***BOMBASTIC?***

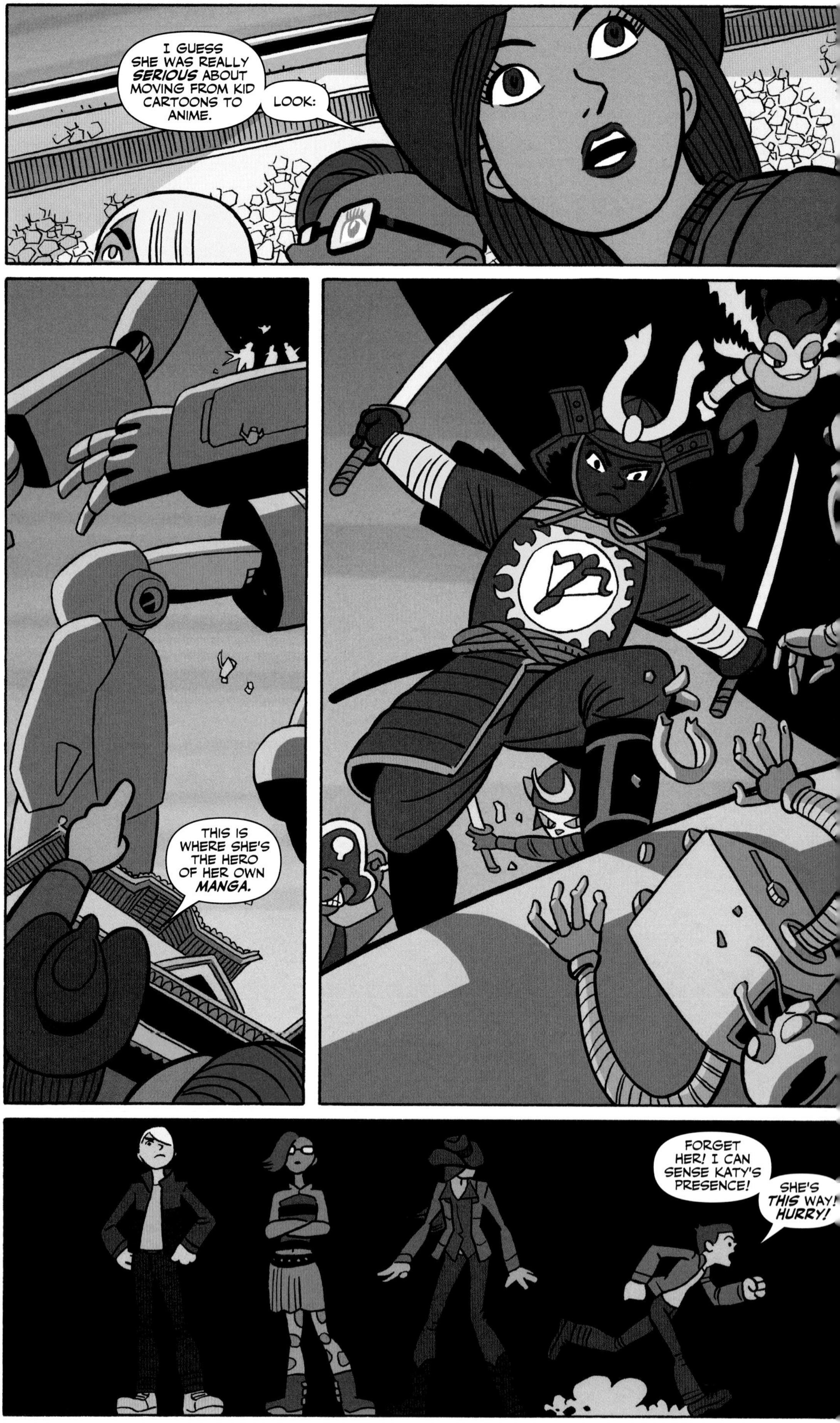
I GUESS SHE WAS REALLY SERIOUS ABOUT MOVING FROM KID CARTOONS TO ANIME.
LOOK:
THIS IS WHERE SHE'S THE HERO OF HER OWN MANGA.
FORGET HER! I CAN SENSE KATY'S PRESENCE!
SHE'S THIS WAY! HURRY!

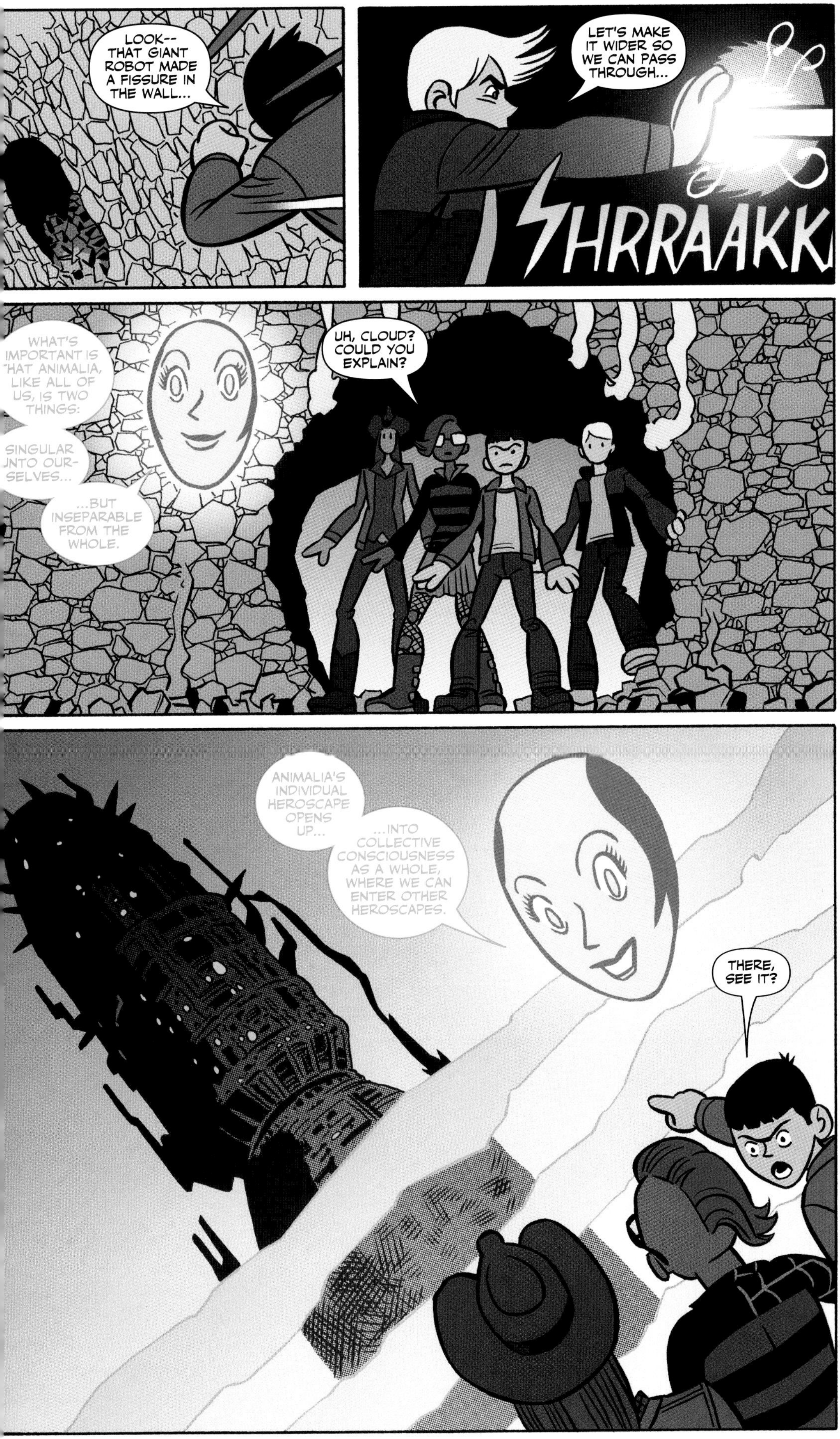
LOOK-- THAT GIANT ROBOT MADE A FISSURE IN THE WALL...
LET'S MAKE IT WIDER SO WE CAN PASS THROUGH...
SHRRAAKK
WHAT'S IMPORTANT IS THAT ANIMALIA, LIKE ALL OF US, IS TWO THINGS:
SINGULAR INTO OURSELVES...
...BUT INSEPARABLE FROM THE WHOLE.
UH, CLOUD? COULD YOU EXPLAIN?
ANIMALIA'S INDIVIDUAL HEROSCAPE OPENS UP...
...INTO COLLECTIVE CONSCIOUSNESS AS A WHOLE, WHERE WE CAN ENTER OTHER HEROSCAPES.
THERE, SEE IT?

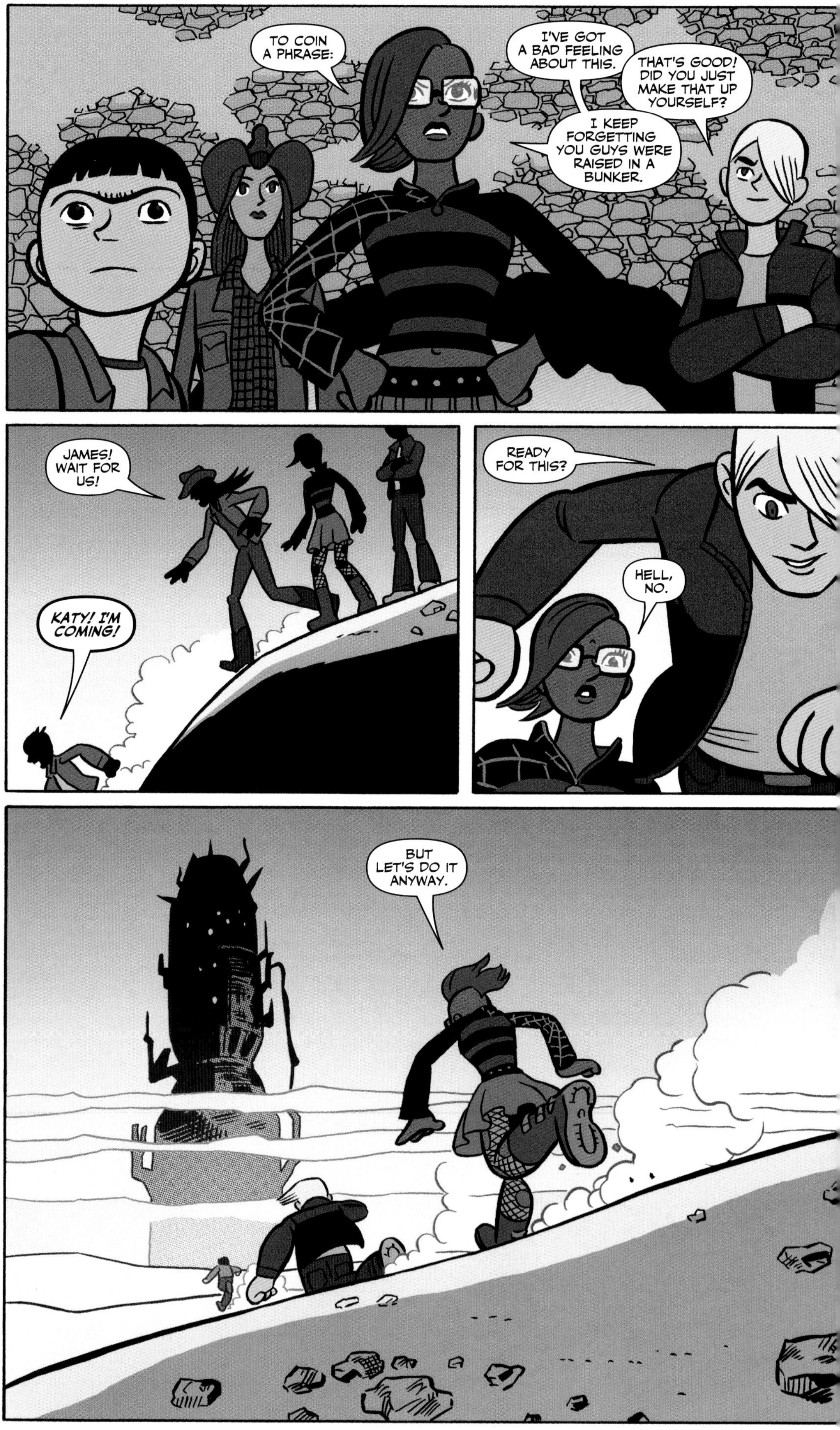
TO COIN A PHRASE:
I'VE GOT A BAD FEELING ABOUT THIS.
THAT'S GOOD! DID YOU JUST MAKE THAT UP YOURSELF?
I KEEP FORGETTING YOU GUYS WERE RAISED IN A BUNKER.
JAMES! WAIT FOR US!
KATY! I'M COMING!
READY FOR THIS?
HELL, NO.
BUT LET'S DO IT ANYWAY.

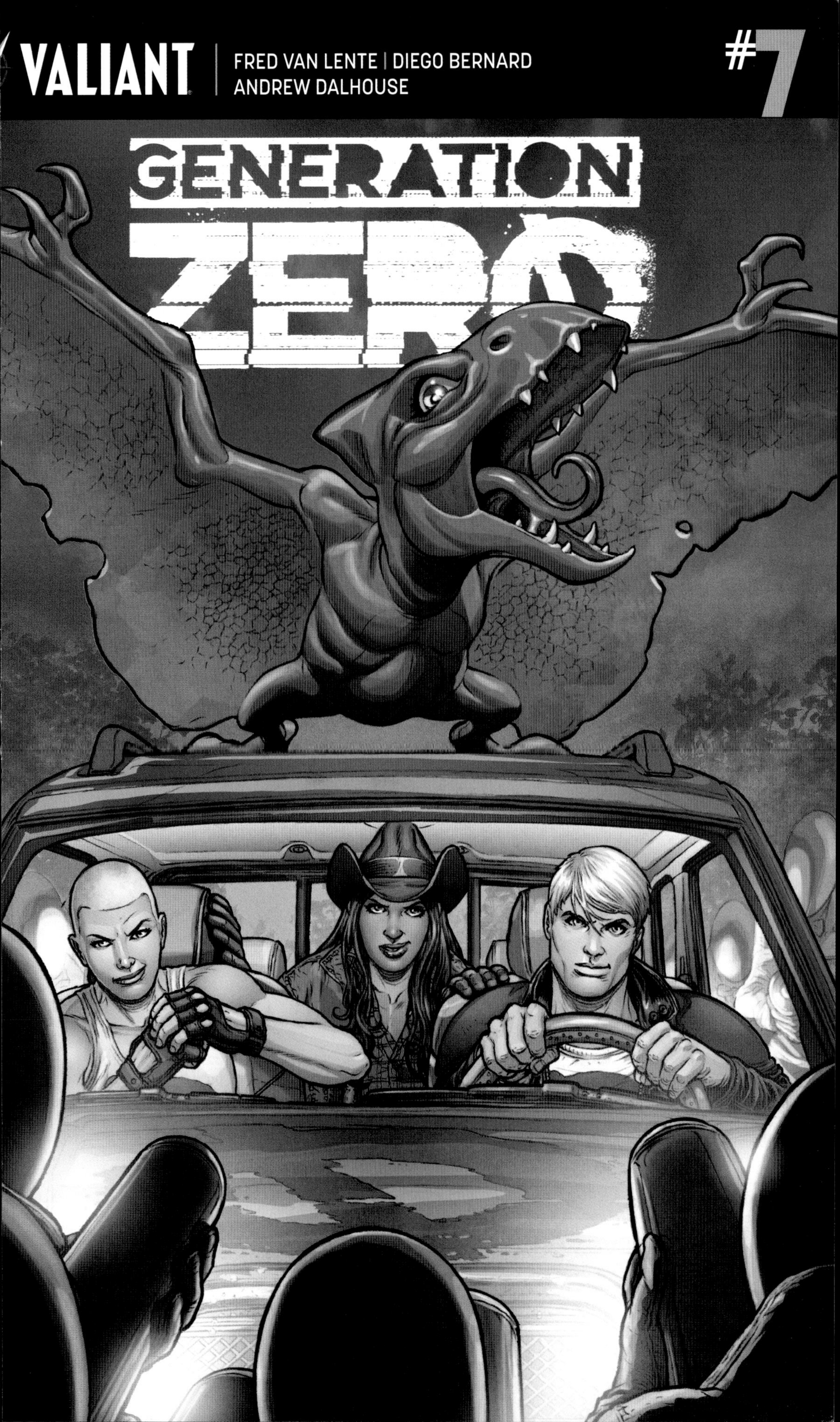
VALIANT
FRED VAN LENTE | DIEGO BERNARD
ANDREW DALHOUSE
#7
GENERATION
ZERO

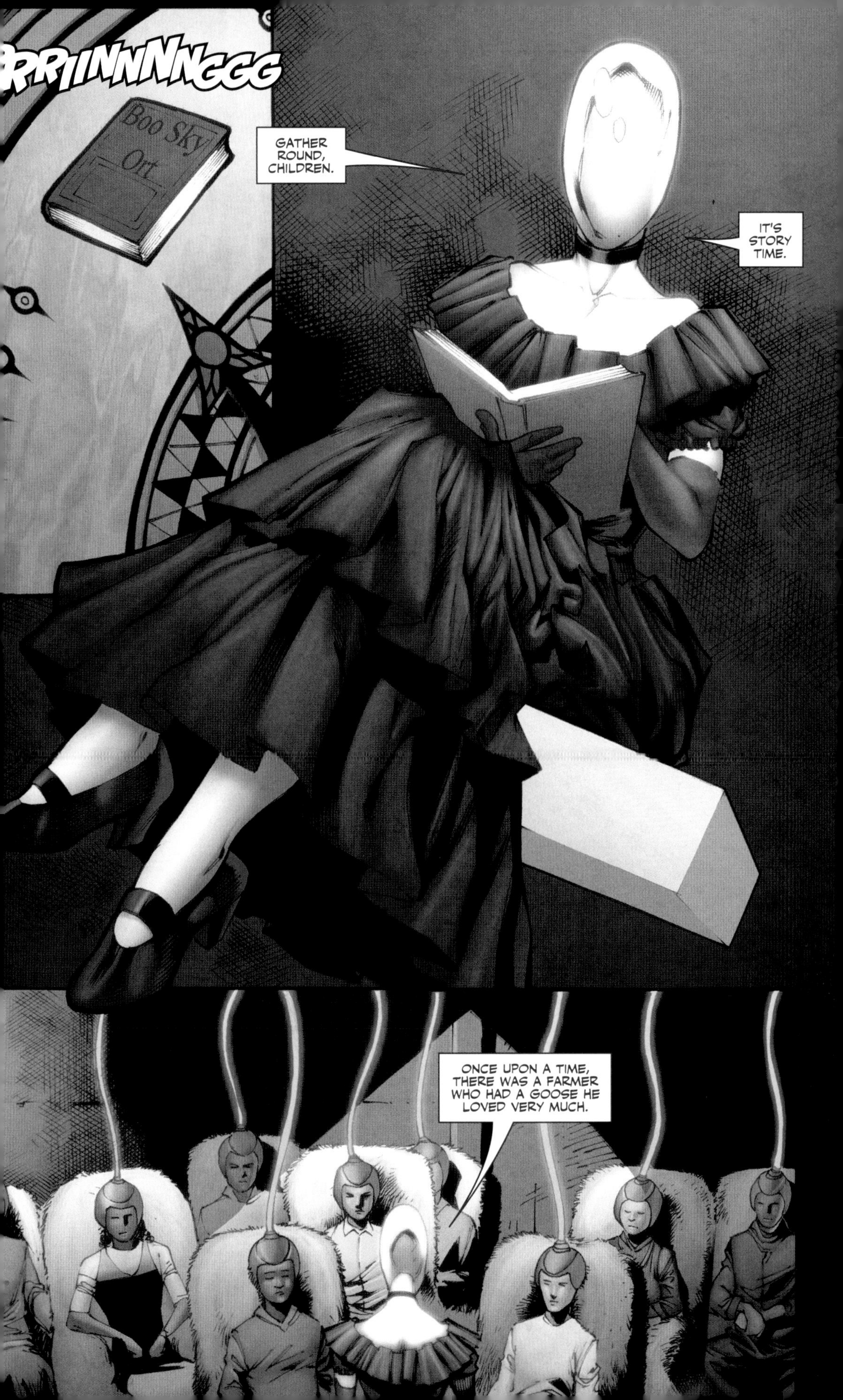

RRIINNNNGGG
Boo Sky
Ort.
GATHER ROUND, CHILDREN.
IT'S STORY TIME.
ONCE UPON A TIME, THERE WAS A FARMER WHO HAD A GOOSE HE LOVED VERY MUCH.

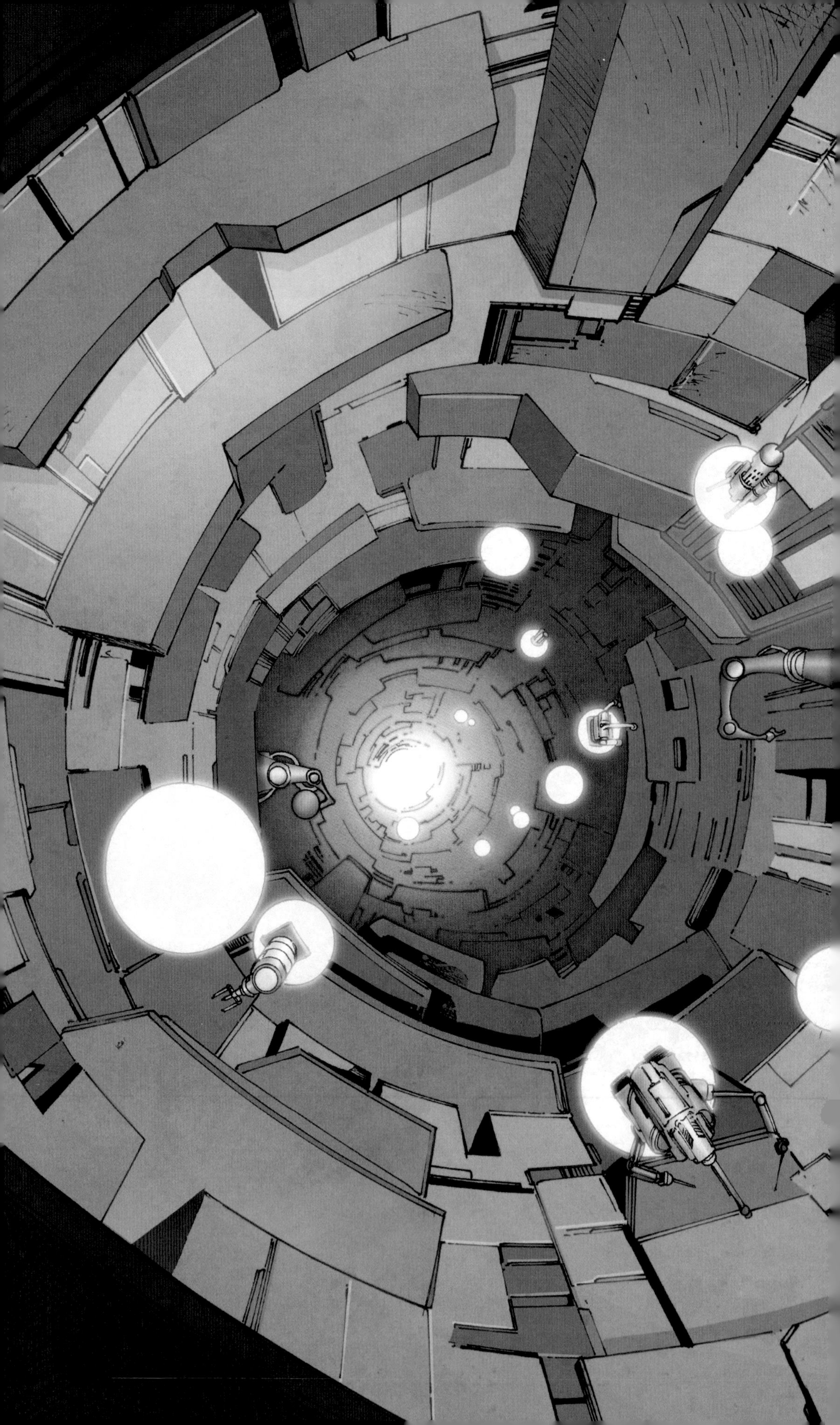

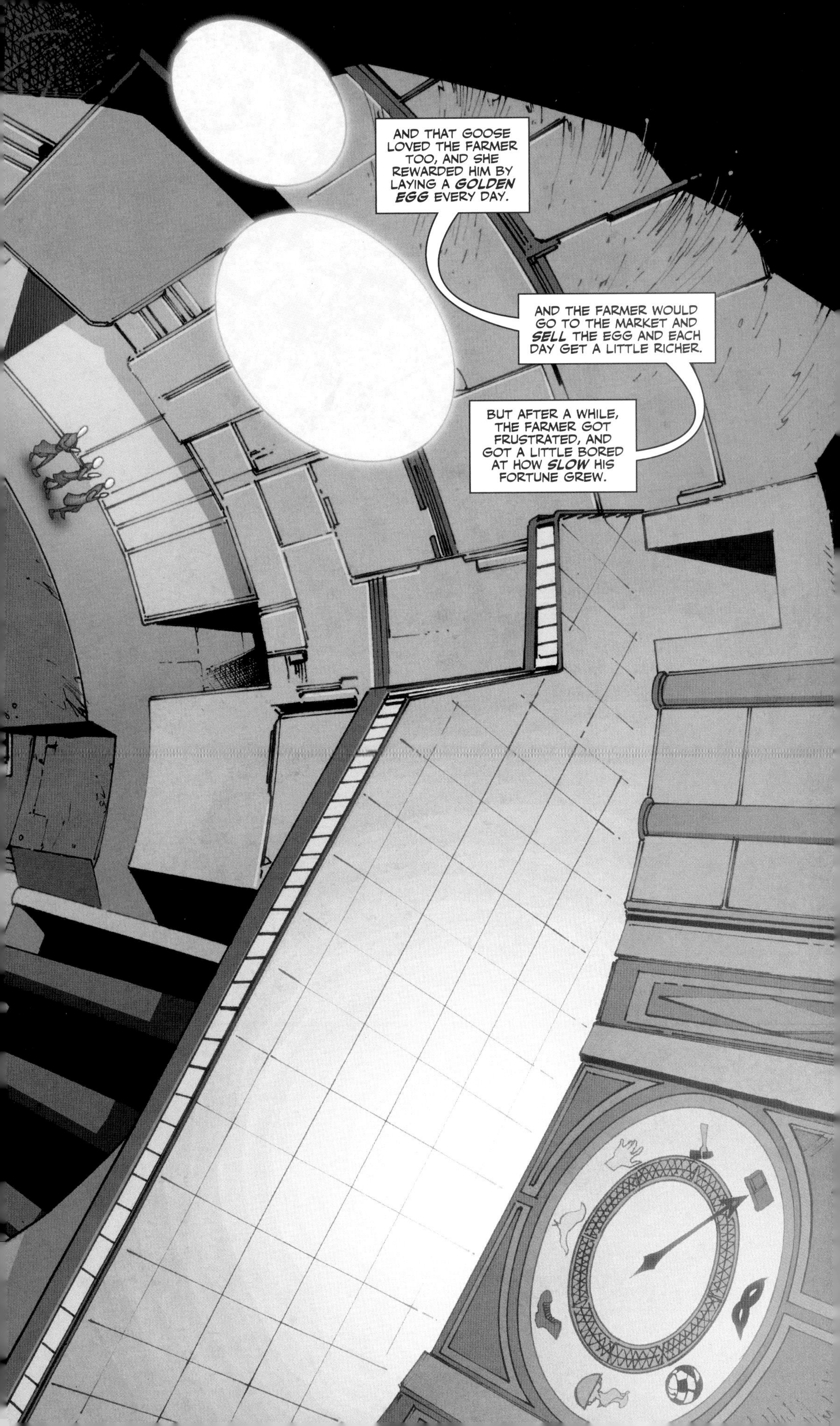
AND THAT GOOSE LOVED THE FARMER TOO, AND SHE REWARDED HIM BY LAYING A ***GOLDEN EGG*** EVERY DAY.
AND THE FARMER WOULD GO TO THE MARKET AND ***SELL*** THE EGG AND EACH DAY GET A LITTLE RICHER.
BUT AFTER A WHILE, THE FARMER GOT FRUSTRATED, AND GOT A LITTLE BORED AT HOW ***SLOW*** HIS FORTUNE GREW.

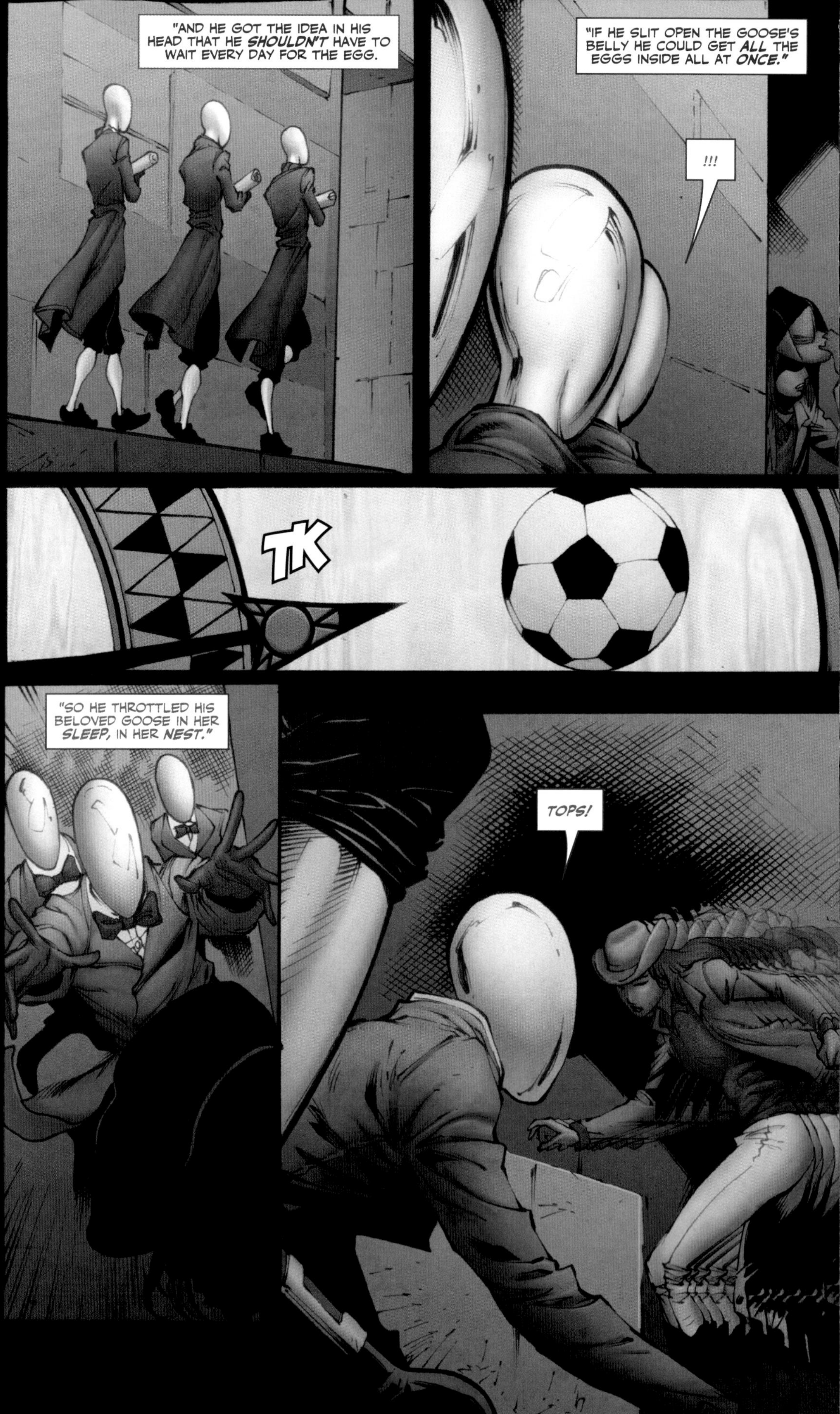
"AND HE GOT THE IDEA IN HIS HEAD THAT HE SHOULDN'T HAVE TO WAIT EVERY DAY FOR THE EGG.
"IF HE SLIT OPEN THE GOOSE'S BELLY HE COULD GET ALL THE EGGS INSIDE ALL AT ONCE."
!!!
TK
"SO HE THROTTLED HIS BELOVED GOOSE IN HER SLEEP, IN HER NEST."
TOPS!

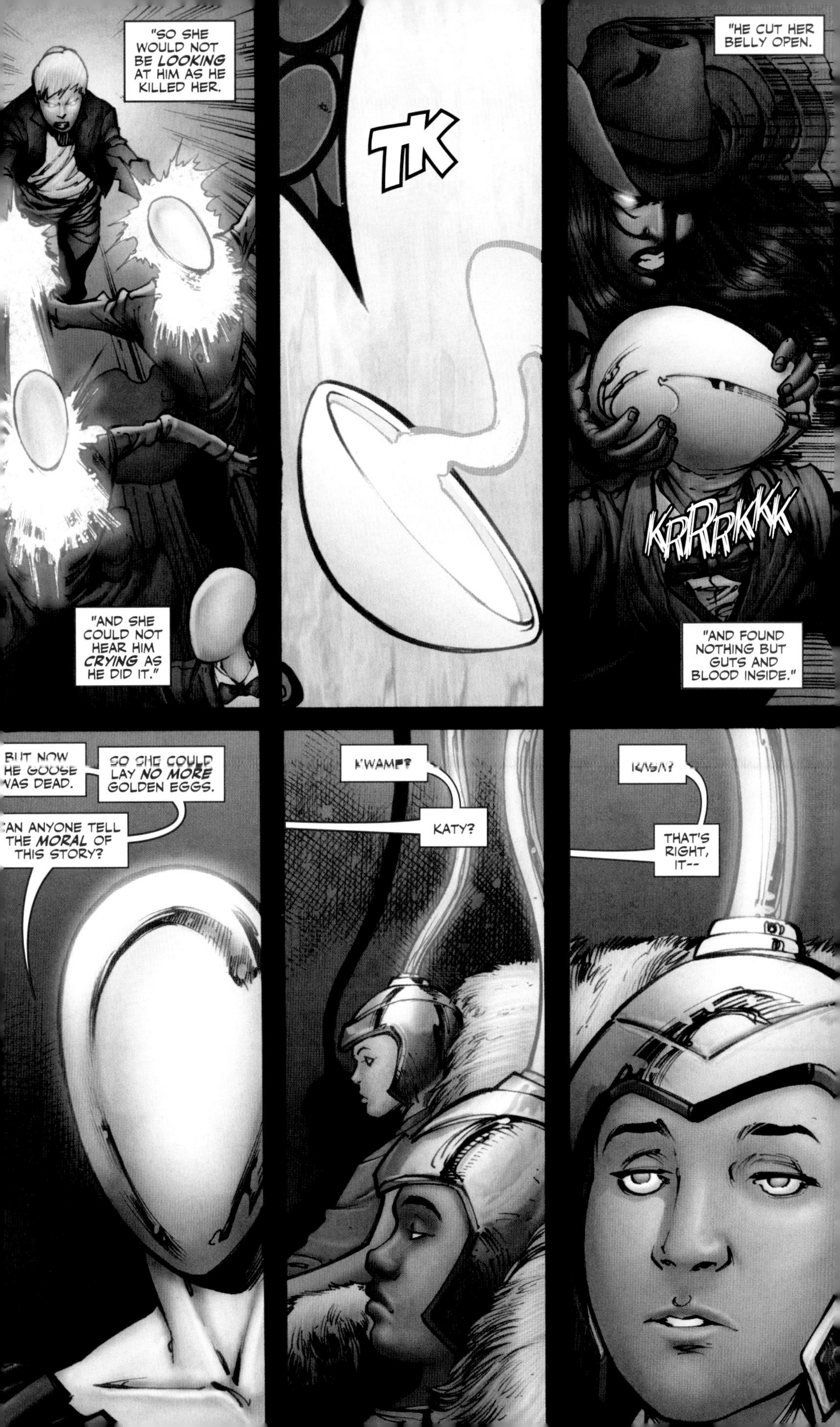
"SO SHE WOULD NOT BE *LOOKING* AT HIM AS HE KILLED HER.
"AND SHE COULD NOT HEAR HIM *CRYING* AS HE DID IT."
TK
"HE CUT HER BELLY OPEN.
KRRRKKK
"AND FOUND NOTHING BUT GUTS AND BLOOD INSIDE."
BUT NOW HE GOOSE WAS DEAD.
SO SHE COULD LAY *NO MORE* GOLDEN EGGS.
AN ANYONE TELL THE *MORAL* OF THIS STORY?
KWAME?
KATY?
KASA?
THAT'S RIGHT, IT--

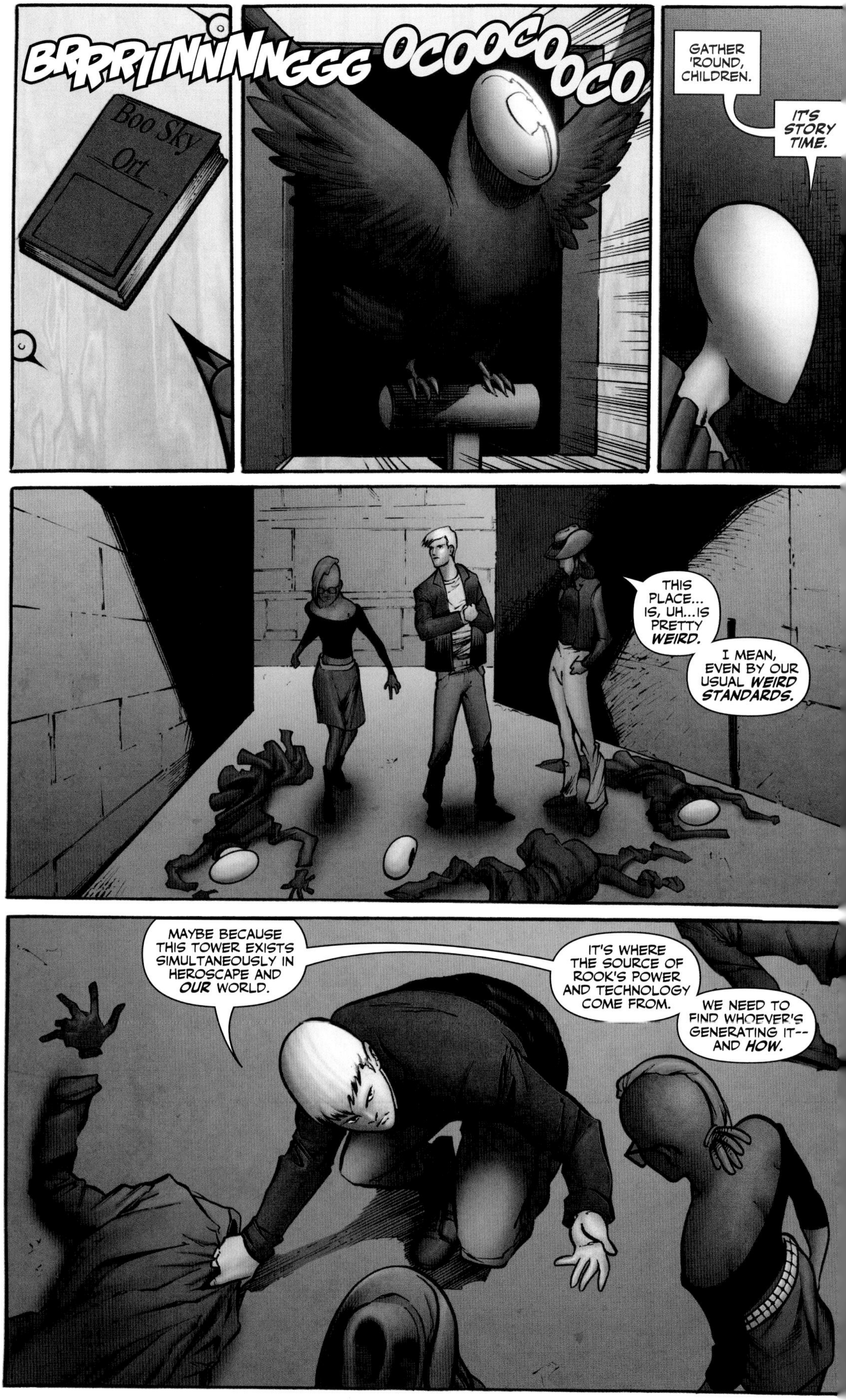
BRRRIINNNNGGG
OCOOCOOCO
Boo Sky Ort
GATHER 'ROUND, CHILDREN.
IT'S STORY TIME.
THIS PLACE... IS, UH...IS PRETTY WEIRD.
I MEAN, EVEN BY OUR USUAL WEIRD STANDARDS.
MAYBE BECAUSE THIS TOWER EXISTS SIMULTANEOUSLY IN HEROSCAPE AND OUR WORLD.
IT'S WHERE THE SOURCE OF ROOK'S POWER AND TECHNOLOGY COME FROM.
WE NEED TO FIND WHOEVER'S GENERATING IT-- AND HOW.

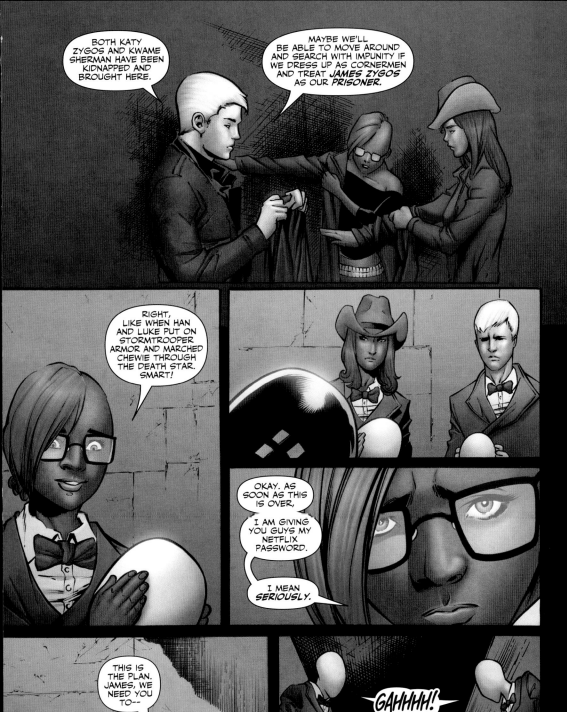

BOTH KATY ZYGOS AND KWAME SHERMAN HAVE BEEN KIDNAPPED AND BROUGHT HERE.

MAYBE WE'LL BE ABLE TO MOVE AROUND AND SEARCH WITH IMPUNITY IF WE DRESS UP AS CORNERMEN AND TREAT *JAMES ZYGOS* AS OUR *PRISONER.*

RIGHT, LIKE WHEN HAN AND LUKE PUT ON STORMTROOPER ARMOR AND MARCHED CHEWIE THROUGH THE DEATH STAR. SMART!

OKAY. AS SOON AS THIS IS OVER,

I AM GIVING YOU GUYS MY NETFLIX PASSWORD.

I MEAN *SERIOUSLY.*

THIS IS THE PLAN. JAMES, WE NEED YOU TO--

GAHHHH!

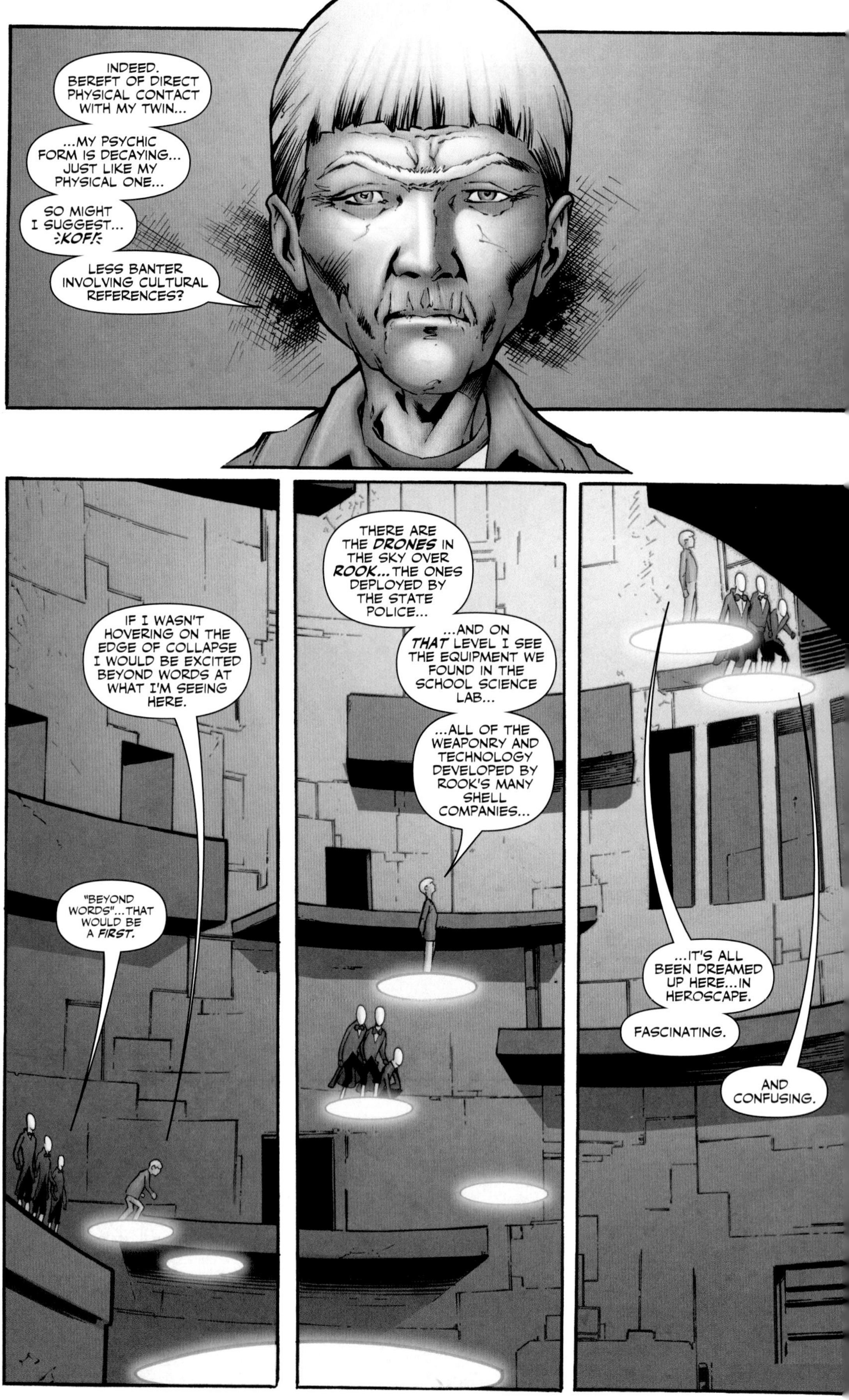
INDEED. BEREFT OF DIRECT PHYSICAL CONTACT WITH MY TWIN...
...MY PSYCHIC FORM IS DECAYING... JUST LIKE MY PHYSICAL ONE...
SO MIGHT I SUGGEST... KOF!
LESS BANTER INVOLVING CULTURAL REFERENCES?
IF I WASN'T HOVERING ON THE EDGE OF COLLAPSE I WOULD BE EXCITED BEYOND WORDS AT WHAT I'M SEEING HERE.
"BEYOND WORDS"...THAT WOULD BE A FIRST.
THERE ARE THE DRONES IN THE SKY OVER ROOK...THE ONES DEPLOYED BY THE STATE POLICE...
...AND ON THAT LEVEL I SEE THE EQUIPMENT WE FOUND IN THE SCHOOL SCIENCE LAB...
...ALL OF THE WEAPONRY AND TECHNOLOGY DEVELOPED BY ROOK'S MANY SHELL COMPANIES...
...IT'S ALL BEEN DREAMED UP HERE...IN HEROSCAPE.
FASCINATING.
AND CONFUSING.

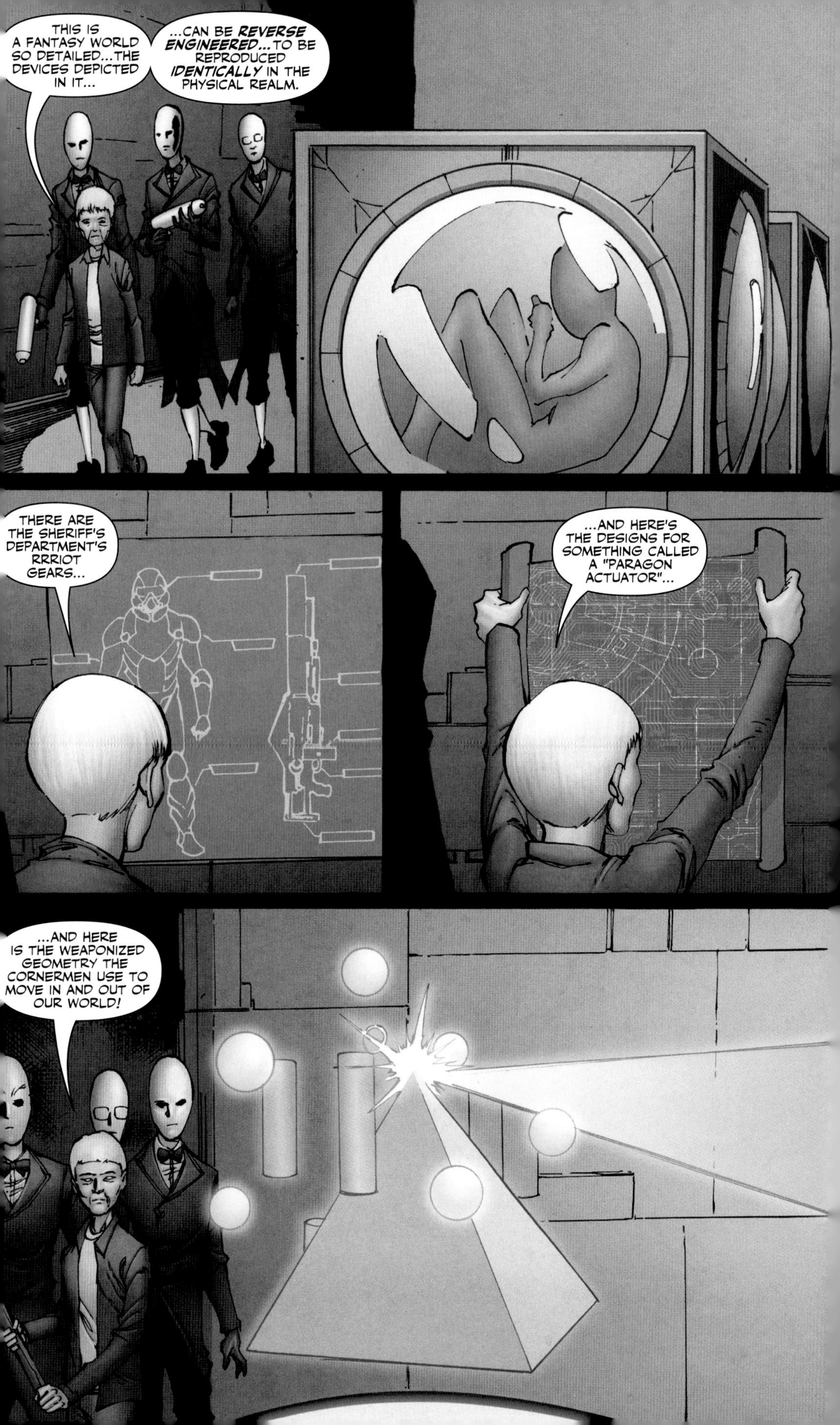
THIS IS A FANTASY WORLD SO DETAILED...THE DEVICES DEPICTED IN IT...
...CAN BE REVERSE ENGINEERED...TO BE REPRODUCED IDENTICALLY IN THE PHYSICAL REALM.
THERE ARE THE SHERIFF'S DEPARTMENT'S RRRIOT GEARS...
...AND HERE'S THE DESIGNS FOR SOMETHING CALLED A "PARAGON ACTUATOR"...
...AND HERE IS THE WEAPONIZED GEOMETRY THE CORNERMEN USE TO MOVE IN AND OUT OF OUR WORLD!

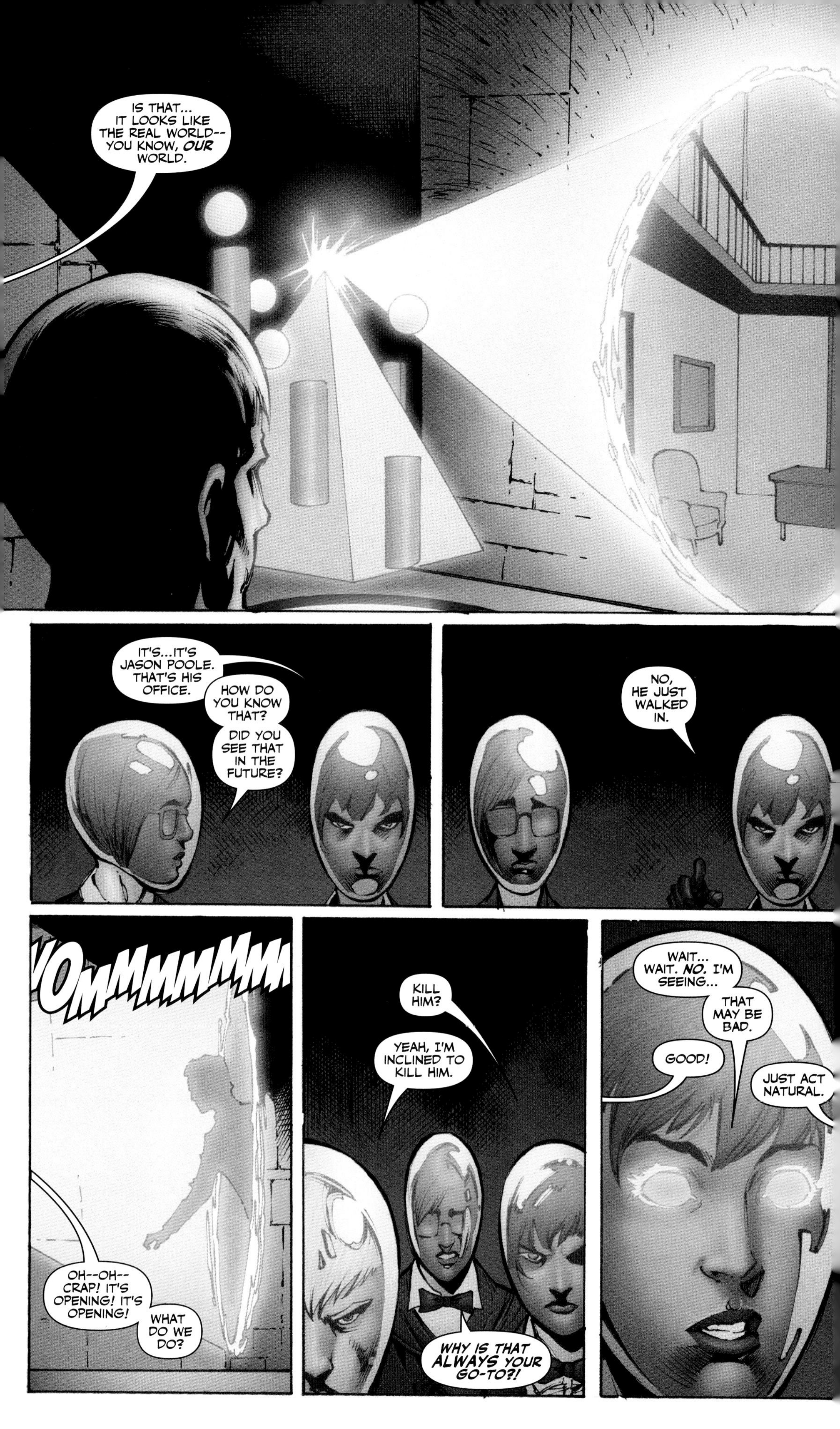
IS THAT... IT LOOKS LIKE THE REAL WORLD-- YOU KNOW, *OUR* WORLD.
IT'S...IT'S JASON POOLE. THAT'S HIS OFFICE.
HOW DO YOU KNOW THAT?
DID YOU SEE THAT IN THE FUTURE?
NO, HE JUST WALKED IN.
VOMMMMMMMM
OH--OH-- CRAP! IT'S OPENING! IT'S OPENING!
WHAT DO WE DO?
KILL HIM?
YEAH, I'M INCLINED TO KILL HIM.
WHY IS THAT ALWAYS YOUR GO-TO?!
WAIT... WAIT. *NO.* I'M SEEING...
THAT MAY BE BAD.
GOOD!
JUST ACT NATURAL.

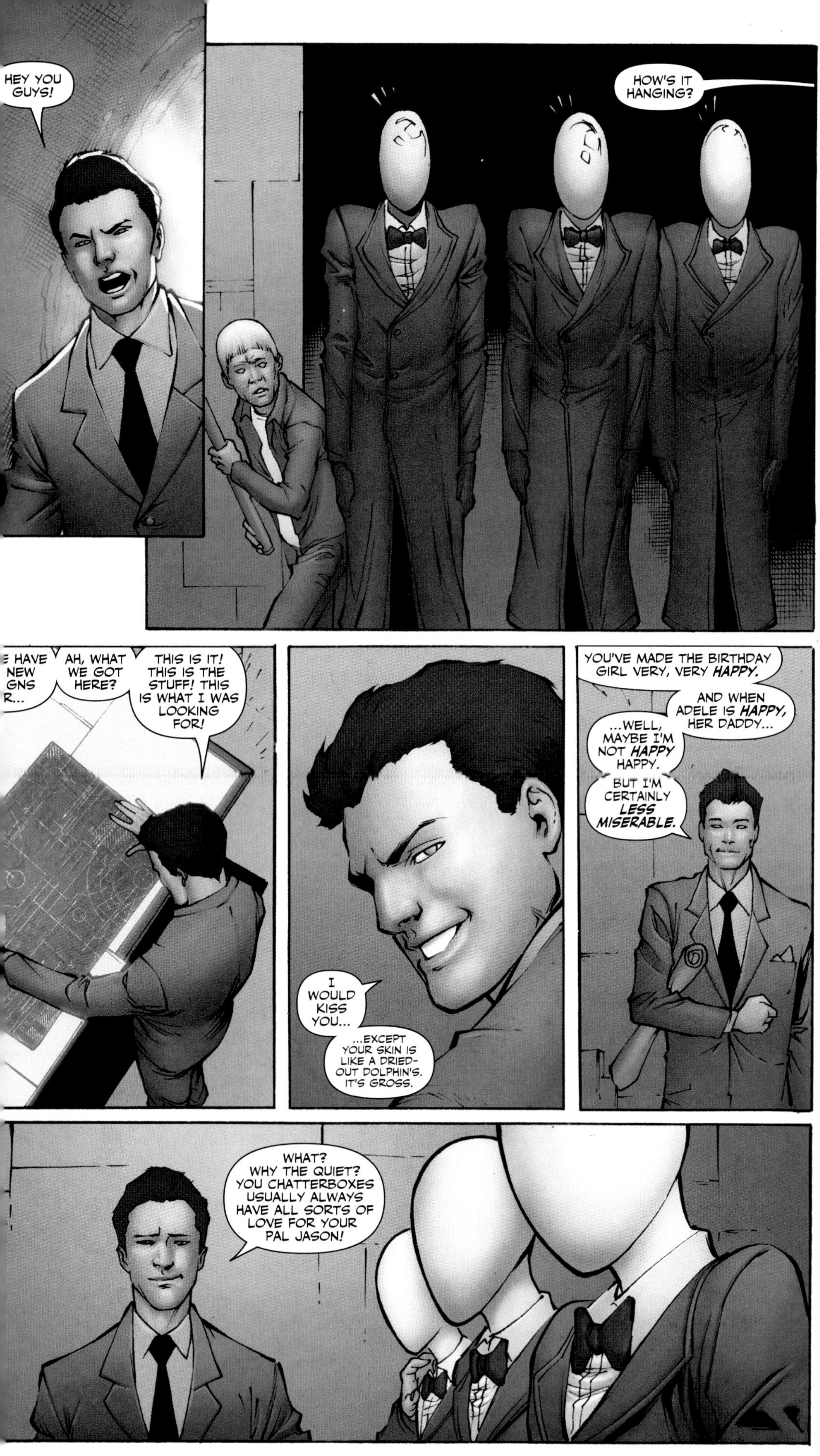
HEY YOU GUYS!
HOW'S IT HANGING?
...E HAVE ...NEW ...GNS ...R...
AH, WHAT WE GOT HERE?
THIS IS IT! THIS IS THE STUFF! THIS IS WHAT I WAS LOOKING FOR!
I WOULD KISS YOU...
...EXCEPT YOUR SKIN IS LIKE A DRIED-OUT DOLPHIN'S. IT'S GROSS.
YOU'VE MADE THE BIRTHDAY GIRL VERY, VERY HAPPY.
AND WHEN ADELE IS HAPPY, HER DADDY...
...WELL, MAYBE I'M NOT HAPPY HAPPY.
BUT I'M CERTAINLY LESS MISERABLE.
WHAT? WHY THE QUIET? YOU CHATTERBOXES USUALLY ALWAYS HAVE ALL SORTS OF LOVE FOR YOUR PAL JASON!

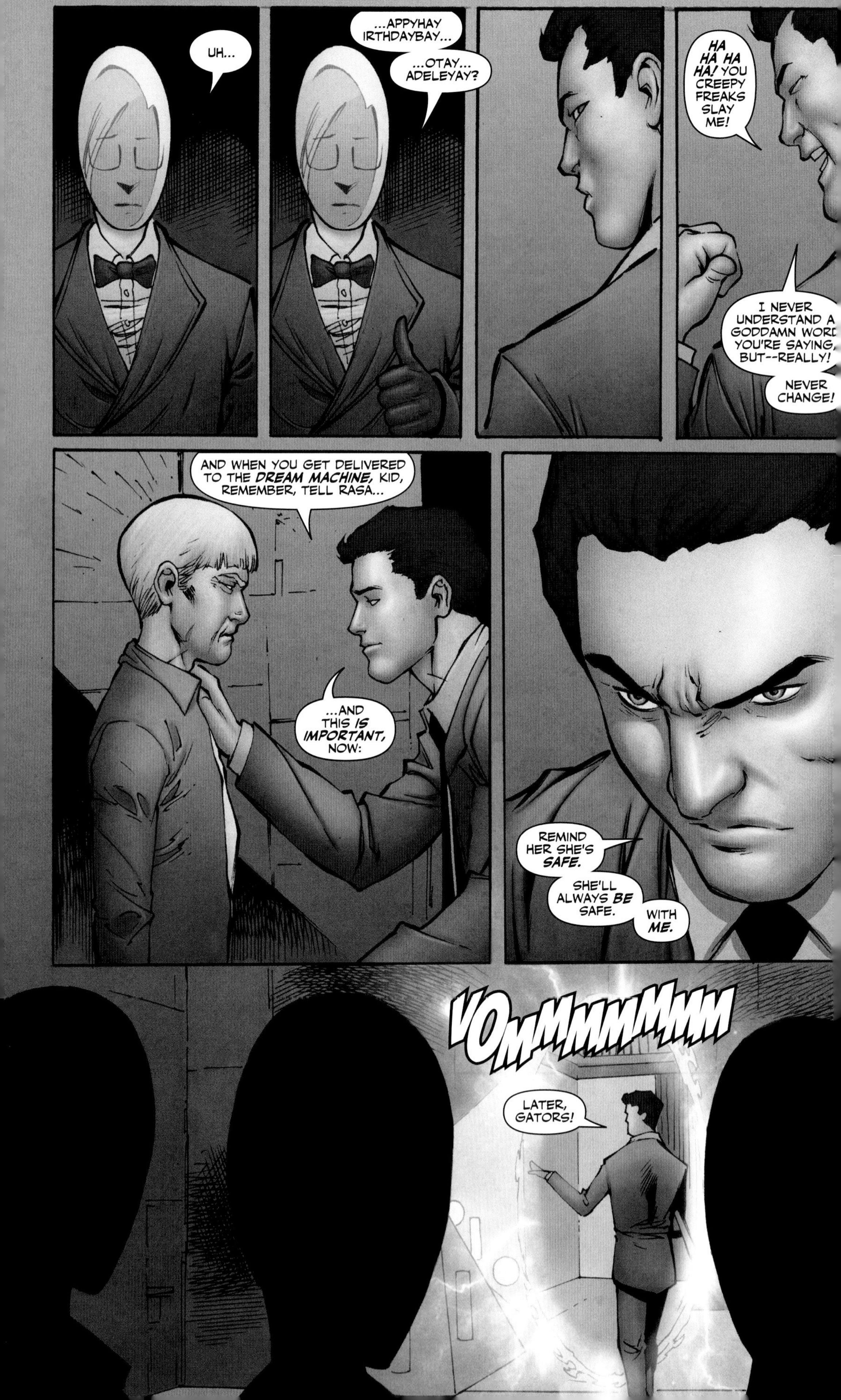
UH...
...APPYHAY IRTHDAYBAY...
...OTAY... ADELEYAY?
HA HA HA HA! YOU CREEPY FREAKS SLAY ME!
I NEVER UNDERSTAND A GODDAMN WORD YOU'RE SAYING, BUT--REALLY!
NEVER CHANGE!
AND WHEN YOU GET DELIVERED TO THE DREAM MACHINE, KID, REMEMBER, TELL RASA...
...AND THIS IS IMPORTANT, NOW:
REMIND HER SHE'S SAFE.
SHE'LL ALWAYS BE SAFE.
WITH ME.
VOMMMMMMM
LATER, GATORS!

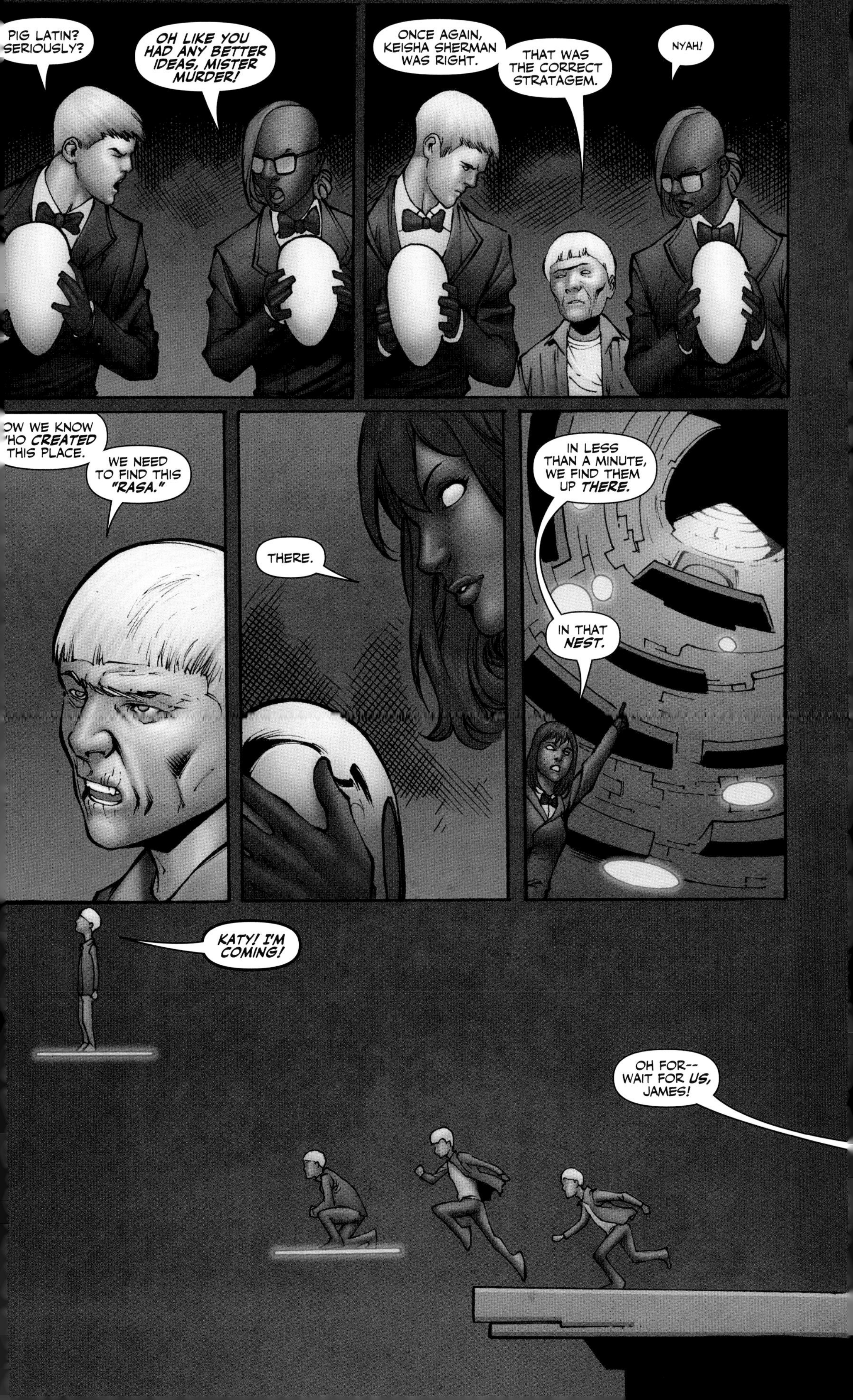
PIG LATIN? SERIOUSLY?
OH LIKE YOU HAD ANY BETTER IDEAS, MISTER MURDER!
ONCE AGAIN, KEISHA SHERMAN WAS RIGHT.
THAT WAS THE CORRECT STRATAGEM.
NYAH!
OW WE KNOW 'HO CREATED THIS PLACE.
WE NEED TO FIND THIS "RASA."
THERE.
IN LESS THAN A MINUTE, WE FIND THEM UP THERE.
IN THAT NEST.
KATY! I'M COMING!
OH FOR-- WAIT FOR US, JAMES!

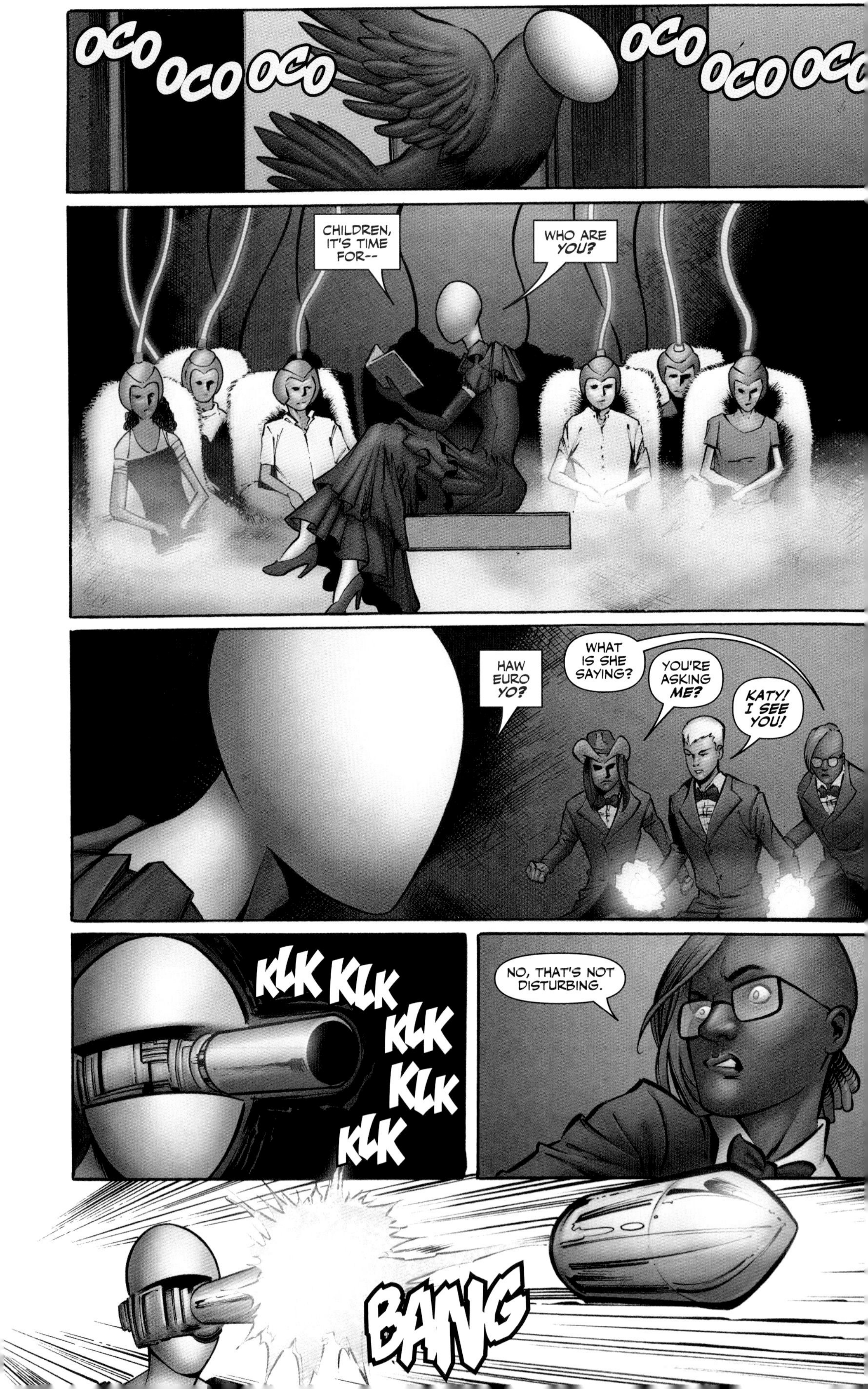
OCO OCO OCO
OCO OCO OCO
CHILDREN, IT'S TIME FOR--
WHO ARE *YOU?*
HAW EURO *YO?*
WHAT IS SHE SAYING?
YOU'RE ASKING *ME?*
KATY! I SEE YOU!
KLK KLK KLK KLK KLK
NO, THAT'S NOT DISTURBING.
BANG

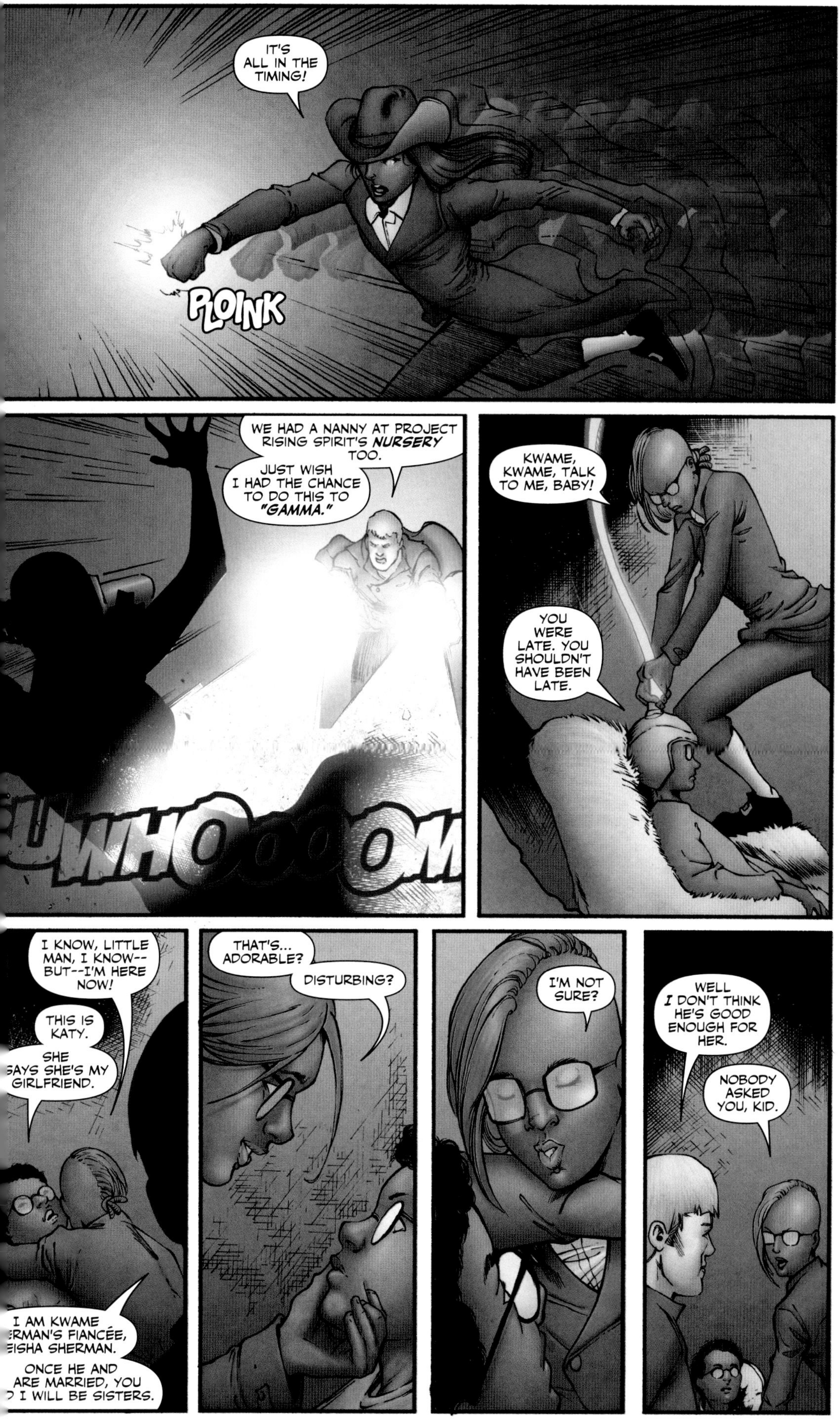
IT'S ALL IN THE TIMING!
PLOINK
WE HAD A NANNY AT PROJECT RISING SPIRIT'S NURSERY TOO.
JUST WISH I HAD THE CHANCE TO DO THIS TO "GAMMA."
WHOOOOOM
KWAME, KWAME, TALK TO ME, BABY!
YOU WERE LATE. YOU SHOULDN'T HAVE BEEN LATE.
I KNOW, LITTLE MAN, I KNOW-- BUT--I'M HERE NOW!
THIS IS KATY.
SHE SAYS SHE'S MY GIRLFRIEND.
I AM KWAME ERMAN'S FIANCÉE, EISHA SHERMAN.
ONCE HE AND ARE MARRIED, YOU I WILL BE SISTERS.
THAT'S... ADORABLE?
DISTURBING?
I'M NOT SURE?
WELL I DON'T THINK HE'S GOOD ENOUGH FOR HER.
NOBODY ASKED YOU, KID.

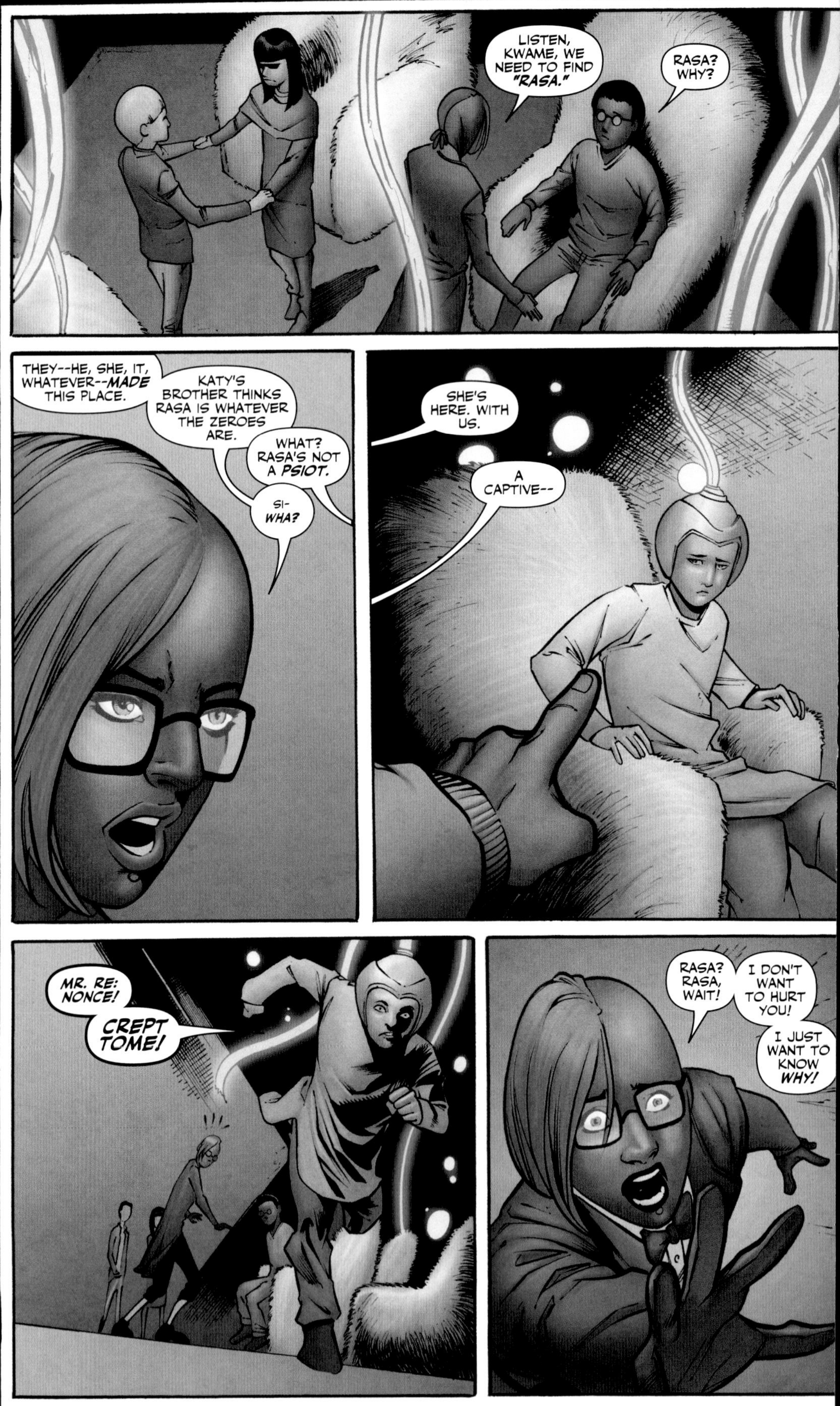
LISTEN, KWAME, WE NEED TO FIND "RASA."
RASA? WHY?
THEY--HE, SHE, IT, WHATEVER--MADE THIS PLACE.
KATY'S BROTHER THINKS RASA IS WHATEVER THE ZEROES ARE.
WHAT? RASA'S NOT A PSIOT.
SI- WHA?
SHE'S HERE. WITH US.
A CAPTIVE--
MR. RE: NONCE!
CREPT TOME!
RASA? RASA, WAIT!
I DON'T WANT TO HURT YOU!
I JUST WANT TO KNOW WHY!

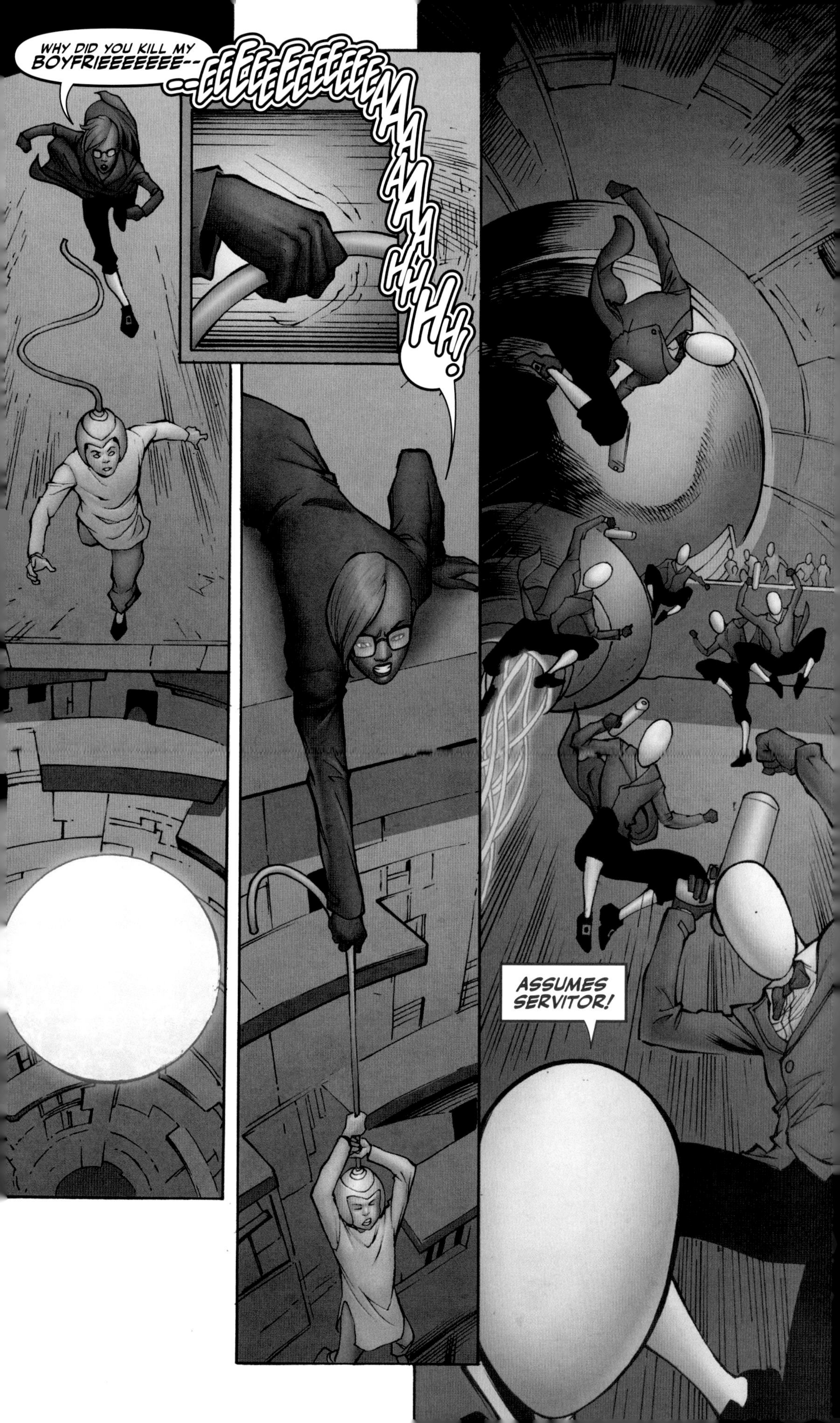
WHY DID YOU KILL MY BOYFRIEEEEEEEE--
--EEEEEEEEEEEEEAAAAAAAHHHHH!
ASSUMES SERVITOR!

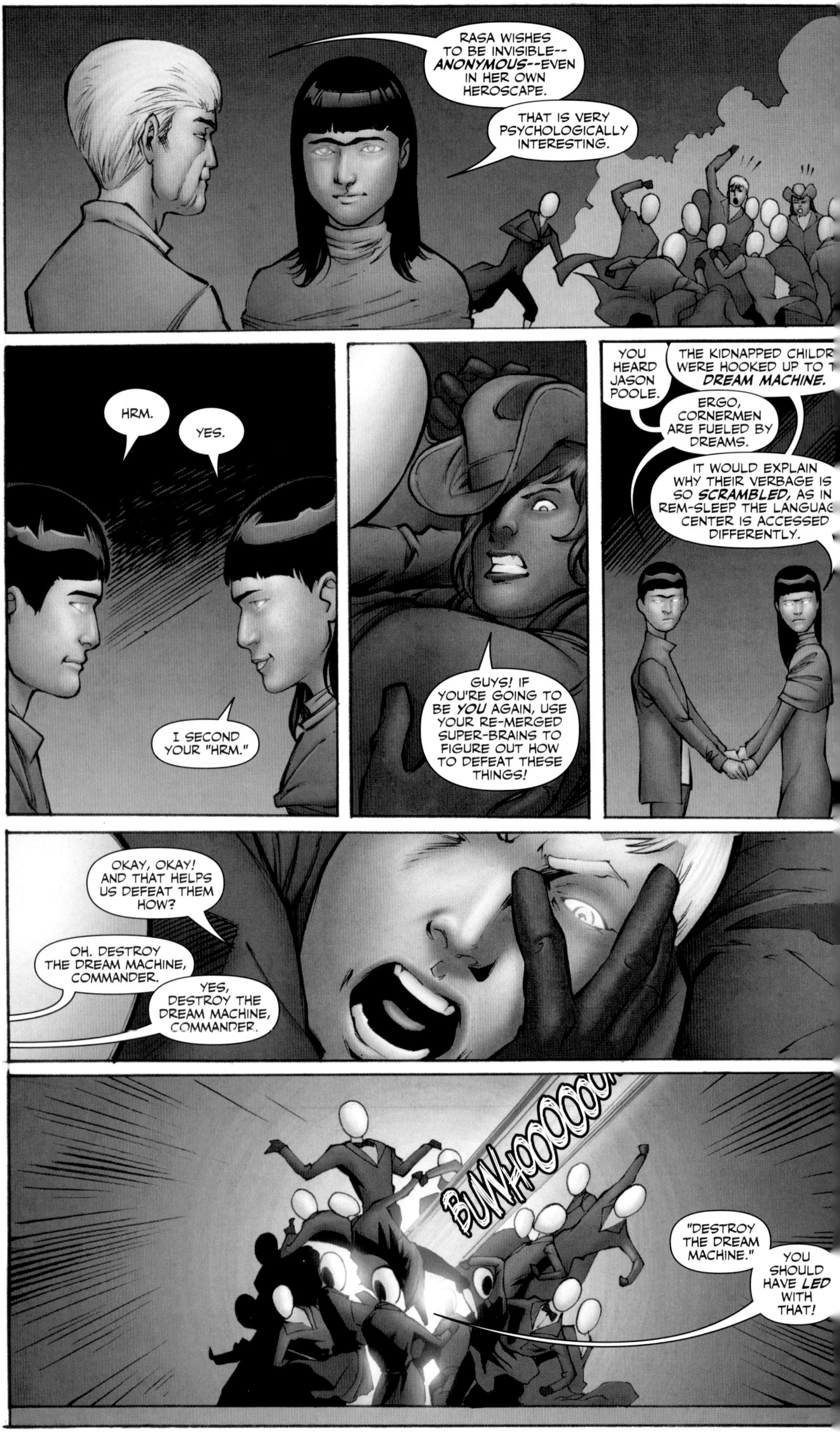
RASA WISHES TO BE INVISIBLE-- ANONYMOUS--EVEN IN HER OWN HEROSCAPE.
THAT IS VERY PSYCHOLOGICALLY INTERESTING.
HRM.
YES.
I SECOND YOUR "HRM."
GUYS! IF YOU'RE GOING TO BE YOU AGAIN, USE YOUR RE-MERGED SUPER-BRAINS TO FIGURE OUT HOW TO DEFEAT THESE THINGS!
YOU HEARD JASON POOLE.
THE KIDNAPPED CHILDR WERE HOOKED UP TO T DREAM MACHINE.
ERGO, CORNERMEN ARE FUELED BY DREAMS.
IT WOULD EXPLAIN WHY THEIR VERBAGE IS SO SCRAMBLED, AS IN REM-SLEEP THE LANGUAG CENTER IS ACCESSED DIFFERENTLY.
OKAY, OKAY! AND THAT HELPS US DEFEAT THEM HOW?
OH. DESTROY THE DREAM MACHINE, COMMANDER.
YES, DESTROY THE DREAM MACHINE, COMMANDER.
BUWHOOOOOO
"DESTROY THE DREAM MACHINE."
YOU SHOULD HAVE LED WITH THAT!

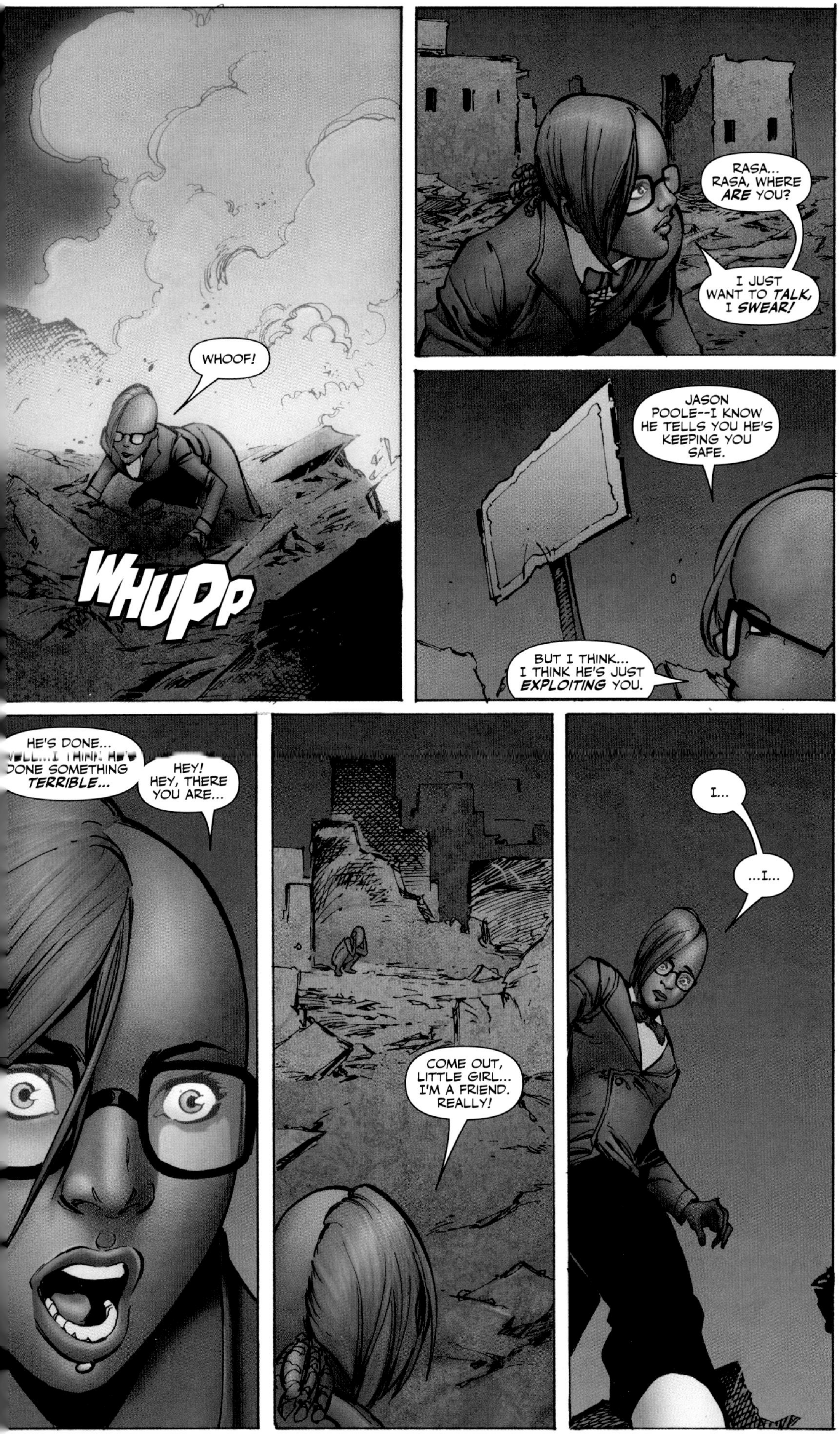
WHOOF!
WHUPP
RASA... RASA, WHERE ARE YOU?
I JUST WANT TO TALK, I SWEAR!
JASON POOLE--I KNOW HE TELLS YOU HE'S KEEPING YOU SAFE.
BUT I THINK... I THINK HE'S JUST EXPLOITING YOU.
HE'S DONE... WELL...I THINK HE'S DONE SOMETHING TERRIBLE...
HEY! HEY, THERE YOU ARE...
COME OUT, LITTLE GIRL... I'M A FRIEND. REALLY!
I...
...I...

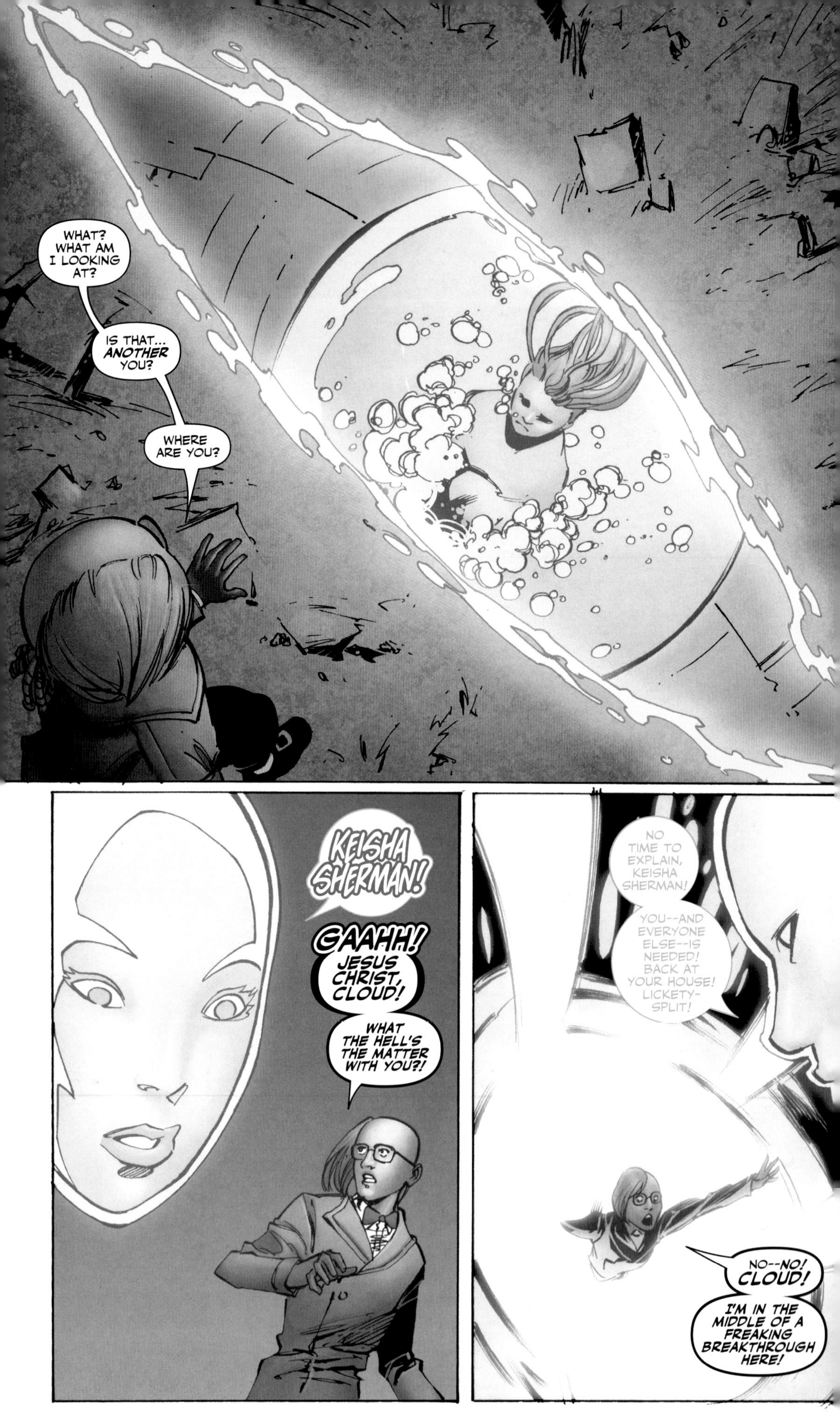
WHAT? WHAT AM I LOOKING AT?
IS THAT... ANOTHER YOU?
WHERE ARE YOU?
KEISHA SHERMAN!
GAAHH! JESUS CHRIST, CLOUD!
WHAT THE HELL'S THE MATTER WITH YOU?!
NO TIME TO EXPLAIN, KEISHA SHERMAN!
YOU--AND EVERYONE ELSE--IS NEEDED! BACK AT YOUR HOUSE! LICKETY-SPLIT!
NO--NO! CLOUD!
I'M IN THE MIDDLE OF A FREAKING BREAKTHROUGH HERE!

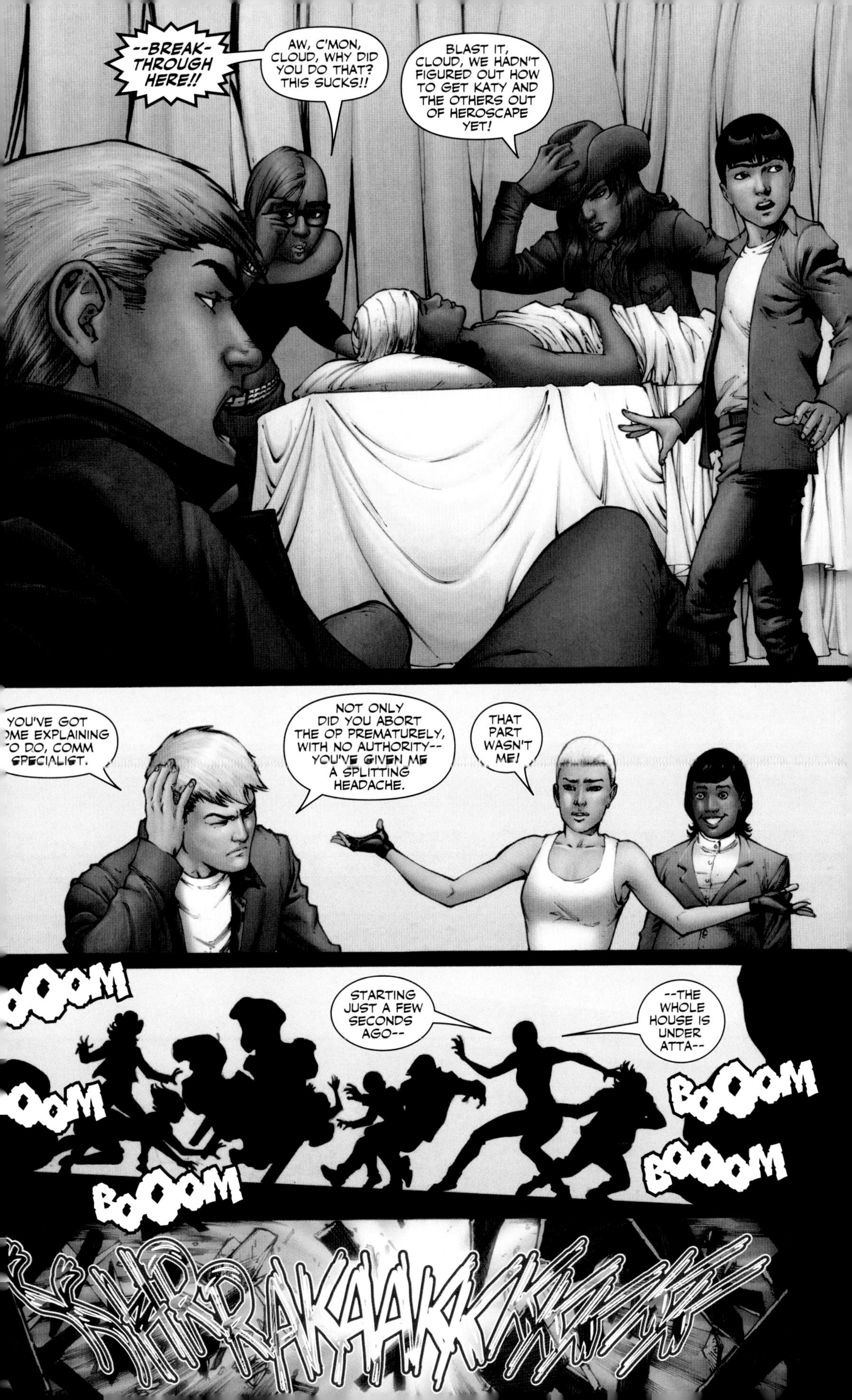
--BREAK-THROUGH HERE!!
AW, C'MON, CLOUD, WHY DID YOU DO THAT? THIS SUCKS!!
BLAST IT, CLOUD, WE HADN'T FIGURED OUT HOW TO GET KATY AND THE OTHERS OUT OF HEROSCAPE YET!
YOU'VE GOT OME EXPLAINING TO DO, COMM SPECIALIST.
NOT ONLY DID YOU ABORT THE OP PREMATURELY, WITH NO AUTHORITY-- YOU'VE GIVEN ME A SPLITTING HEADACHE.
THAT PART WASN'T ME!
OOOM
OOM
STARTING JUST A FEW SECONDS AGO--
--THE WHOLE HOUSE IS UNDER ATTA--
BOOOM
BOOOM
BOOOM
SHRAKAAAKKKK

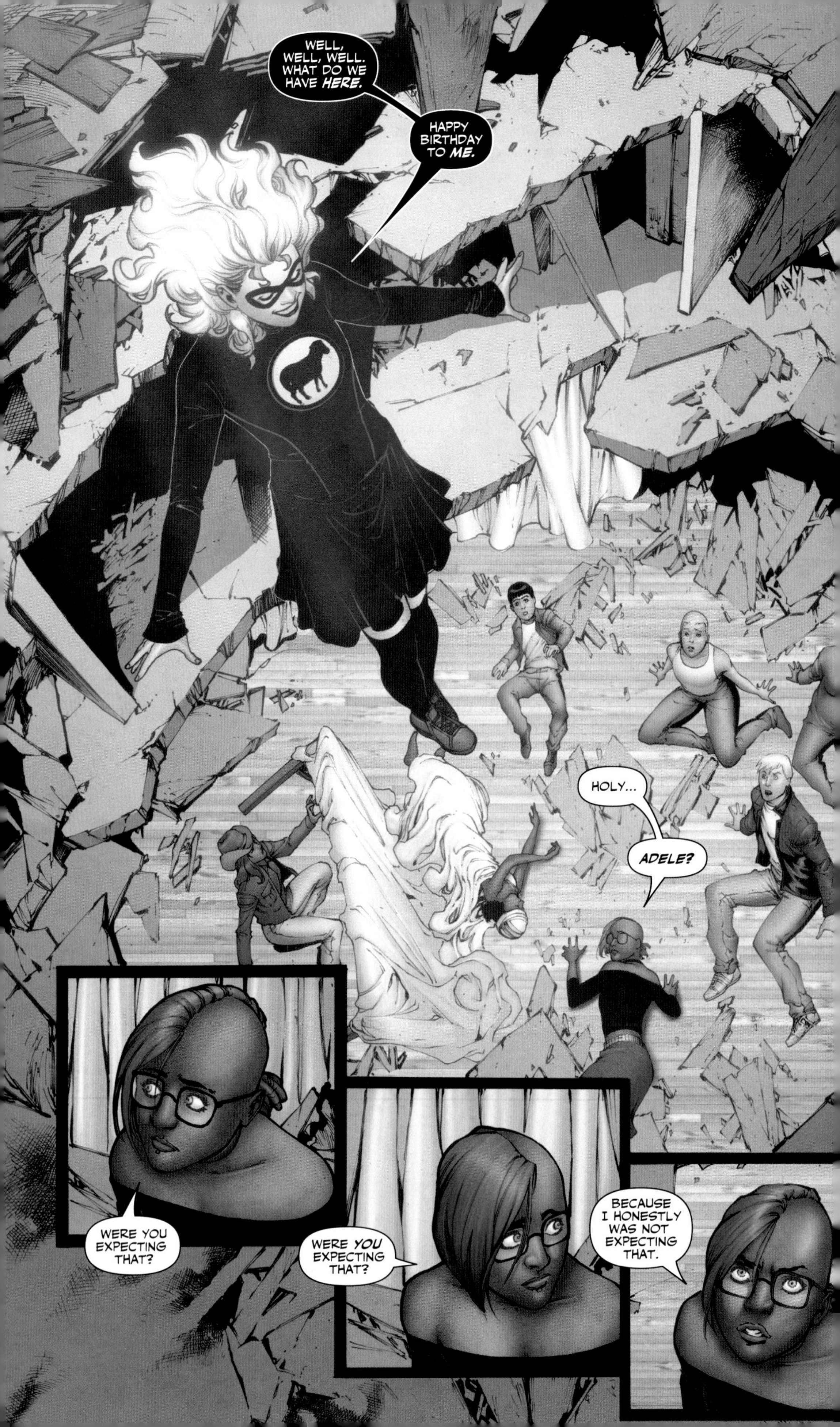
WELL, WELL, WELL. WHAT DO WE HAVE *HERE.*
HAPPY BIRTHDAY TO *ME.*
HOLY...
ADELE?
WERE YOU EXPECTING THAT?
WERE *YOU* EXPECTING THAT?
BECAUSE I HONESTLY WAS NOT EXPECTING THAT.

VALIANT

FRED VAN LENTE | DIEGO BERNARD
JUAN CASTRO | ANDREW DALHOUSE

#8

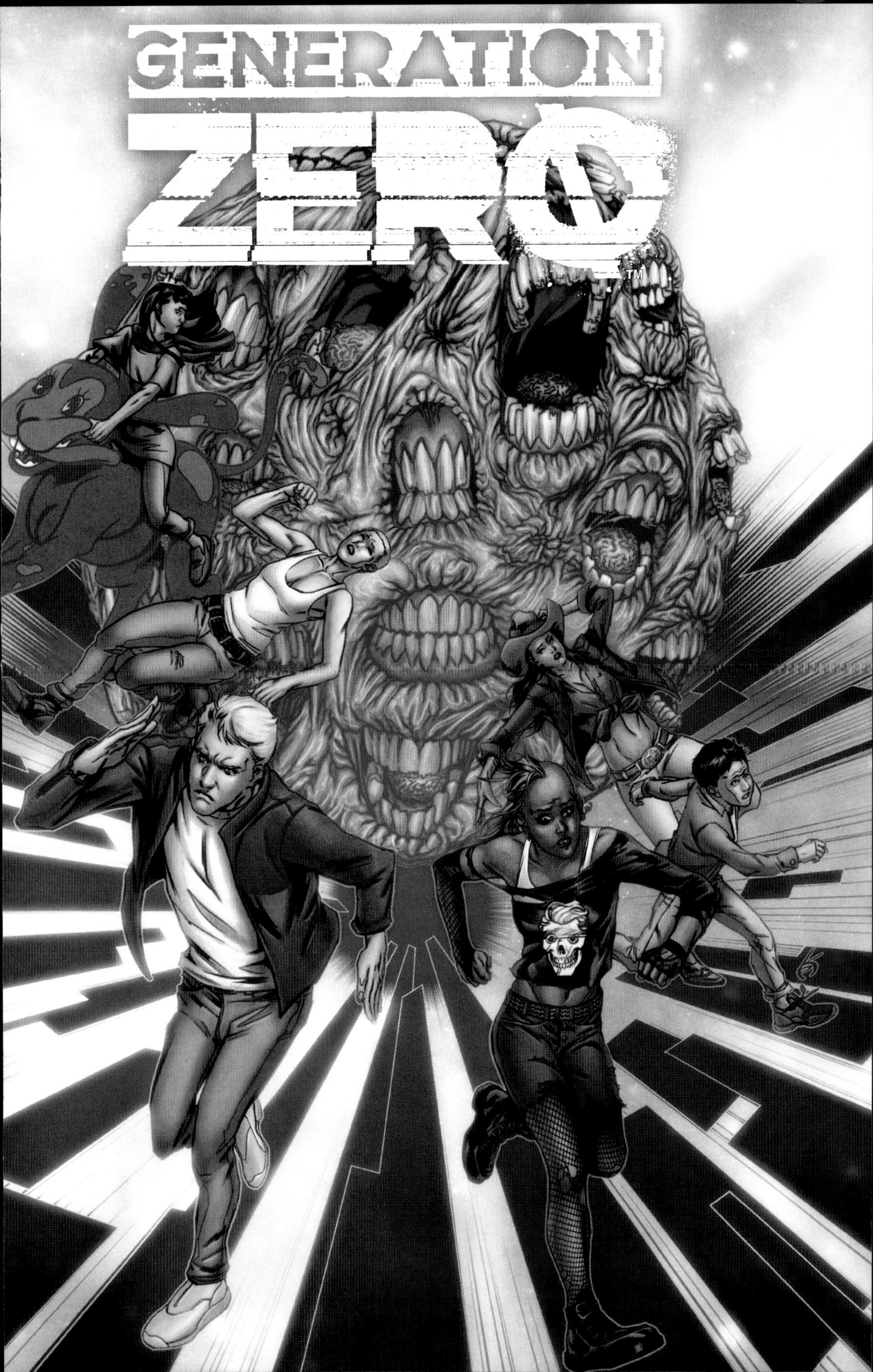
GENERATION
ZERO™

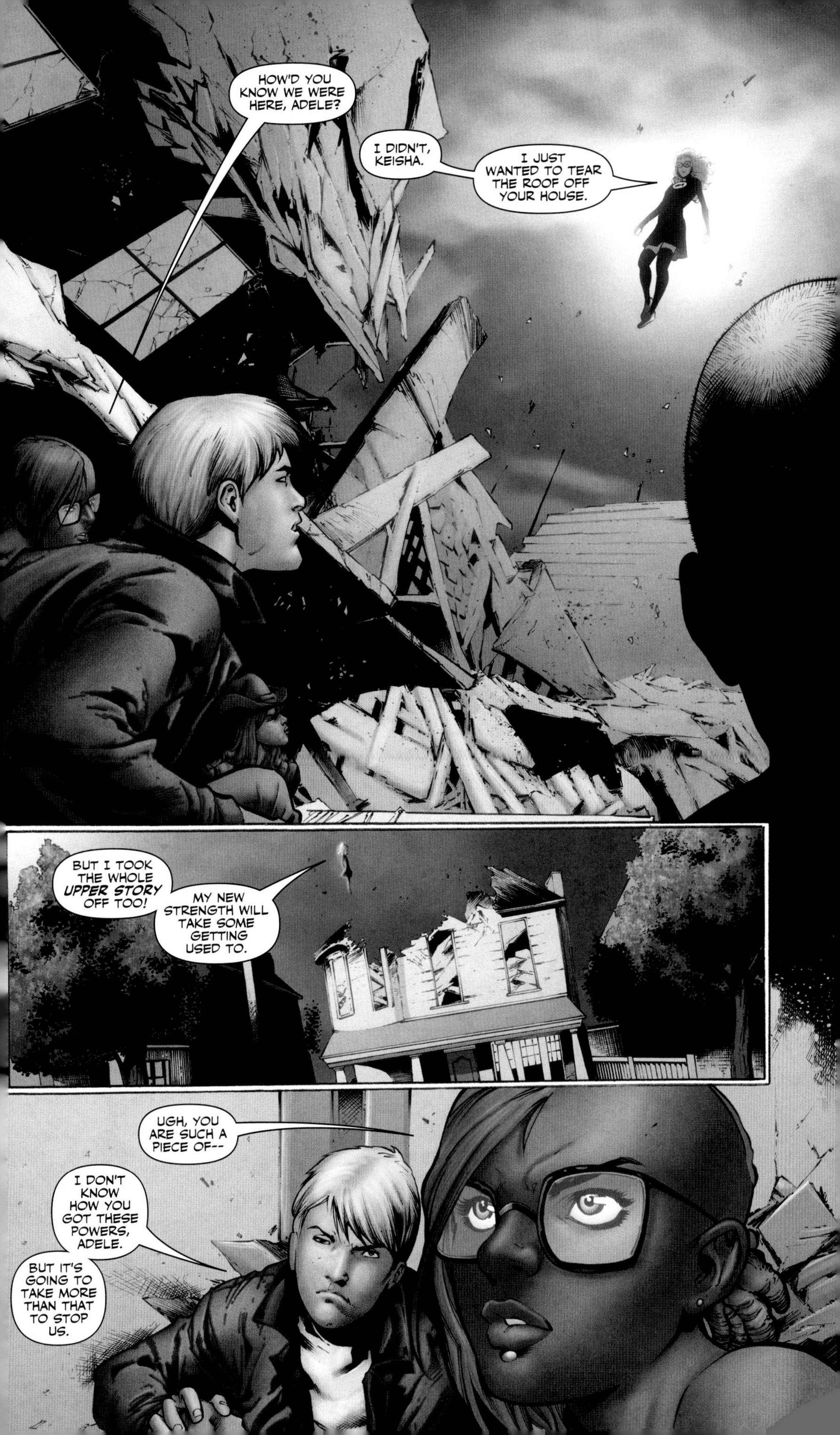
HOW'D YOU KNOW WE WERE HERE, ADELE?
I DIDN'T, KEISHA.
I JUST WANTED TO TEAR THE ROOF OFF YOUR HOUSE.
BUT I TOOK THE WHOLE *UPPER STORY* OFF TOO!
MY NEW STRENGTH WILL TAKE SOME GETTING USED TO.
UGH, YOU ARE SUCH A PIECE OF--
I DON'T KNOW HOW YOU GOT THESE POWERS, ADELE.
BUT IT'S GOING TO TAKE MORE THAN THAT TO STOP US.

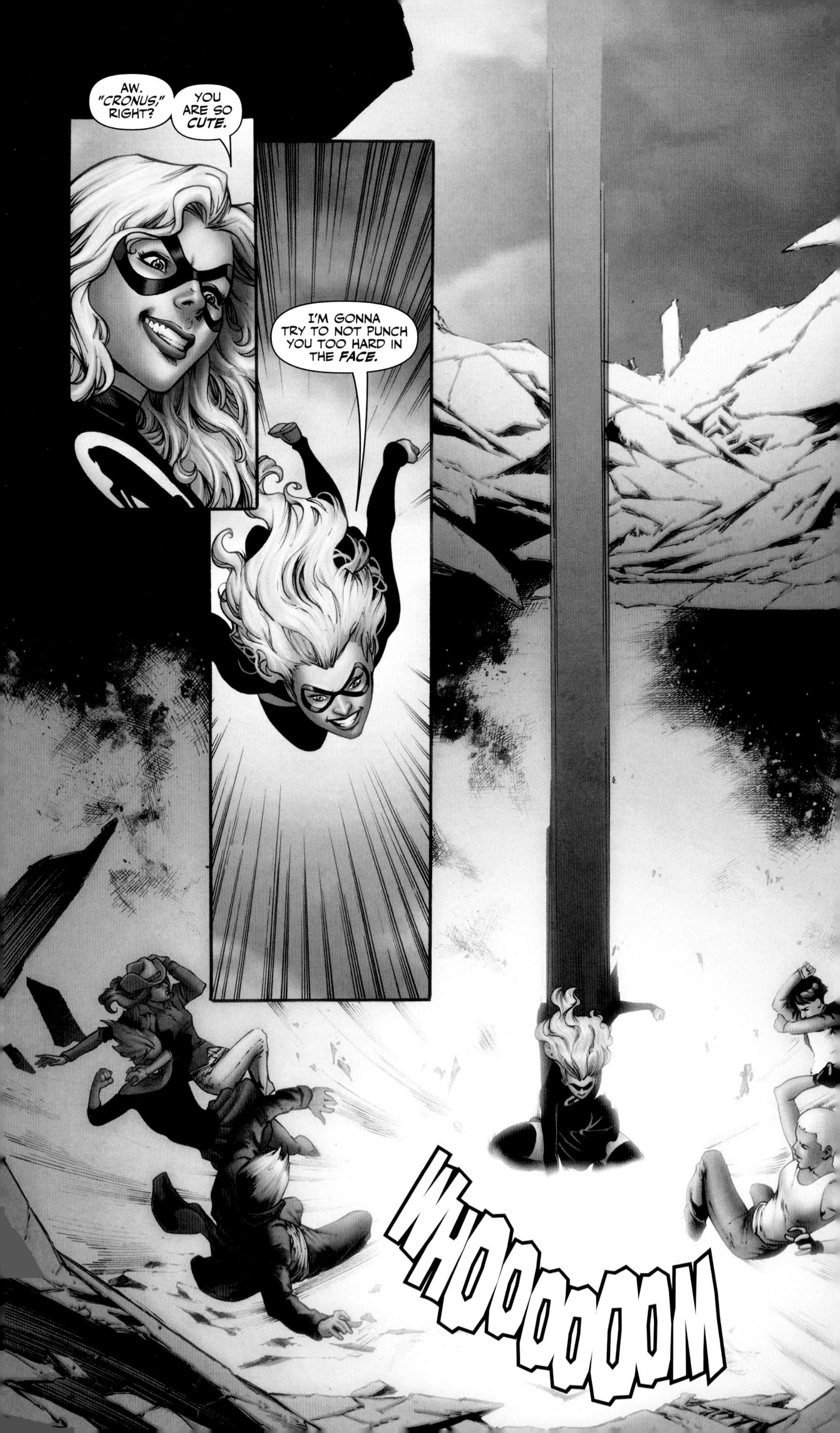
AW. "CRONUS," RIGHT?
YOU ARE SO CUTE.
I'M GONNA TRY TO NOT PUNCH YOU TOO HARD IN THE FACE.
WHOOOOOOM

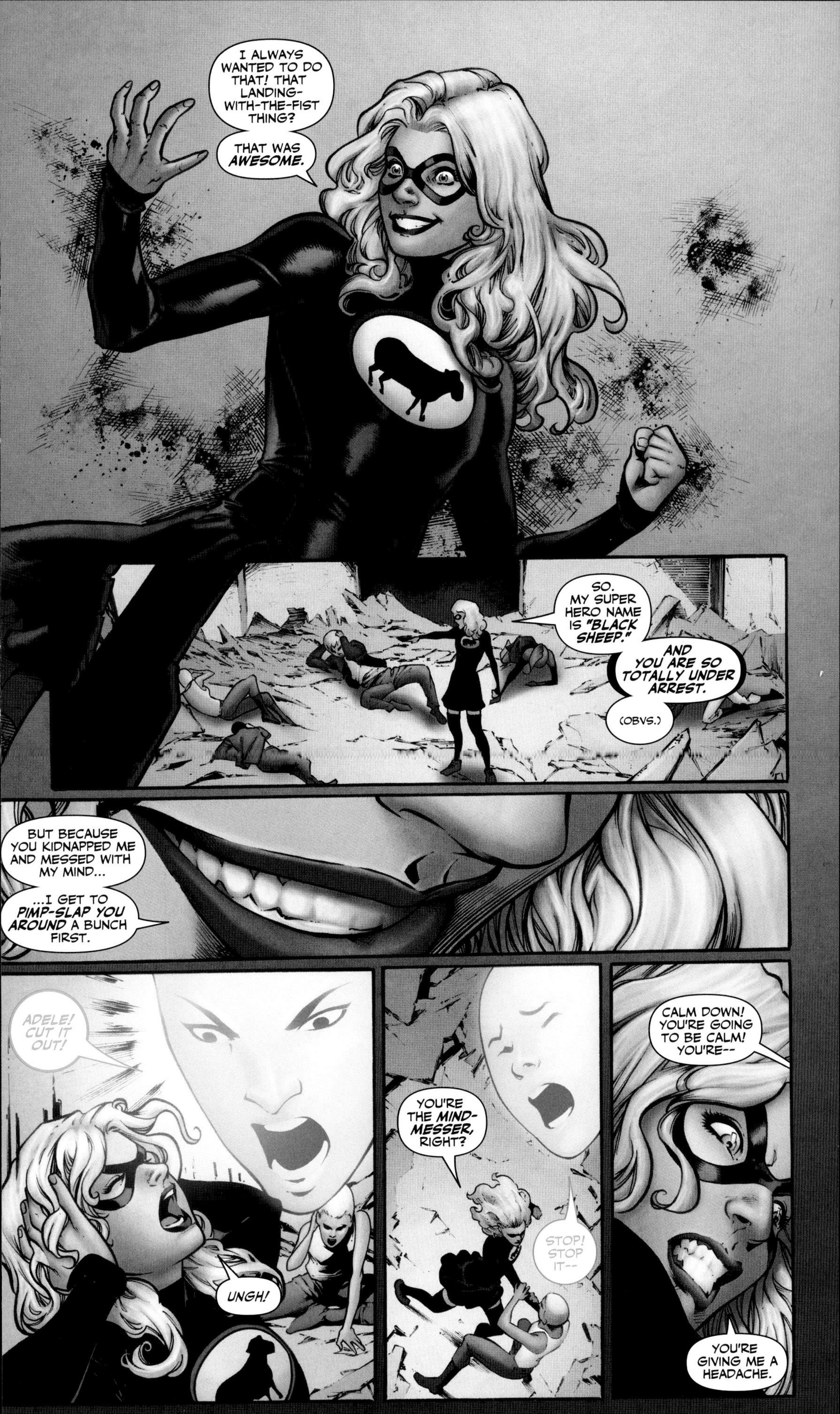
I ALWAYS WANTED TO DO THAT! THAT LANDING-WITH-THE-FIST THING?
THAT WAS AWESOME.
SO. MY SUPER HERO NAME IS "BLACK SHEEP."
AND YOU ARE SO TOTALLY UNDER ARREST.
(OBVS.)
BUT BECAUSE YOU KIDNAPPED ME AND MESSED WITH MY MIND...
...I GET TO PIMP-SLAP YOU AROUND A BUNCH FIRST.
ADELE! CUT IT OUT!
UNGH!
YOU'RE THE MIND-MESSER, RIGHT?
STOP! STOP IT--
CALM DOWN! YOU'RE GOING TO BE CALM! YOU'RE--
YOU'RE GIVING ME A HEADACHE.

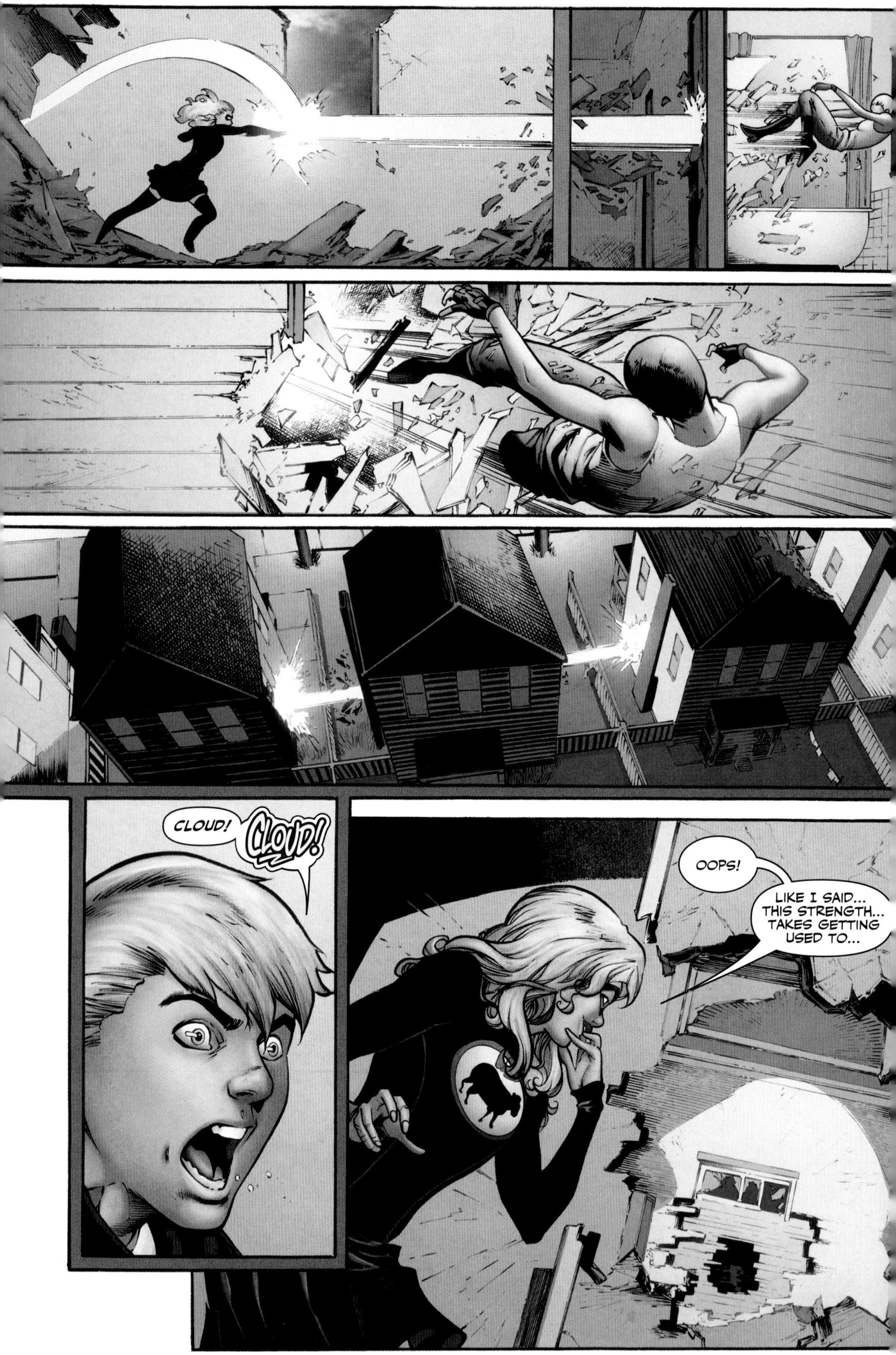
CLOUD!
CLOUD!
OOPS!
LIKE I SAID... THIS STRENGTH... TAKES GETTING USED TO...

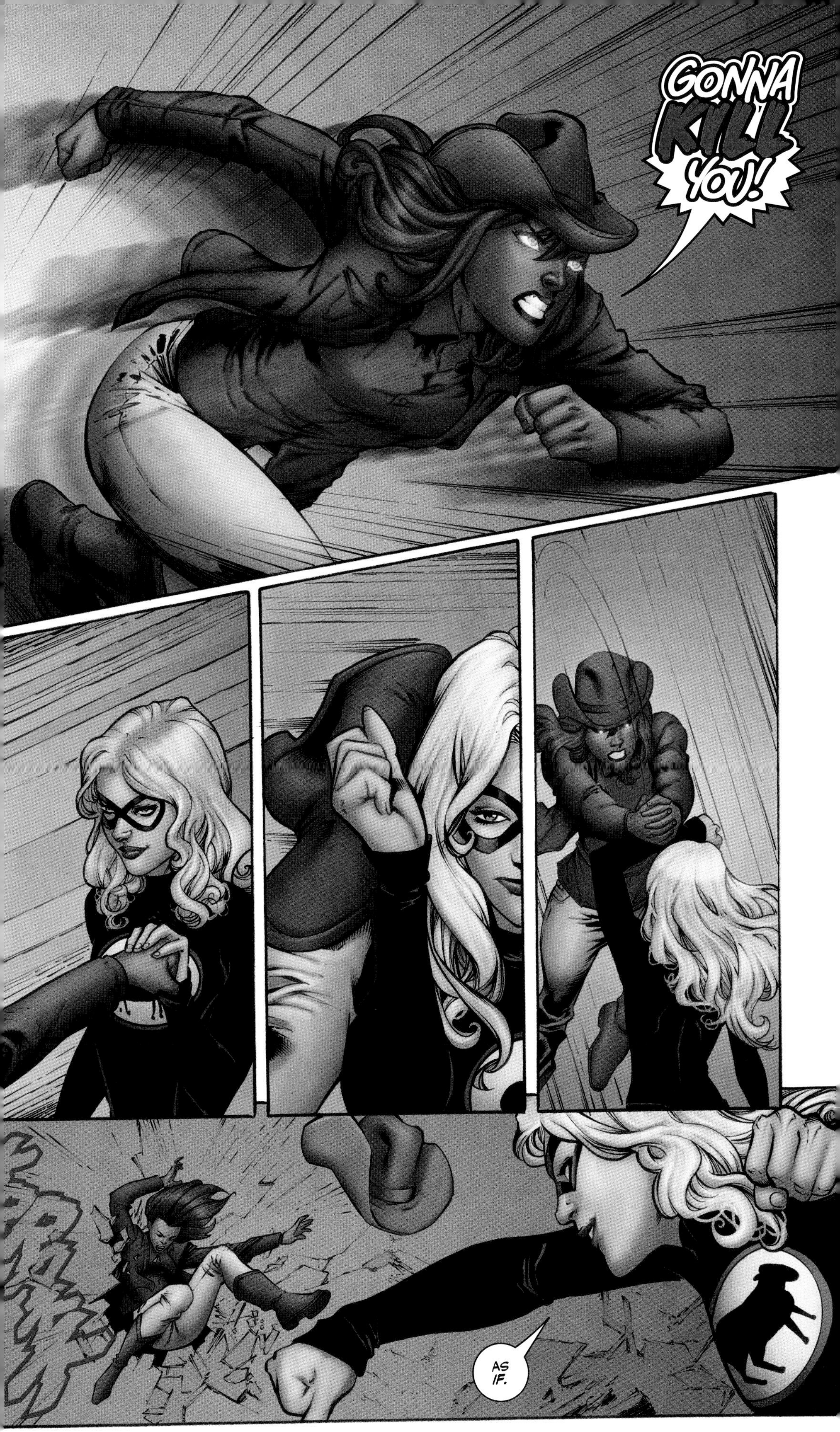
GONNA KILL YOU!
AS IF.

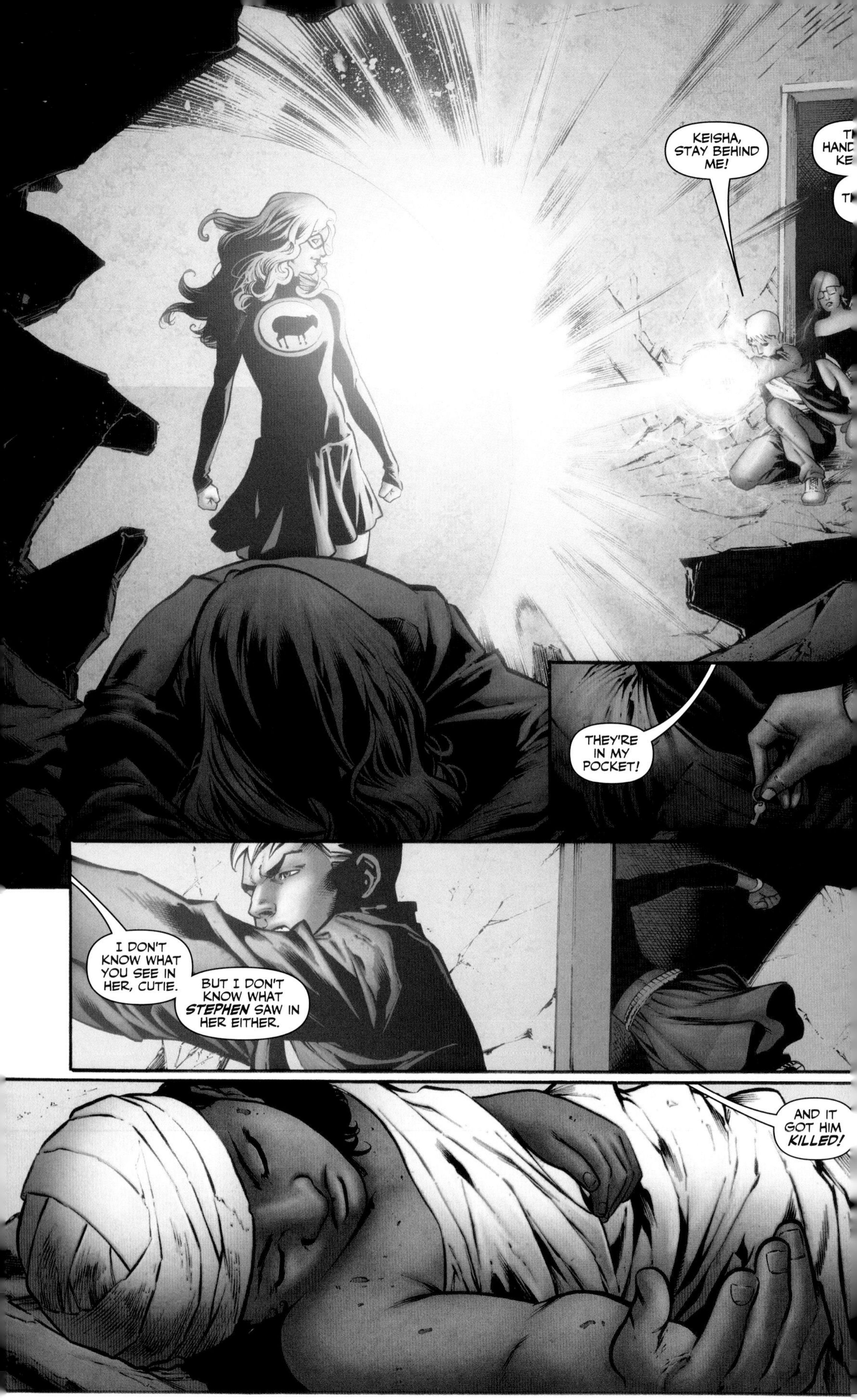
KEISHA, STAY BEHIND ME!
THEY'RE IN MY POCKET!
I DON'T KNOW WHAT YOU SEE IN HER, CUTIE.
BUT I DON'T KNOW WHAT STEPHEN SAW IN HER EITHER.
AND IT GOT HIM KILLED!

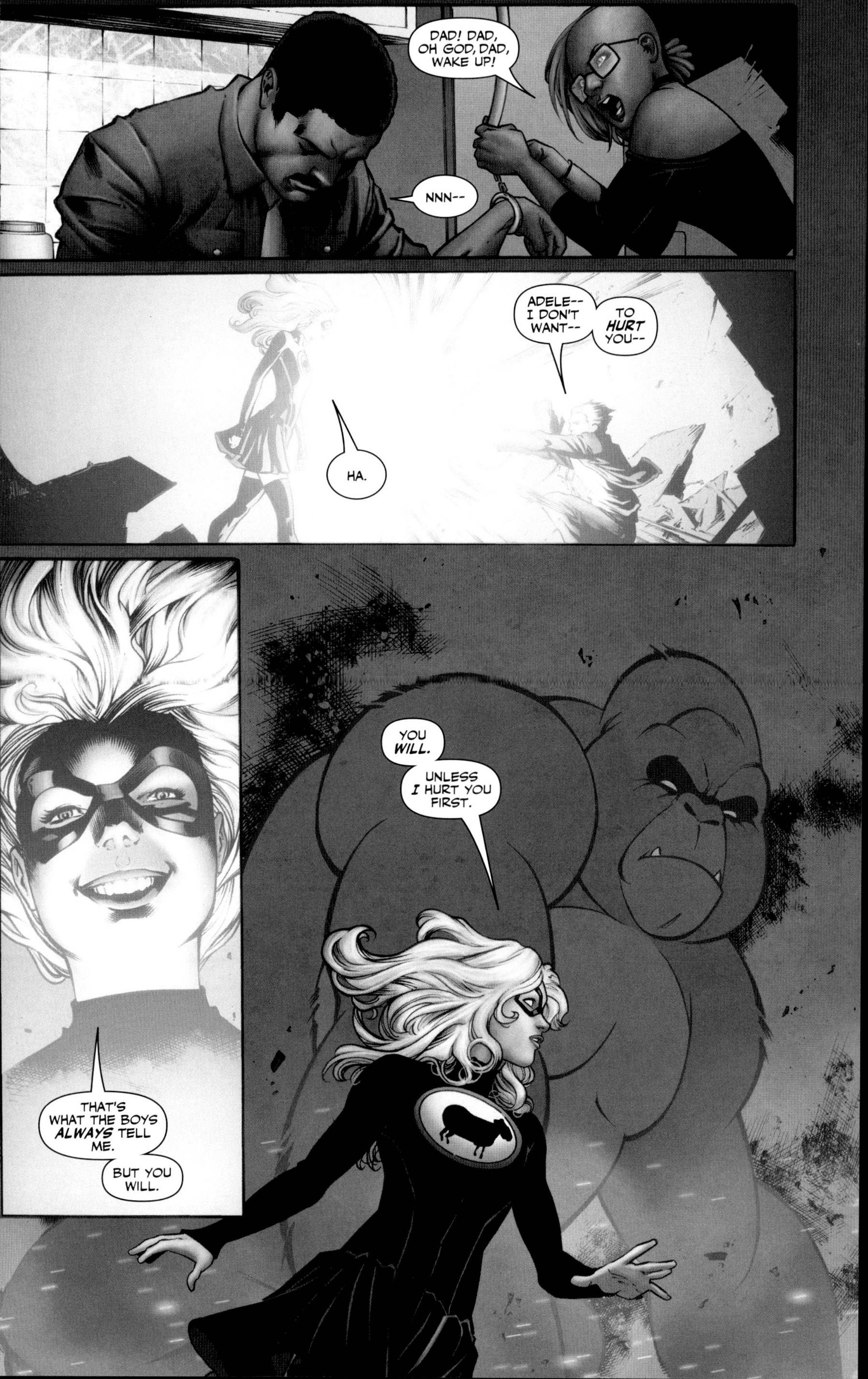
DAD! DAD, OH GOD, DAD, WAKE UP!
NNN--
ADELE-- I DON'T WANT--
TO *HURT* YOU--
HA.
YOU *WILL.*
UNLESS *I* HURT YOU FIRST.
THAT'S WHAT THE BOYS *ALWAYS* TELL ME.
BUT YOU WILL.

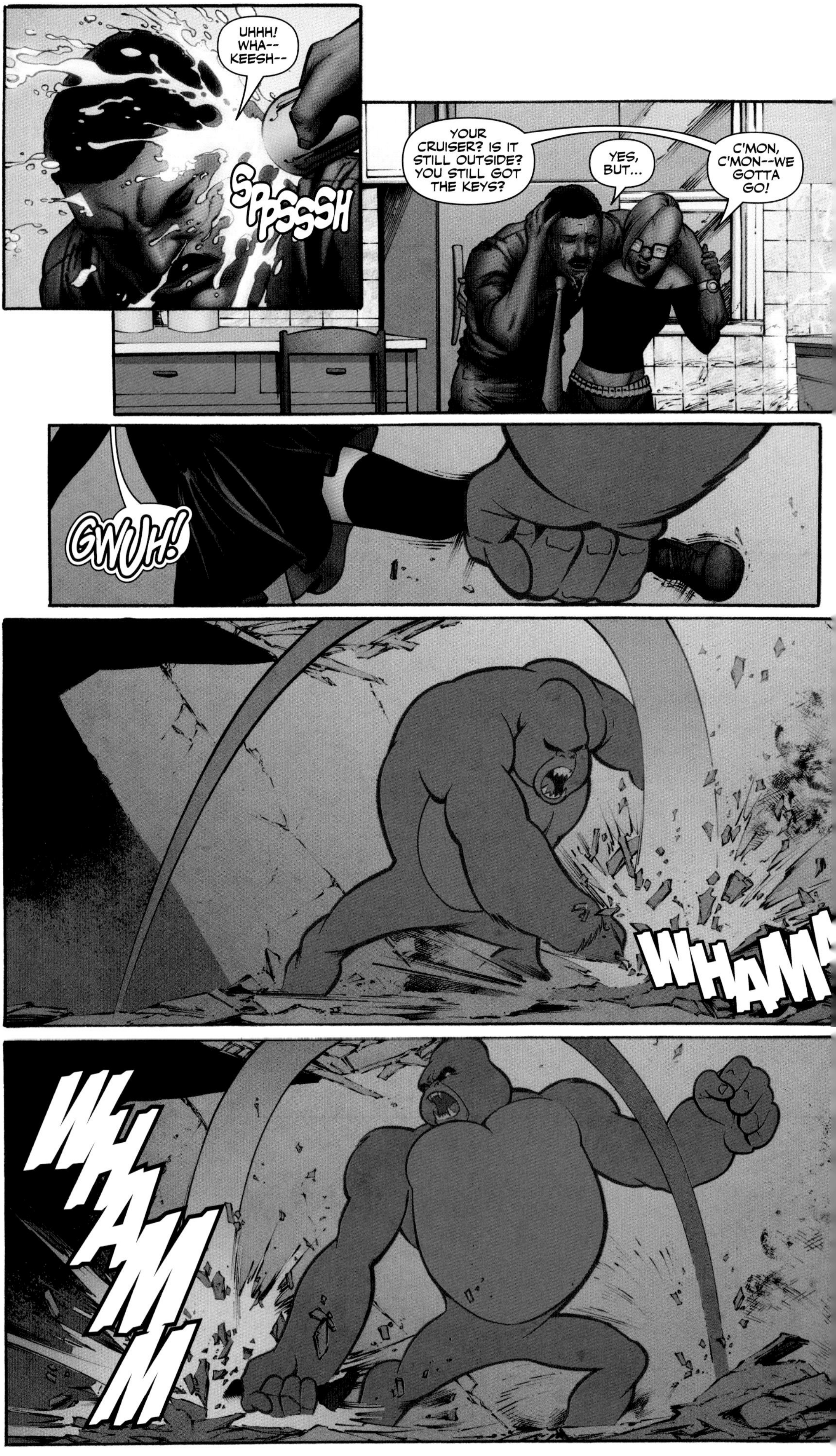
UHHH! WHA-- KEESH--
SPPSSSH
YOUR CRUISER? IS IT STILL OUTSIDE? YOU STILL GOT THE KEYS?
YES, BUT...
C'MON, C'MON--WE GOTTA GO!
GWUH!
WHAM
WHAM

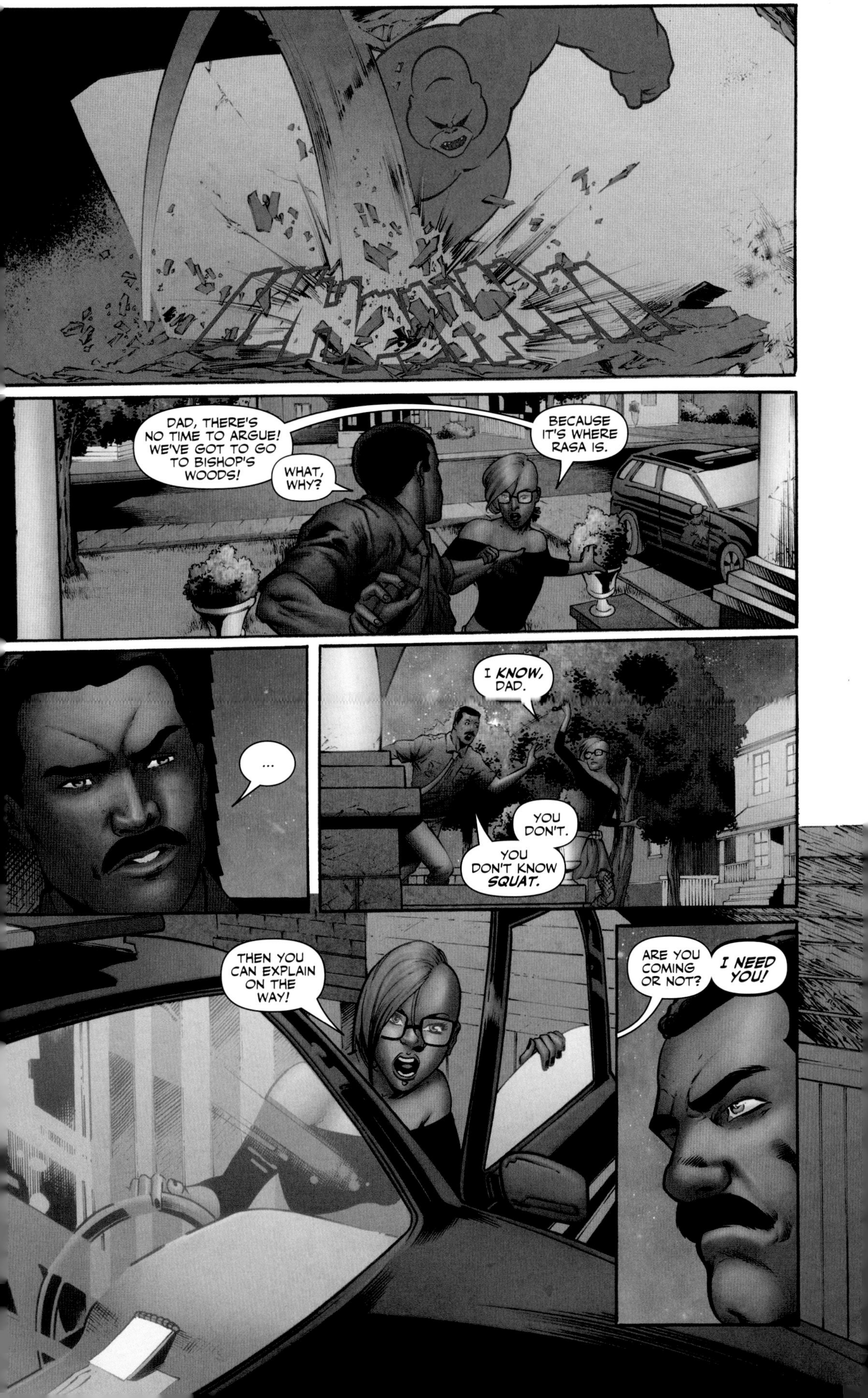
DAD, THERE'S NO TIME TO ARGUE! WE'VE GOT TO GO TO BISHOP'S WOODS!
WHAT, WHY?
BECAUSE IT'S WHERE RASA IS.
...
I KNOW, DAD.
YOU DON'T.
YOU DON'T KNOW SQUAT.
THEN YOU CAN EXPLAIN ON THE WAY!
ARE YOU COMING OR NOT?
I NEED YOU!

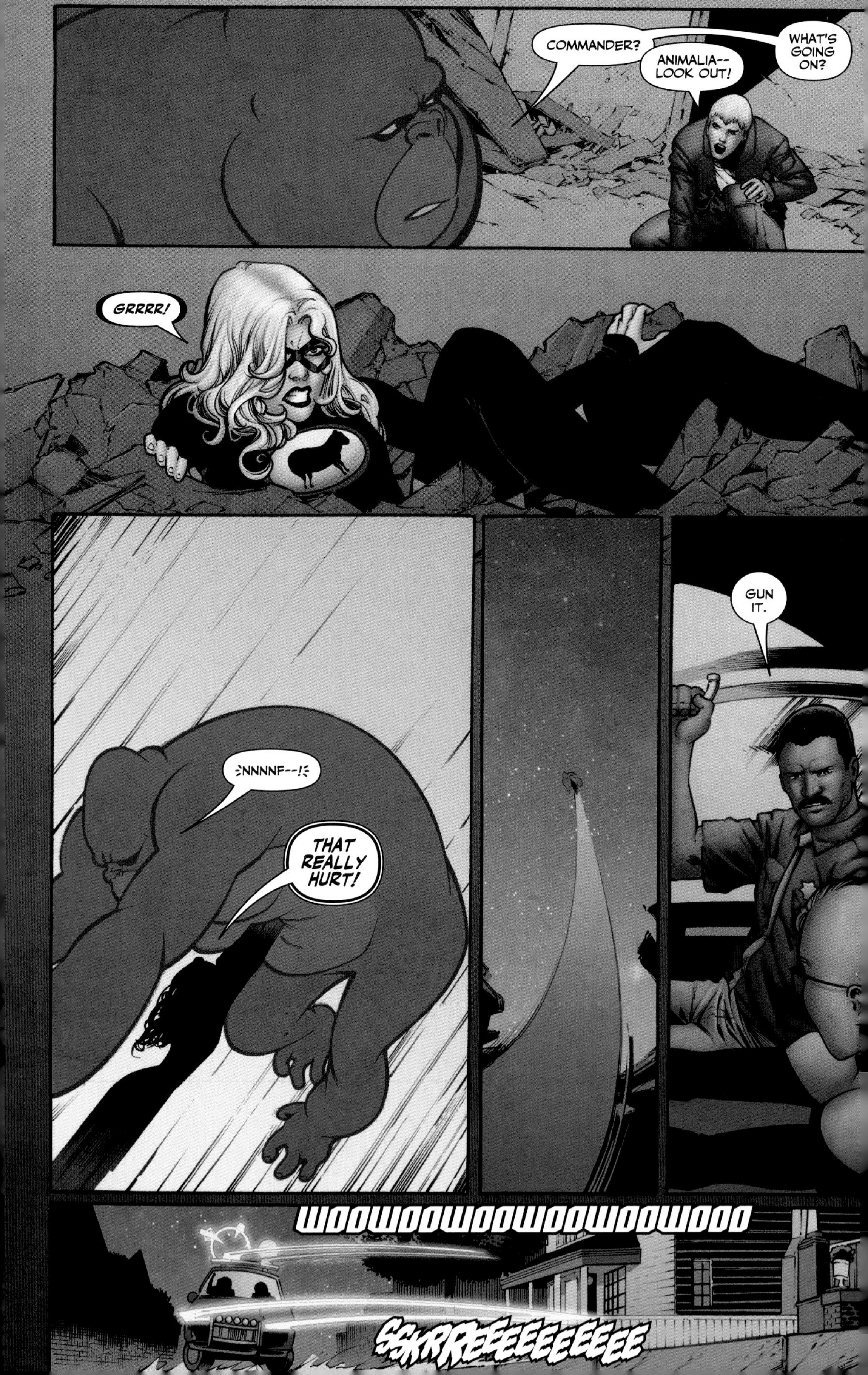

COMMANDER?
WHAT'S GOING ON?
ANIMALIA-- LOOK OUT!
GRRRR!
NNNNF--!
THAT REALLY HURT!
GUN IT.
WOOWOOWOOWOOWOOWOOO
SSKRREEEEEEEEEEEE

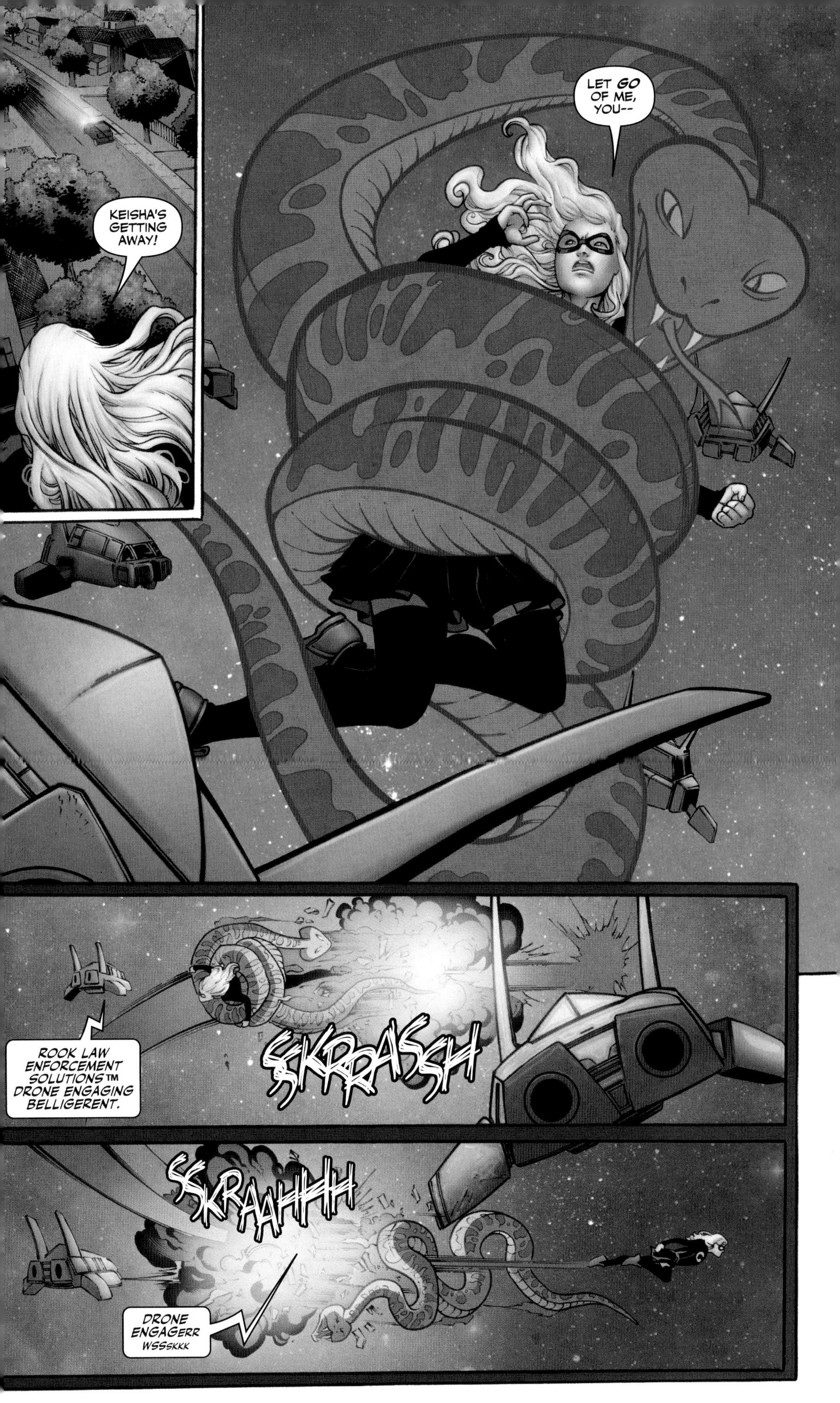
KEISHA'S GETTING AWAY!
LET GO OF ME, YOU--
ROOK LAW ENFORCEMENT SOLUTIONS™ DRONE ENGAGING BELLIGERENT.
SKRASSH
SSKRAAHHH
DRONE ENGAGERR WSSSKKK

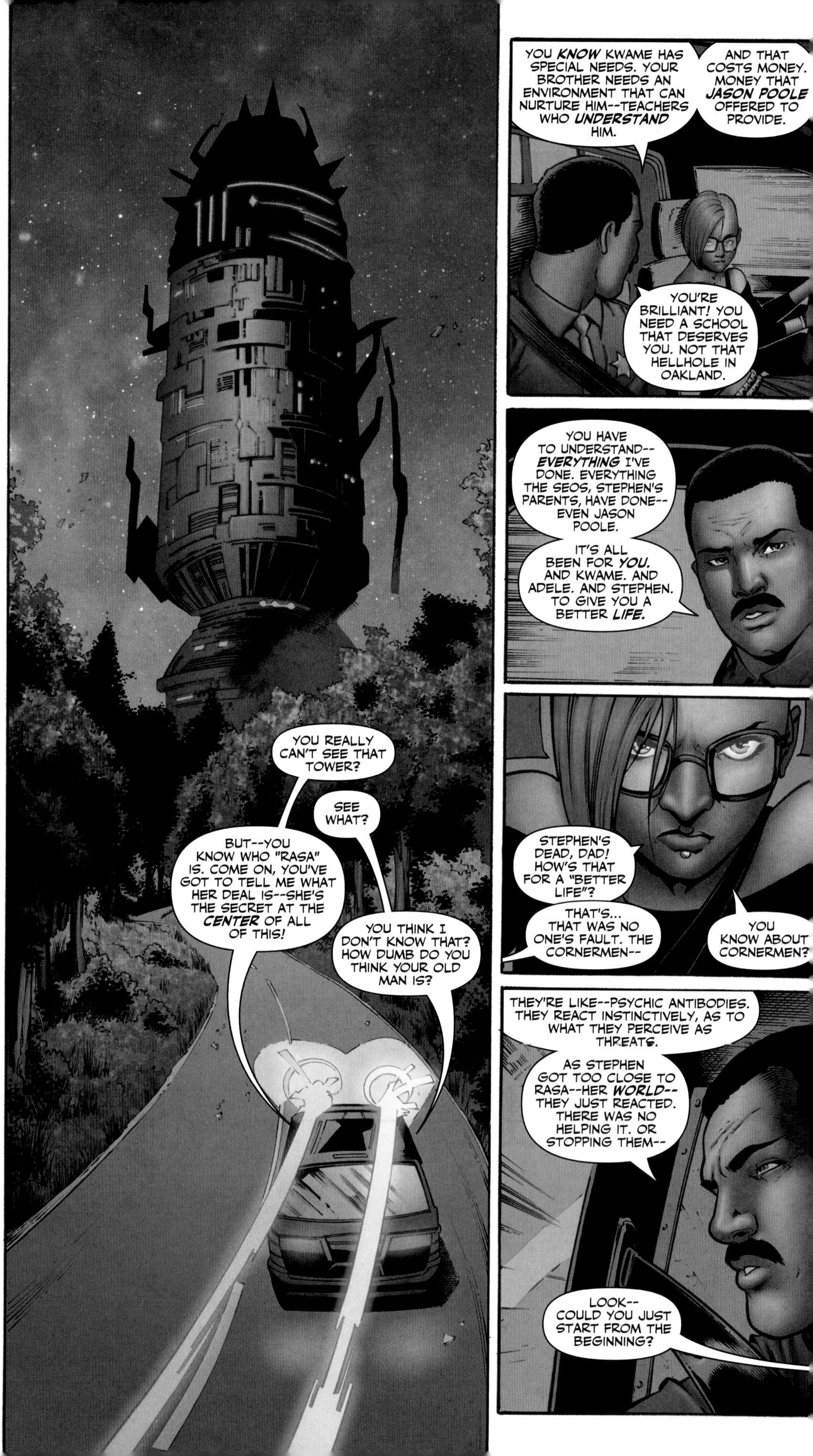
YOU REALLY CAN'T SEE THAT TOWER?
SEE WHAT?
BUT--YOU KNOW WHO "RASA" IS. COME ON, YOU'VE GOT TO TELL ME WHAT HER DEAL IS--SHE'S THE SECRET AT THE CENTER OF ALL OF THIS!
YOU THINK I DON'T KNOW THAT? HOW DUMB DO YOU THINK YOUR OLD MAN IS?
YOU KNOW KWAME HAS SPECIAL NEEDS. YOUR BROTHER NEEDS AN ENVIRONMENT THAT CAN NURTURE HIM--TEACHERS WHO UNDERSTAND HIM.
AND THAT COSTS MONEY. MONEY THAT JASON POOLE OFFERED TO PROVIDE.
YOU'RE BRILLIANT! YOU NEED A SCHOOL THAT DESERVES YOU. NOT THAT HELLHOLE IN OAKLAND.
YOU HAVE TO UNDERSTAND--EVERYTHING I'VE DONE. EVERYTHING THE SEOS, STEPHEN'S PARENTS, HAVE DONE--EVEN JASON POOLE.
IT'S ALL BEEN FOR YOU. AND KWAME. AND ADELE. AND STEPHEN. TO GIVE YOU A BETTER LIFE.
STEPHEN'S DEAD, DAD! HOW'S THAT FOR A "BETTER LIFE"?
THAT'S... THAT WAS NO ONE'S FAULT. THE CORNERMEN--
YOU KNOW ABOUT CORNERMEN?
THEY'RE LIKE--PSYCHIC ANTIBODIES. THEY REACT INSTINCTIVELY, AS TO WHAT THEY PERCEIVE AS THREATS.
AS STEPHEN GOT TOO CLOSE TO RASA--HER WORLD--THEY JUST REACTED. THERE WAS NO HELPING IT. OR STOPPING THEM--
LOOK--COULD YOU JUST START FROM THE BEGINNING?

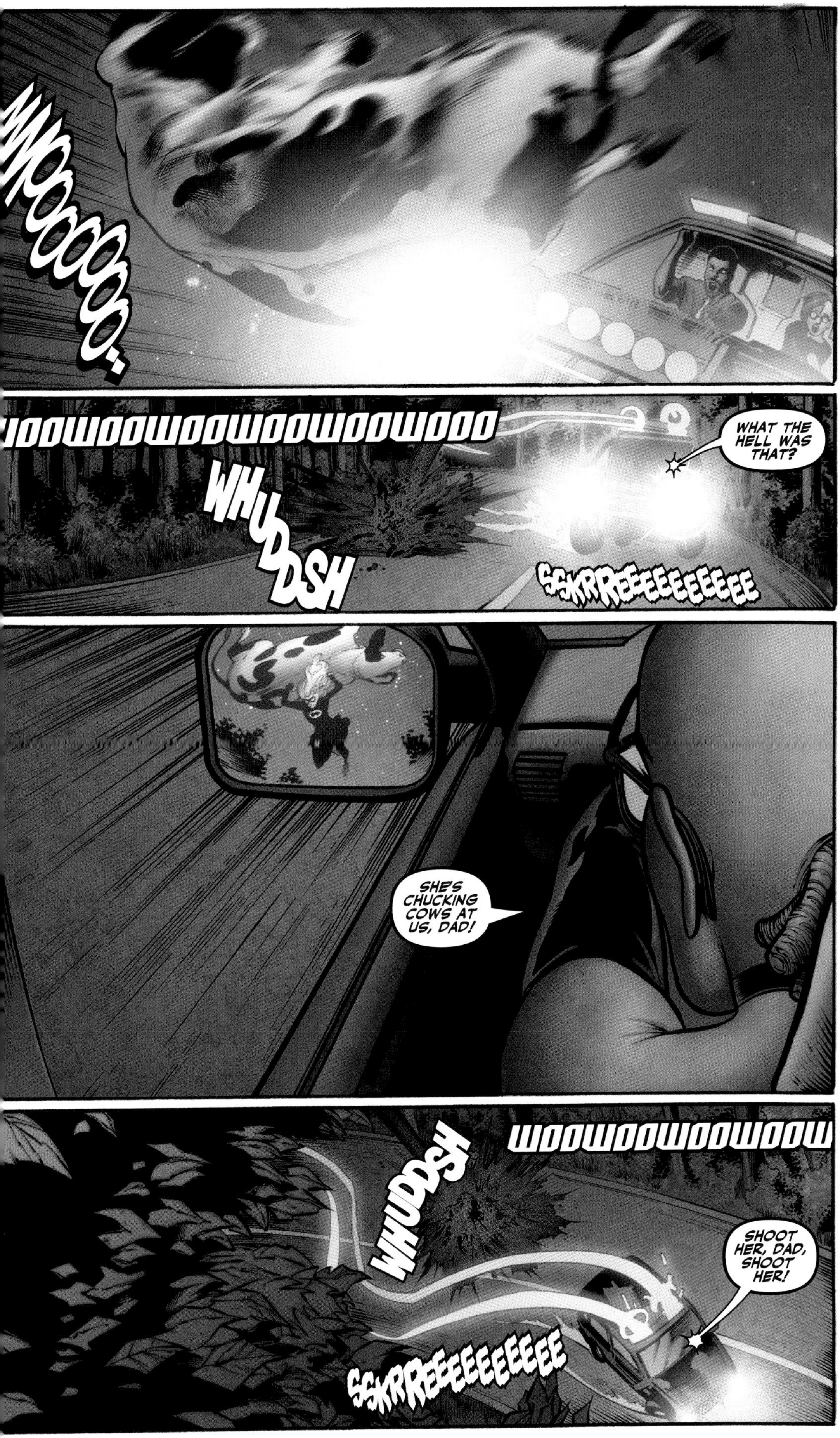
MOOOOOOO...
WOOWOOWOOWOOWOOWOOO
WHUDDSH
WHAT THE HELL WAS THAT?
SSKRREEEEEEEEEEE
SHE'S CHUCKING COWS AT US, DAD!
WOOWOOWOOWOOW
WHUDDSH
SHOOT HER, DAD, SHOOT HER!
SSKRREEEEEEEEEEE

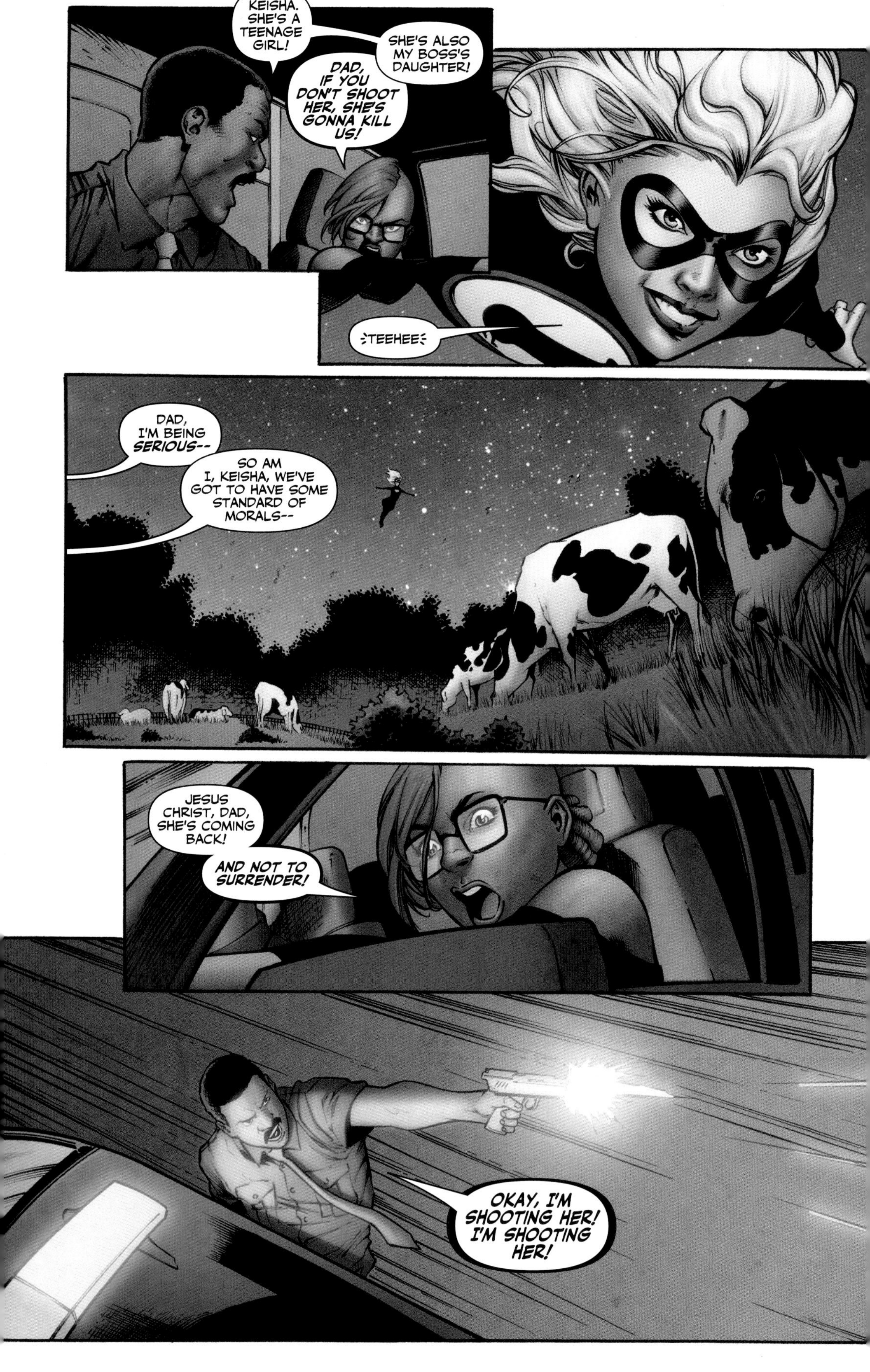
KEISHA. SHE'S A TEENAGE GIRL!
SHE'S ALSO MY BOSS'S DAUGHTER!
DAD, IF YOU DON'T SHOOT HER, SHE'S GONNA KILL US!
TEEHEE
DAD, I'M BEING SERIOUS--
SO AM I, KEISHA, WE'VE GOT TO HAVE SOME STANDARD OF MORALS--
JESUS CHRIST, DAD, SHE'S COMING BACK!
AND NOT TO SURRENDER!
OKAY, I'M SHOOTING HER! I'M SHOOTING HER!

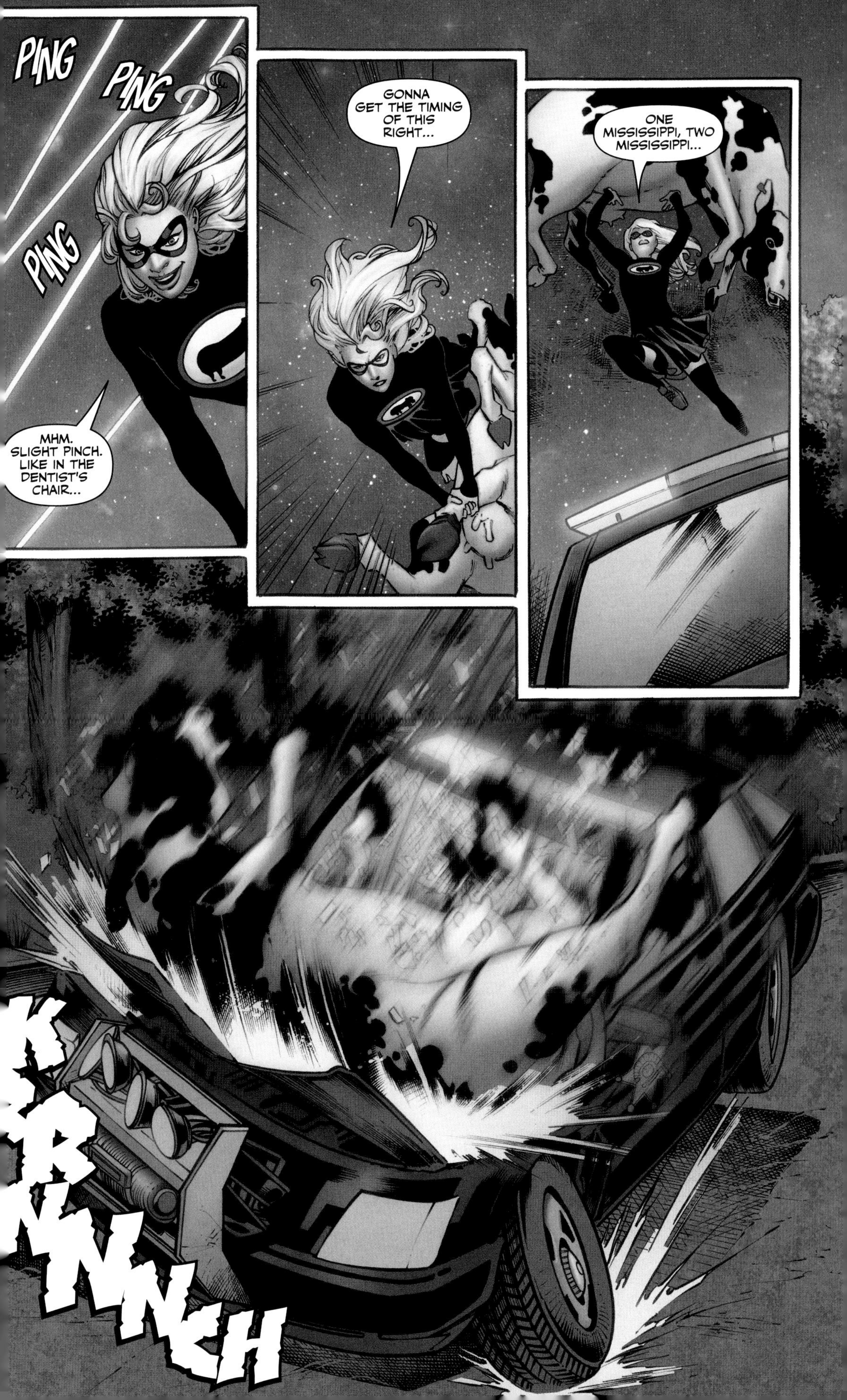
PING
PING
PING
MHM. SLIGHT PINCH. LIKE IN THE DENTIST'S CHAIR...
GONNA GET THE TIMING OF THIS RIGHT...
ONE MISSISSIPPI, TWO MISSISSIPPI...
KRNNNCH

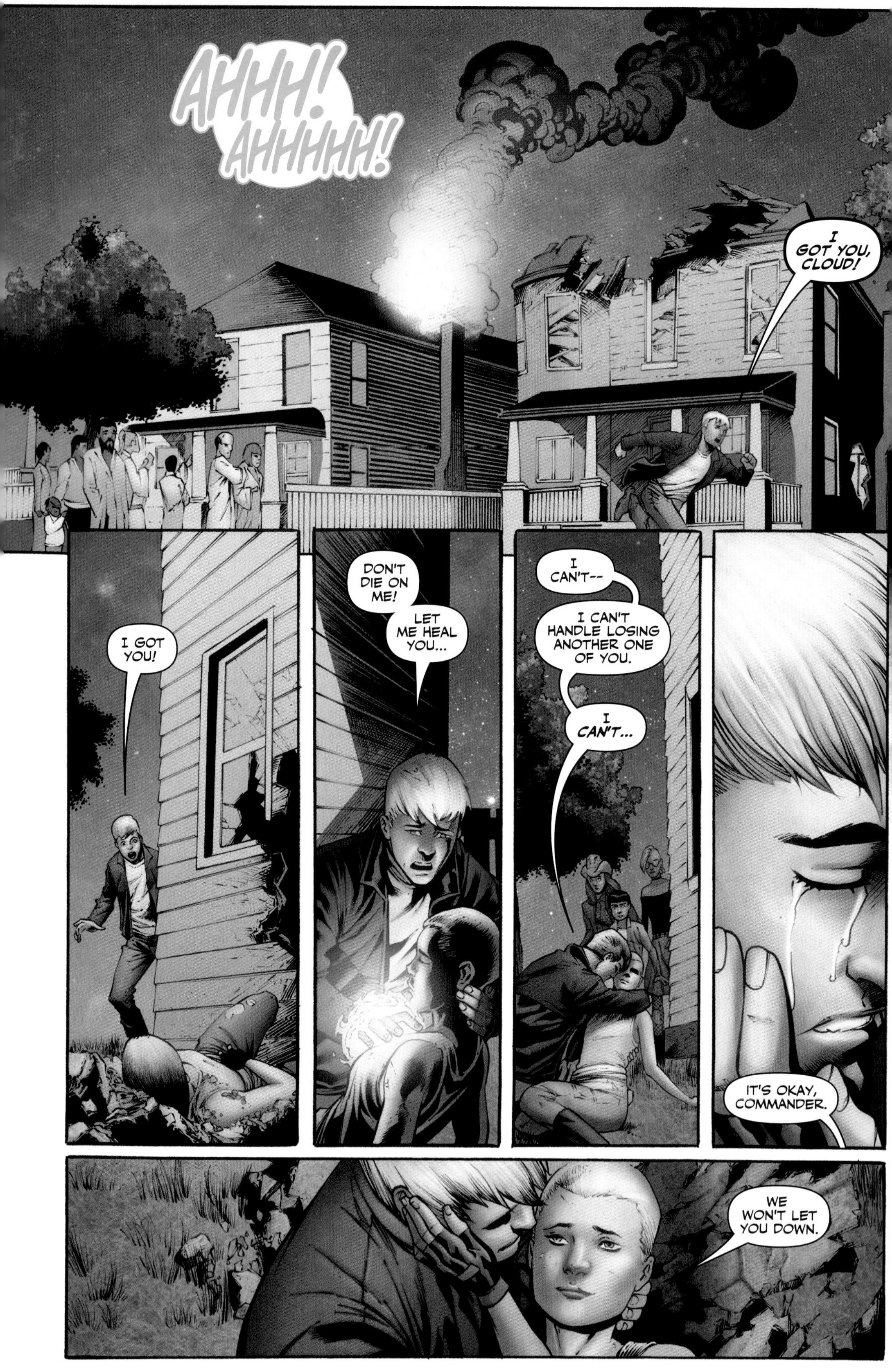
AHHH! AHHHHH!
I GOT YOU, CLOUD!
I GOT YOU!
DON'T DIE ON ME!
LET ME HEAL YOU...
I CAN'T--
I CAN'T HANDLE LOSING ANOTHER ONE OF YOU.
I CAN'T...
IT'S OKAY, COMMANDER.
WE WON'T LET YOU DOWN.

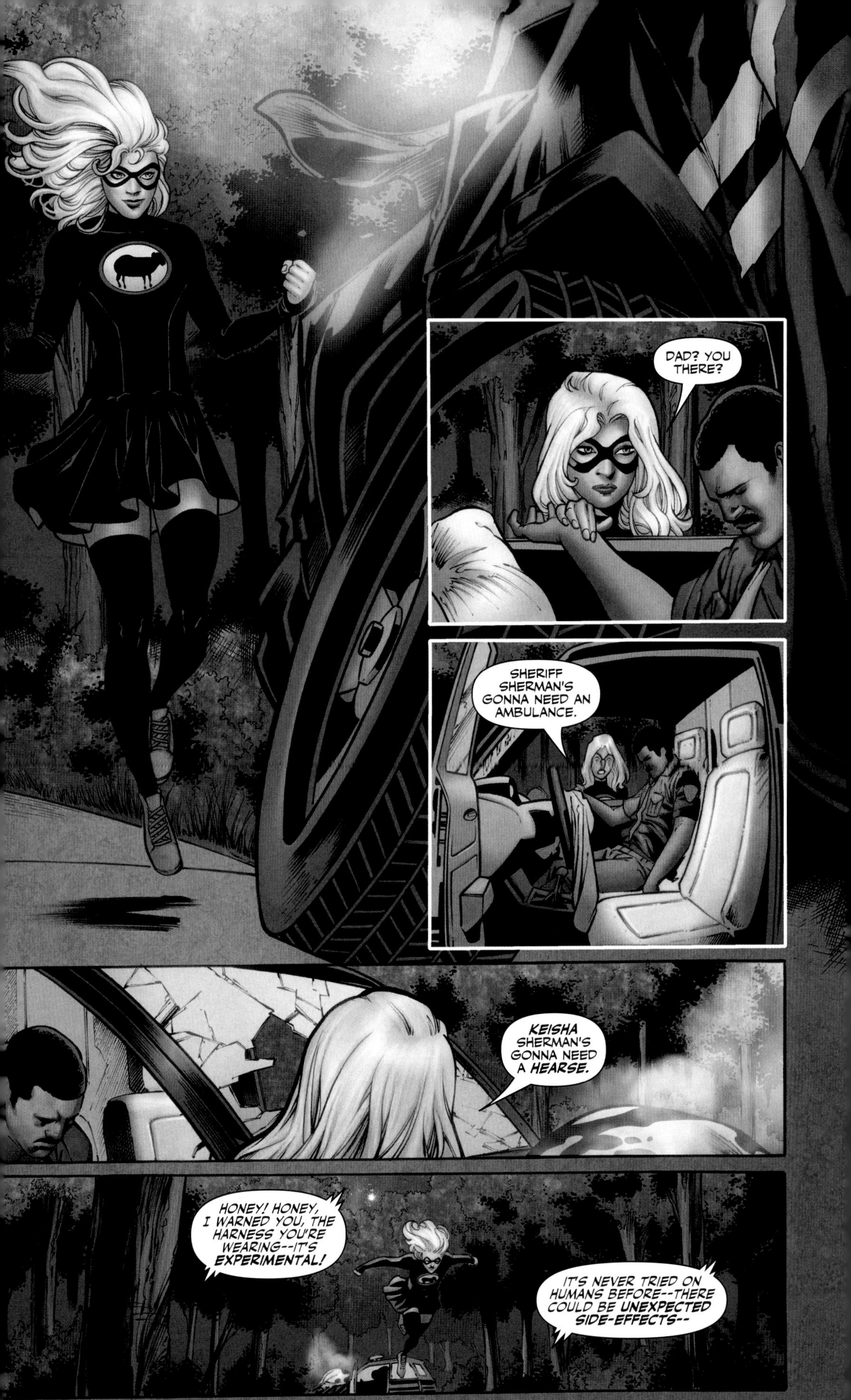
DAD? YOU THERE?
SHERIFF SHERMAN'S GONNA NEED AN AMBULANCE.
KEISHA SHERMAN'S GONNA NEED A HEARSE.
HONEY! HONEY, I WARNED YOU, THE HARNESS YOU'RE WEARING--IT'S EXPERIMENTAL!
IT'S NEVER TRIED ON HUMANS BEFORE--THERE COULD BE UNEXPECTED SIDE-EFFECTS--

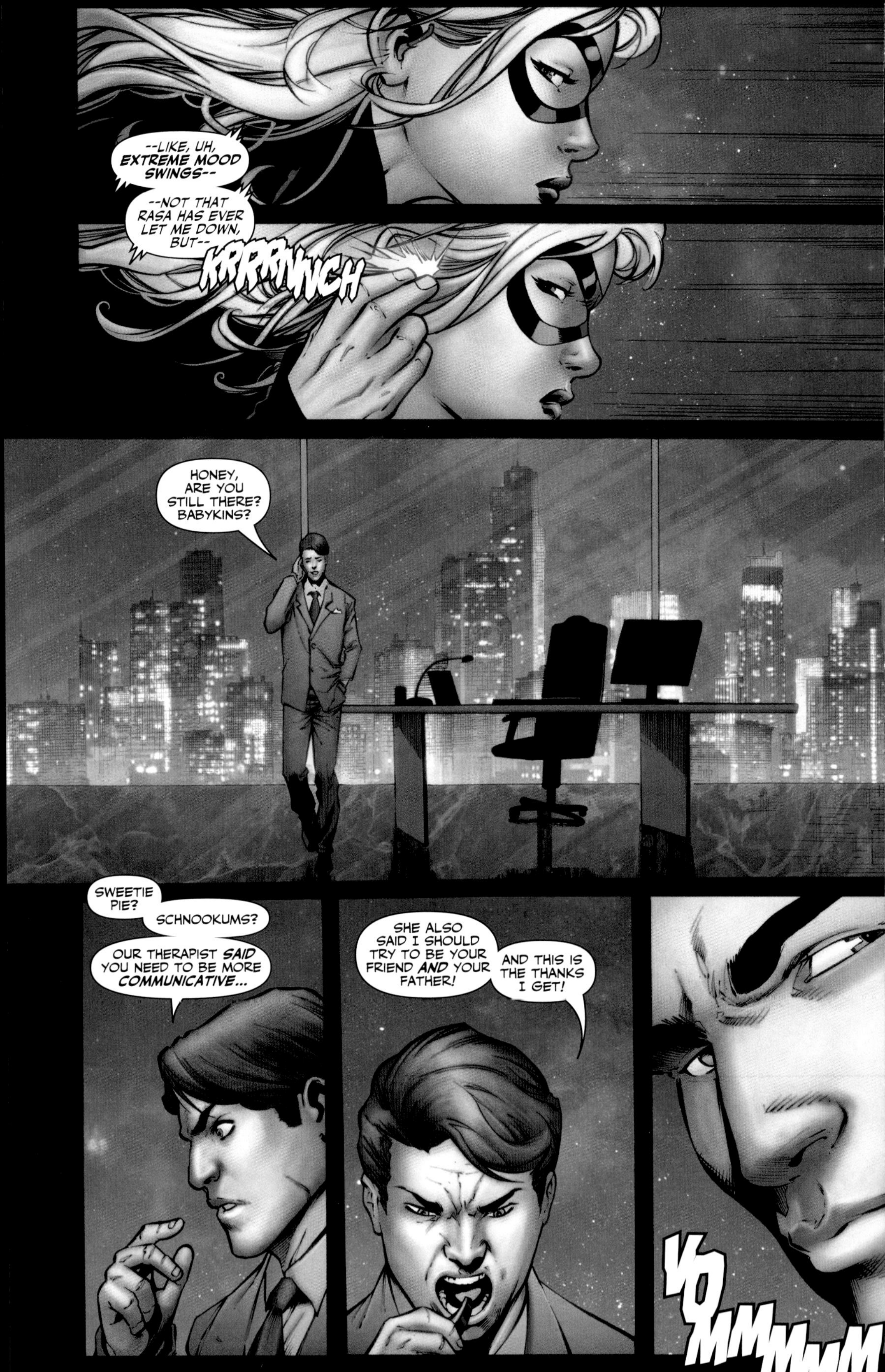
--LIKE, UH, EXTREME MOOD SWINGS--
--NOT THAT RASA HAS EVER LET ME DOWN, BUT--
KRRRNNCH
HONEY, ARE YOU STILL THERE? BABYKINS?
SWEETIE PIE?
SCHNOOKUMS?
OUR THERAPIST SAID YOU NEED TO BE MORE COMMUNICATIVE...
SHE ALSO SAID I SHOULD TRY TO BE YOUR FRIEND AND YOUR FATHER!
AND THIS IS THE THANKS I GET!
VOMMMMMM

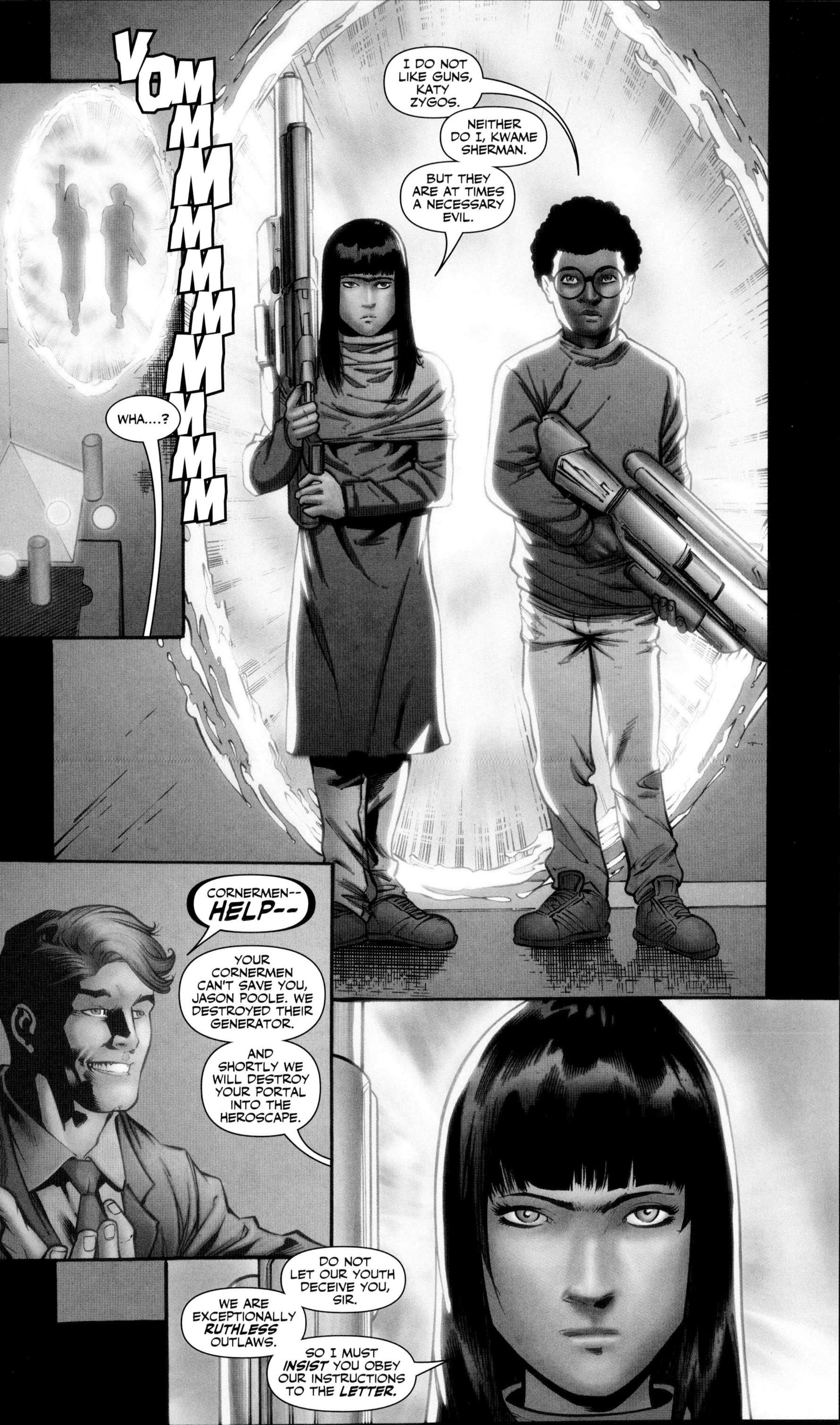
VOMMMMMMMMMMM
WHA....?
I DO NOT LIKE GUNS, KATY ZYGOS.
NEITHER DO I, KWAME SHERMAN.
BUT THEY ARE AT TIMES A NECESSARY EVIL.
CORNERMEN-- HELP--
YOUR CORNERMEN CAN'T SAVE YOU, JASON POOLE. WE DESTROYED THEIR GENERATOR.
AND SHORTLY WE WILL DESTROY YOUR PORTAL INTO THE HEROSCAPE.
DO NOT LET OUR YOUTH DECEIVE YOU, SIR.
WE ARE EXCEPTIONALLY RUTHLESS OUTLAWS.
SO I MUST INSIST YOU OBEY OUR INSTRUCTIONS TO THE LETTER.

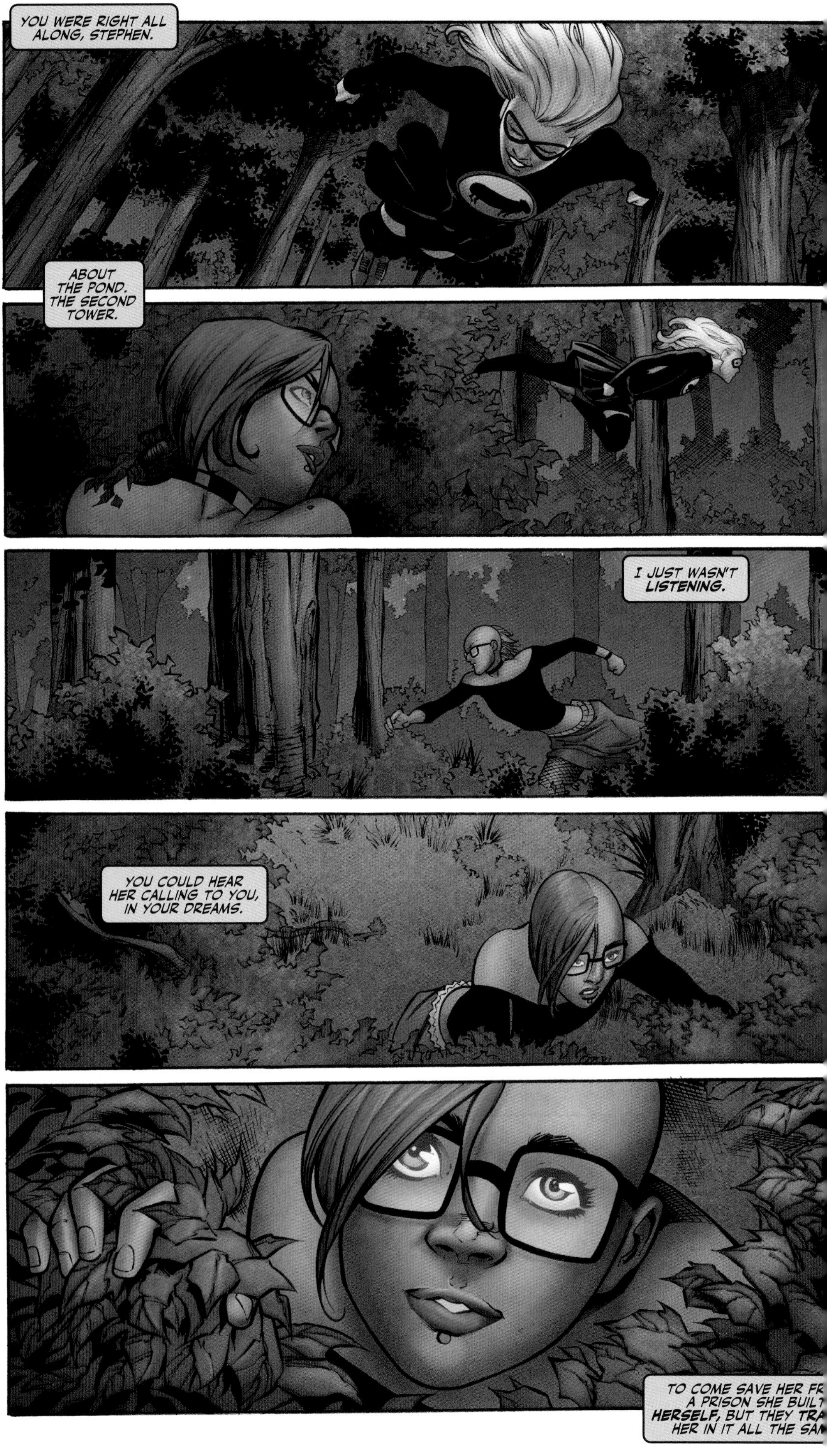
YOU WERE RIGHT ALL ALONG, STEPHEN.
ABOUT THE POND. THE SECOND TOWER.
I JUST WASN'T LISTENING.
YOU COULD HEAR HER CALLING TO YOU, IN YOUR DREAMS.
TO COME SAVE HER FR A PRISON SHE BUILT HERSELF, BUT THEY TRA HER IN IT ALL THE SA

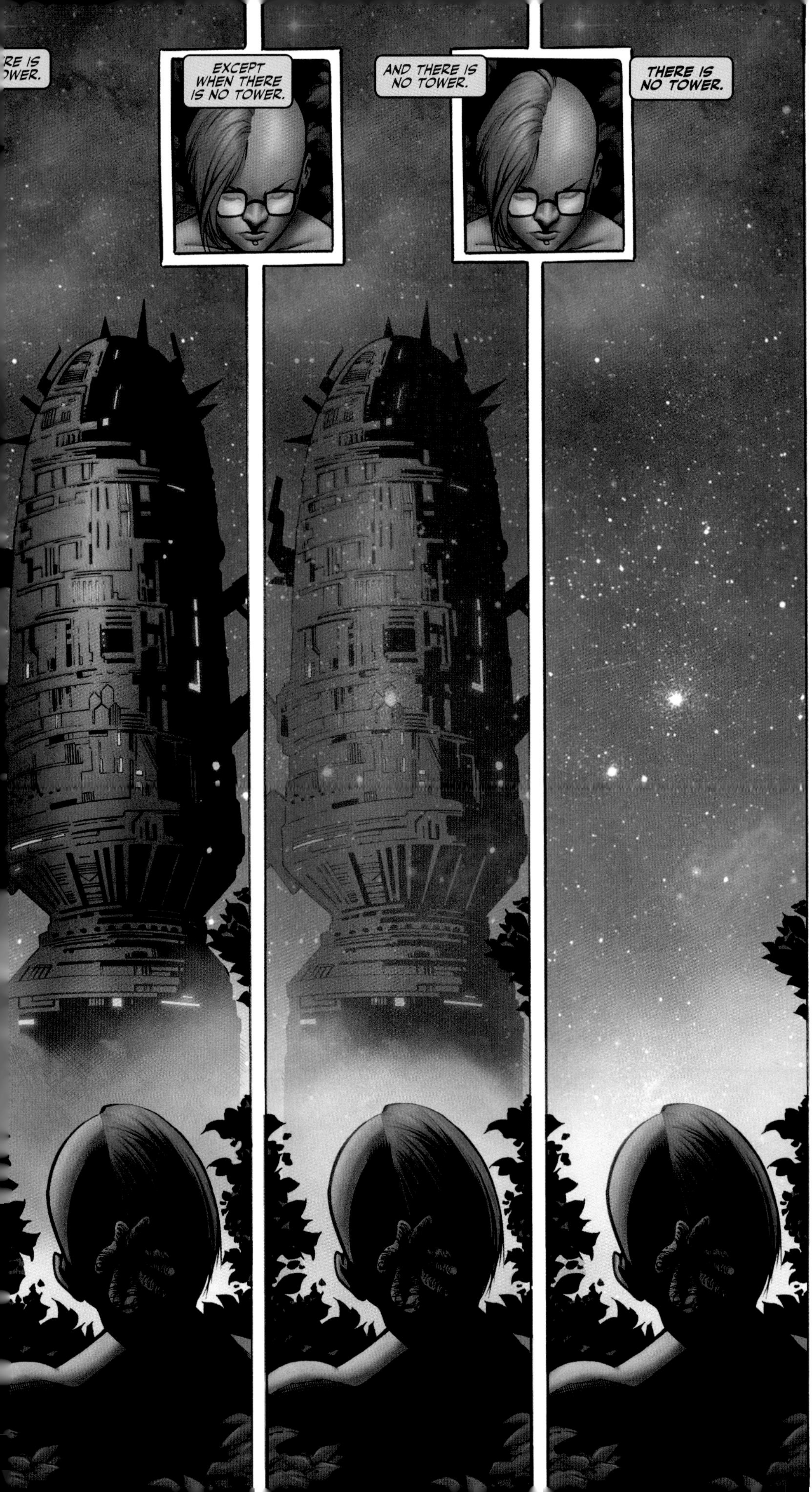
RE IS
WER.
EXCEPT WHEN THERE IS NO TOWER.
AND THERE IS NO TOWER.
THERE IS NO TOWER.

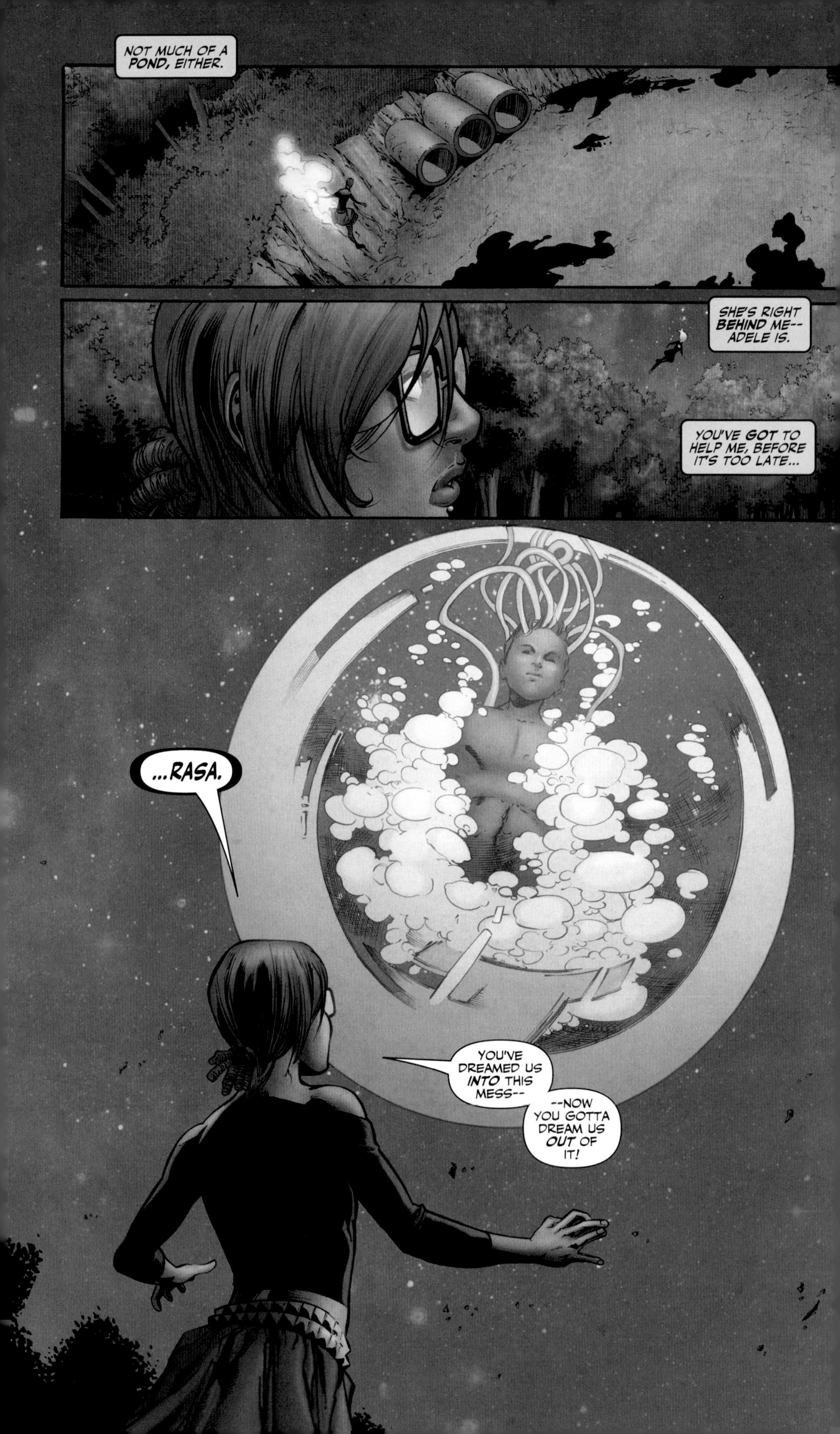
NOT MUCH OF A POND, EITHER.
SHE'S RIGHT BEHIND ME-- ADELE IS.
YOU'VE GOT TO HELP ME, BEFORE IT'S TOO LATE...
...RASA.
YOU'VE DREAMED US INTO THIS MESS--
--NOW YOU GOTTA DREAM US OUT OF IT!

VALIANT

FRED VAN LENTE | DIEGO BERNARD
JUAN CASTRO | ANDREW DALHOUSE

#9

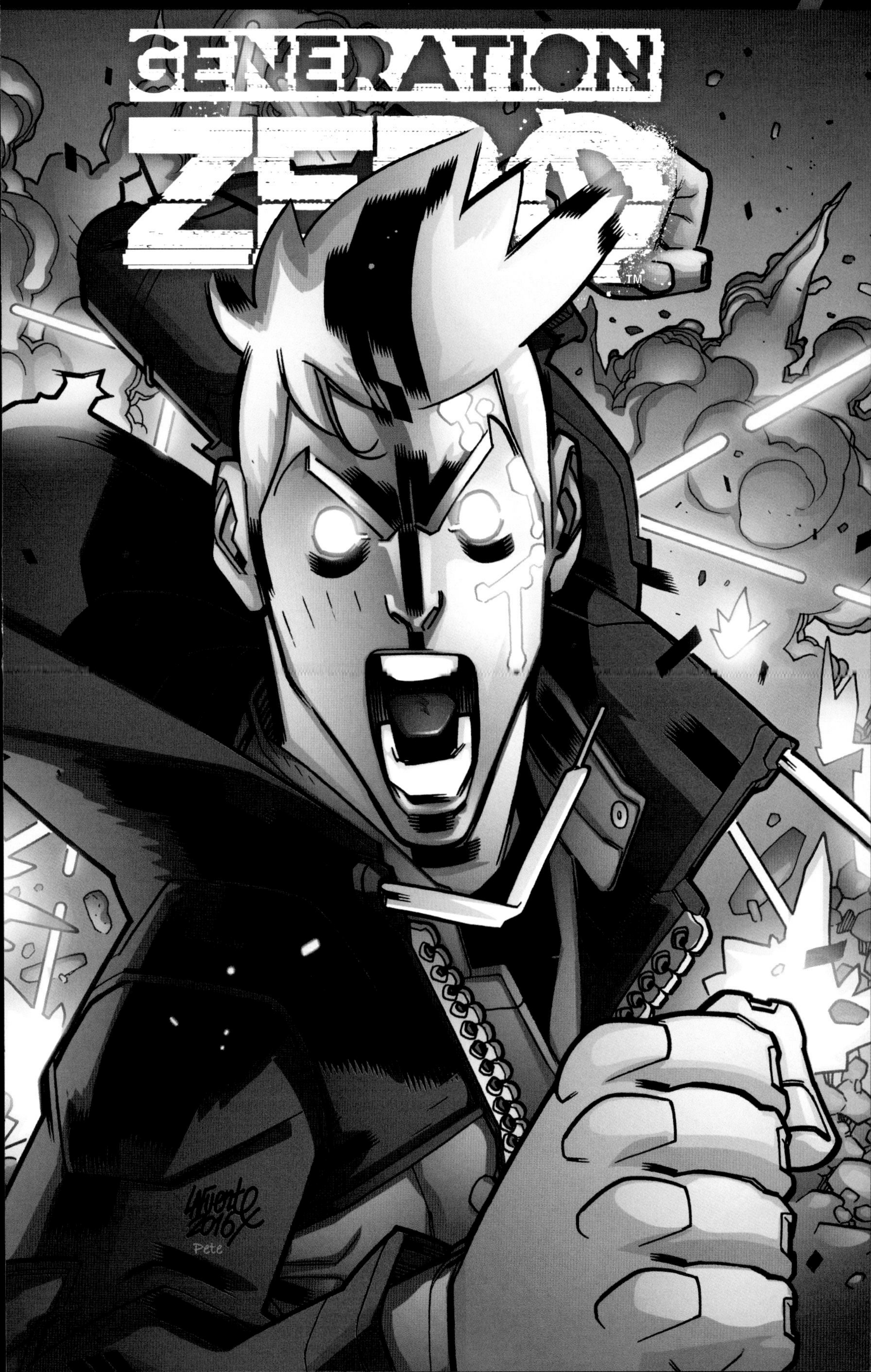
GENERATION ZERO™

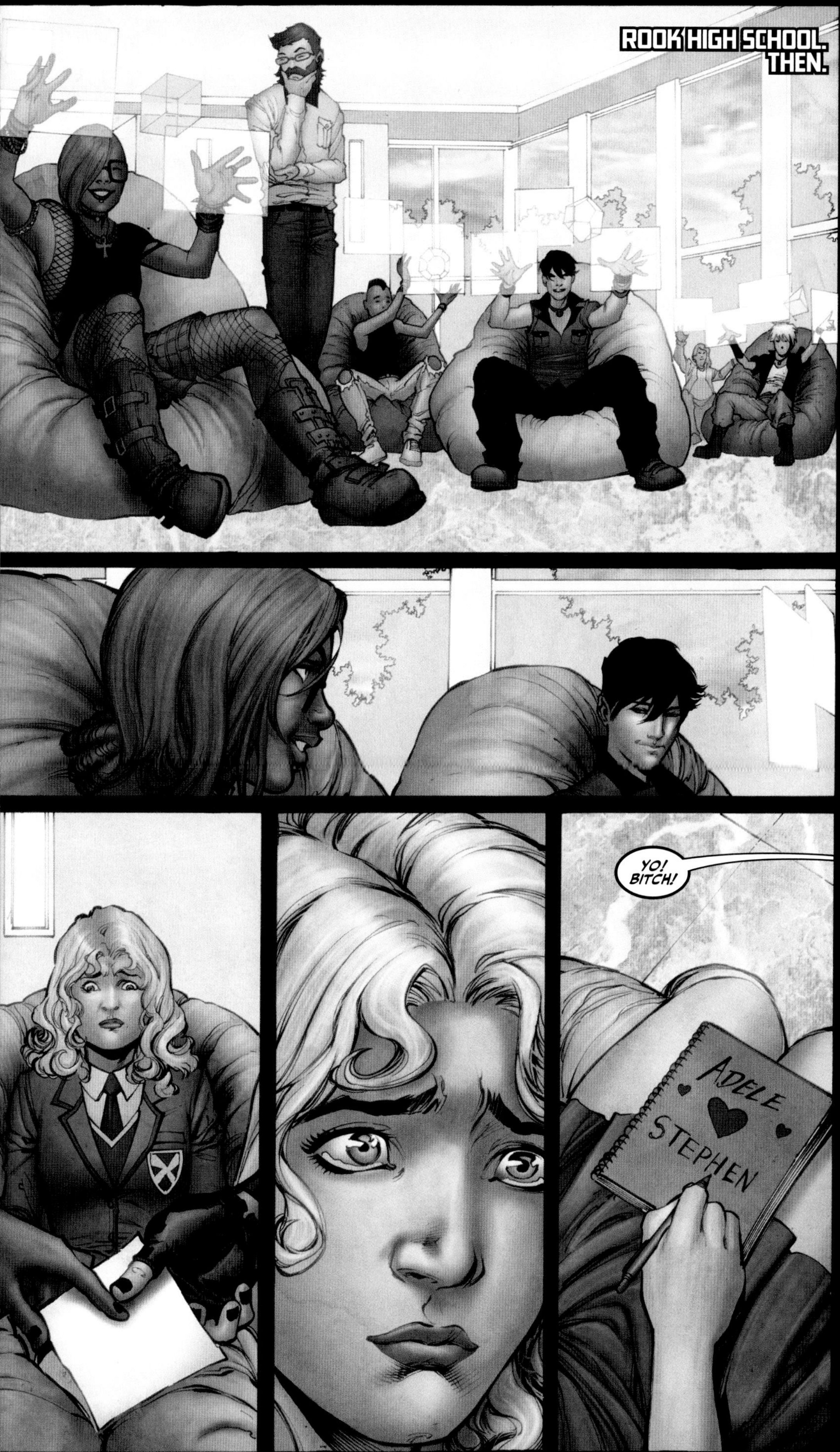

ROOK HIGH SCHOOL.
THEN.
YO! BITCH!
ADELE
STEPHEN

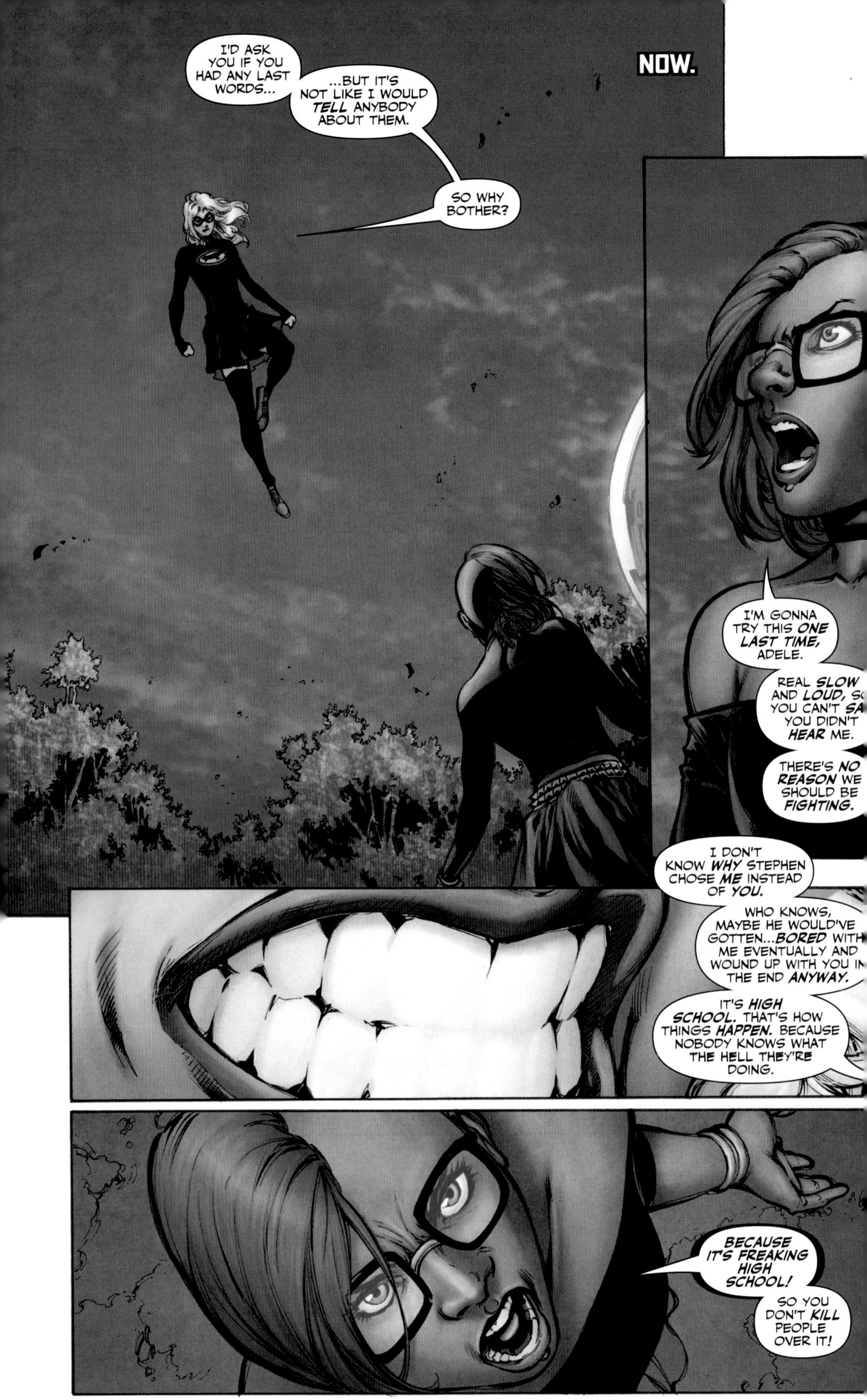
NOW.
I'D ASK YOU IF YOU HAD ANY LAST WORDS...
...BUT IT'S NOT LIKE I WOULD TELL ANYBODY ABOUT THEM.
SO WHY BOTHER?
I'M GONNA TRY THIS ONE LAST TIME, ADELE.
REAL SLOW AND LOUD, SO YOU CAN'T SAY YOU DIDN'T HEAR ME.
THERE'S NO REASON WE SHOULD BE FIGHTING.
I DON'T KNOW WHY STEPHEN CHOSE ME INSTEAD OF YOU.
WHO KNOWS, MAYBE HE WOULD'VE GOTTEN...BORED WITH ME EVENTUALLY AND WOUND UP WITH YOU IN THE END ANYWAY.
IT'S HIGH SCHOOL. THAT'S HOW THINGS HAPPEN. BECAUSE NOBODY KNOWS WHAT THE HELL THEY'RE DOING.
BECAUSE IT'S FREAKING HIGH SCHOOL!
SO YOU DON'T KILL PEOPLE OVER IT!

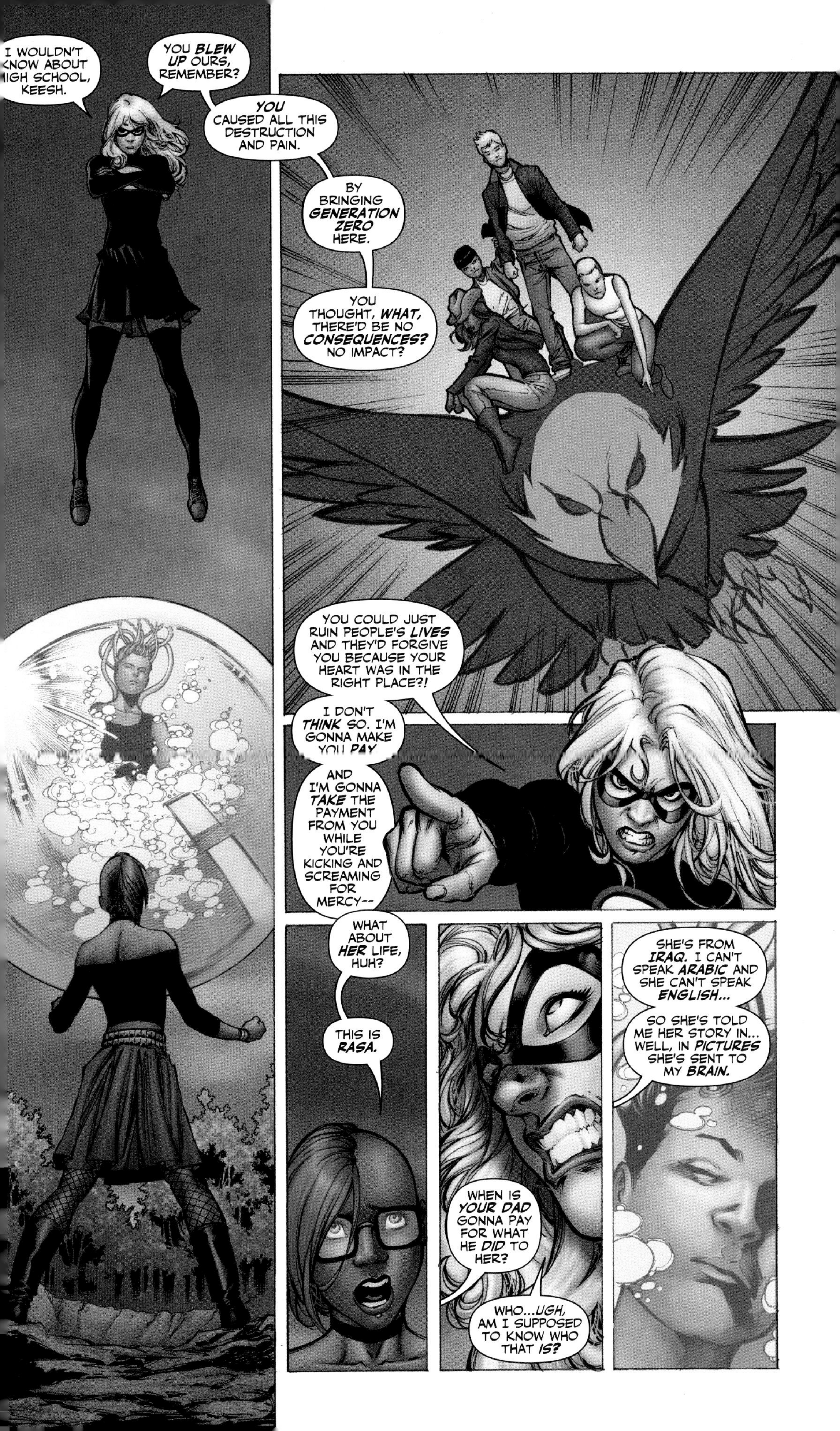

I WOULDN'T KNOW ABOUT HIGH SCHOOL, KEESH.
YOU BLEW UP OURS, REMEMBER?
YOU CAUSED ALL THIS DESTRUCTION AND PAIN.
BY BRINGING GENERATION ZERO HERE.
YOU THOUGHT, WHAT, THERE'D BE NO CONSEQUENCES? NO IMPACT?
YOU COULD JUST RUIN PEOPLE'S LIVES AND THEY'D FORGIVE YOU BECAUSE YOUR HEART WAS IN THE RIGHT PLACE?!
I DON'T THINK SO. I'M GONNA MAKE YOU PAY.
AND I'M GONNA TAKE THE PAYMENT FROM YOU WHILE YOU'RE KICKING AND SCREAMING FOR MERCY--
WHAT ABOUT HER LIFE, HUH?
THIS IS RASA.
WHEN IS YOUR DAD GONNA PAY FOR WHAT HE DID TO HER?
WHO...UGH, AM I SUPPOSED TO KNOW WHO THAT IS?
SHE'S FROM IRAQ. I CAN'T SPEAK ARABIC AND SHE CAN'T SPEAK ENGLISH...
SO SHE'S TOLD ME HER STORY IN... WELL, IN PICTURES SHE'S SENT TO MY BRAIN.

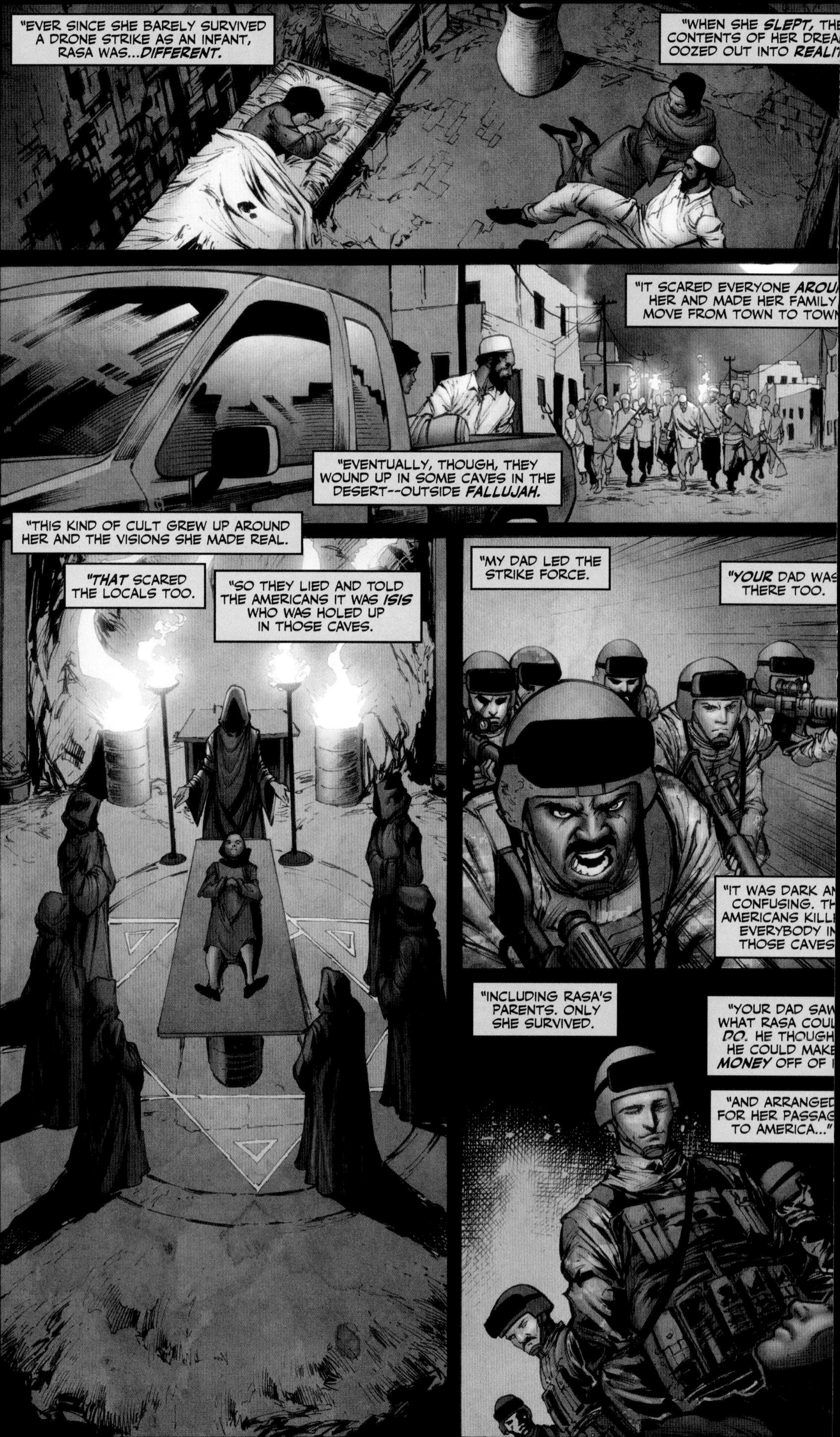

"EVER SINCE SHE BARELY SURVIVED A DRONE STRIKE AS AN INFANT, RASA WAS...DIFFERENT.
"WHEN SHE SLEPT, THE CONTENTS OF HER DREA OOZED OUT INTO REALIT
"IT SCARED EVERYONE AROU HER AND MADE HER FAMILY MOVE FROM TOWN TO TOWN
"EVENTUALLY, THOUGH, THEY WOUND UP IN SOME CAVES IN THE DESERT--OUTSIDE FALLUJAH.
"THIS KIND OF CULT GREW UP AROUND HER AND THE VISIONS SHE MADE REAL.
"THAT SCARED THE LOCALS TOO.
"SO THEY LIED AND TOLD THE AMERICANS IT WAS ISIS WHO WAS HOLED UP IN THOSE CAVES.
"MY DAD LED THE STRIKE FORCE.
"YOUR DAD WAS THERE TOO.
"IT WAS DARK AN CONFUSING. TH AMERICANS KILL EVERYBODY IN THOSE CAVES
"INCLUDING RASA'S PARENTS. ONLY SHE SURVIVED.
"YOUR DAD SAW WHAT RASA COUL DO. HE THOUGH HE COULD MAKE MONEY OFF OF I
"AND ARRANGED FOR HER PASSAG TO AMERICA..."

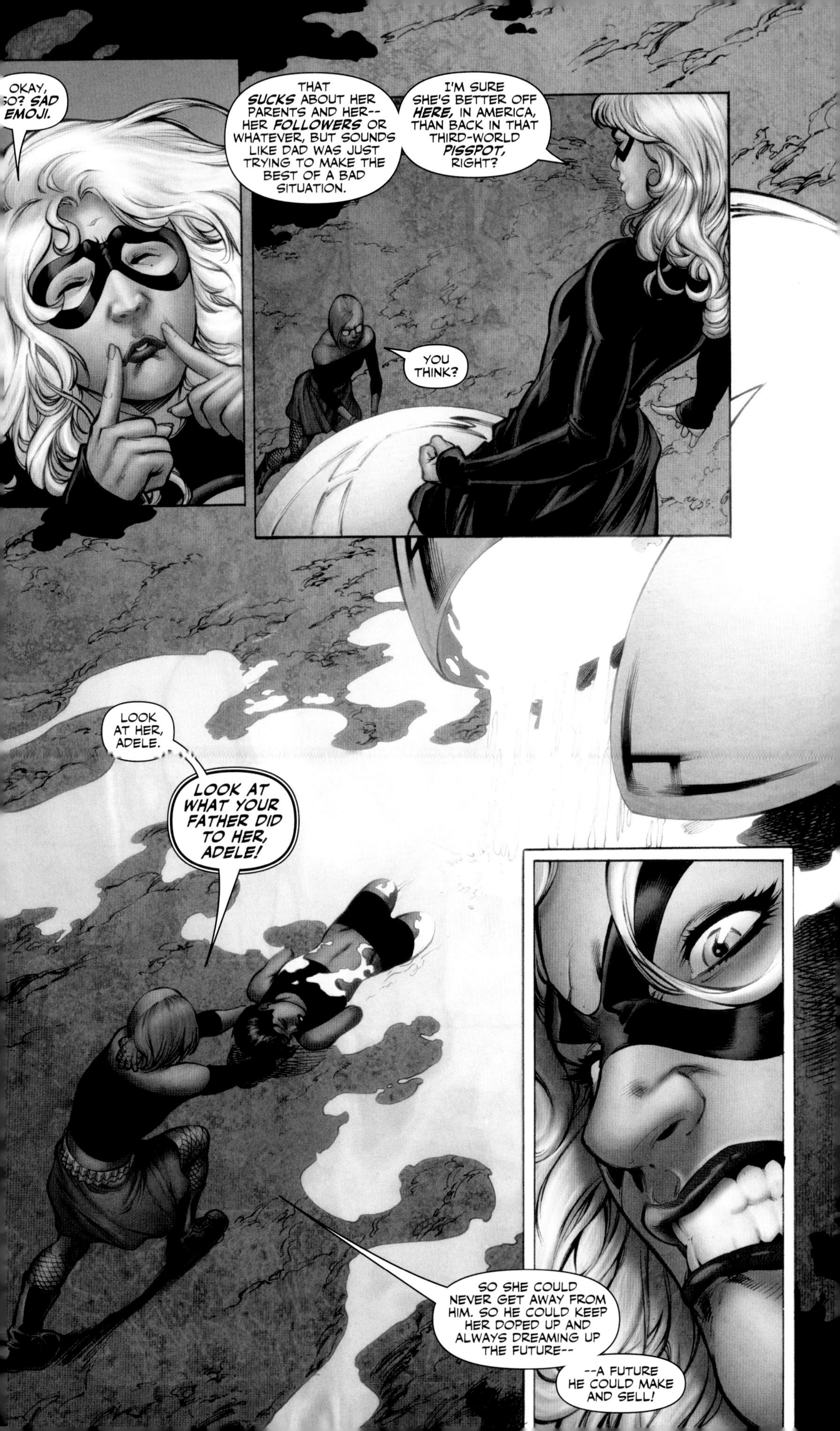
OKAY, SO? SAD EMOJI.
THAT SUCKS ABOUT HER PARENTS AND HER-- HER FOLLOWERS OR WHATEVER, BUT SOUNDS LIKE DAD WAS JUST TRYING TO MAKE THE BEST OF A BAD SITUATION.
I'M SURE SHE'S BETTER OFF HERE, IN AMERICA, THAN BACK IN THAT THIRD-WORLD PISSPOT, RIGHT?
YOU THINK?
LOOK AT HER, ADELE.
LOOK AT WHAT YOUR FATHER DID TO HER, ADELE!
SO SHE COULD NEVER GET AWAY FROM HIM. SO HE COULD KEEP HER DOPED UP AND ALWAYS DREAMING UP THE FUTURE--
--A FUTURE HE COULD MAKE AND SELL!

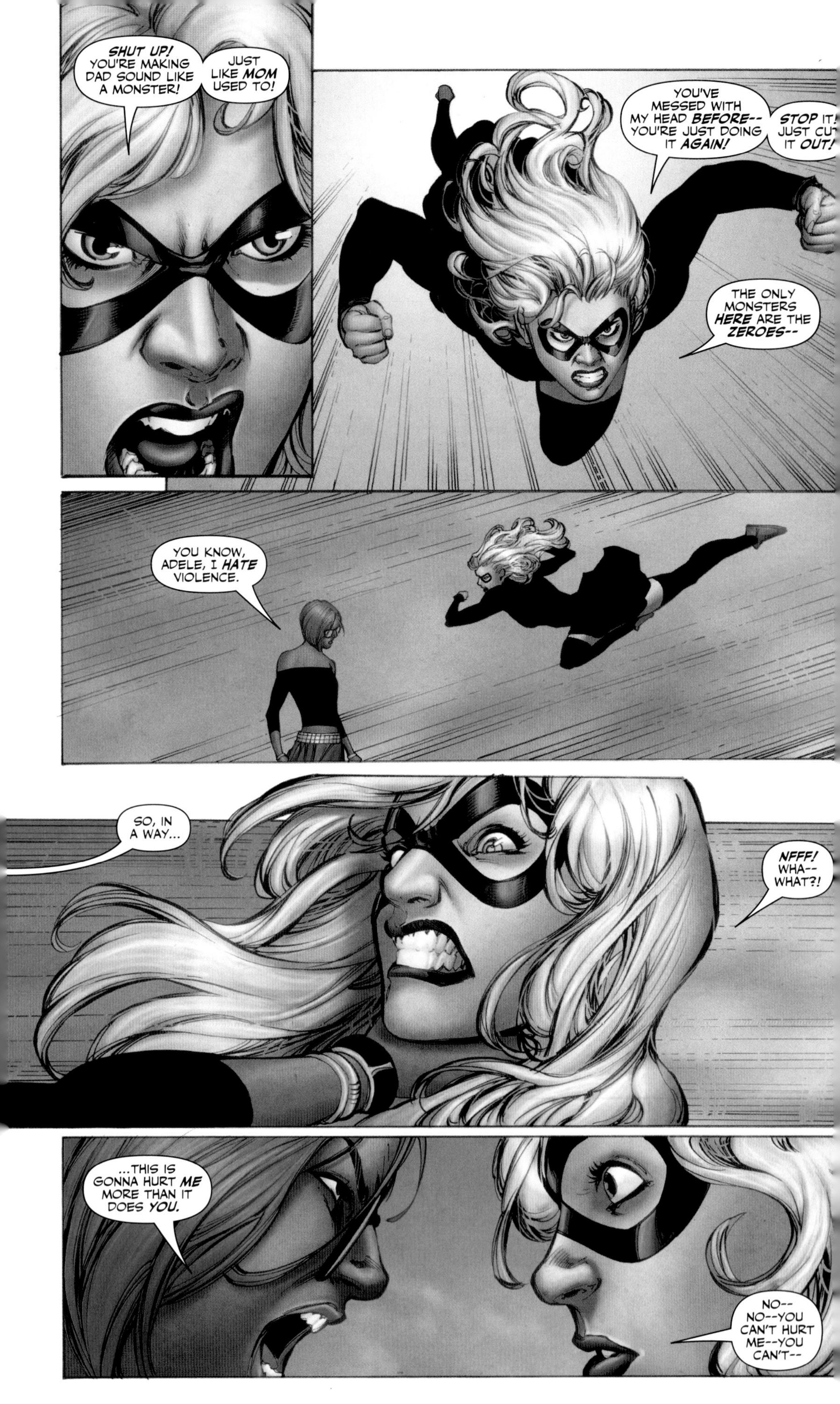
SHUT UP! YOU'RE MAKING DAD SOUND LIKE A MONSTER!
JUST LIKE MOM USED TO!
YOU'VE MESSED WITH MY HEAD BEFORE-- YOU'RE JUST DOING IT AGAIN!
STOP IT! JUST CUT IT OUT!
THE ONLY MONSTERS HERE ARE THE ZEROES--
YOU KNOW, ADELE, I HATE VIOLENCE.
SO, IN A WAY...
NFFF! WHA-- WHAT?!
...THIS IS GONNA HURT ME MORE THAN IT DOES YOU.
NO-- NO--YOU CAN'T HURT ME--YOU CAN'T--

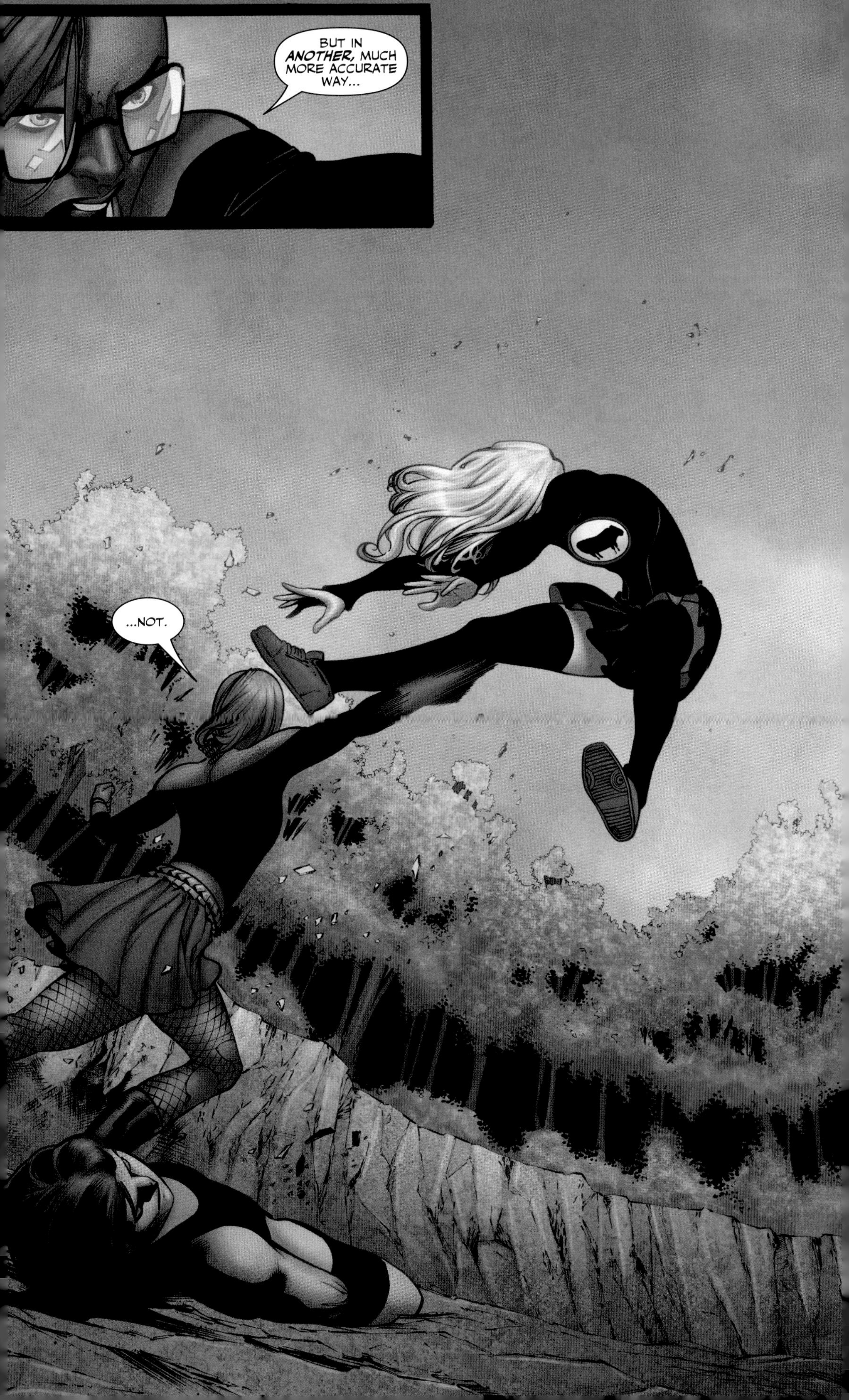
BUT IN ANOTHER, MUCH MORE ACCURATE WAY...
...NOT.

WHOOOM

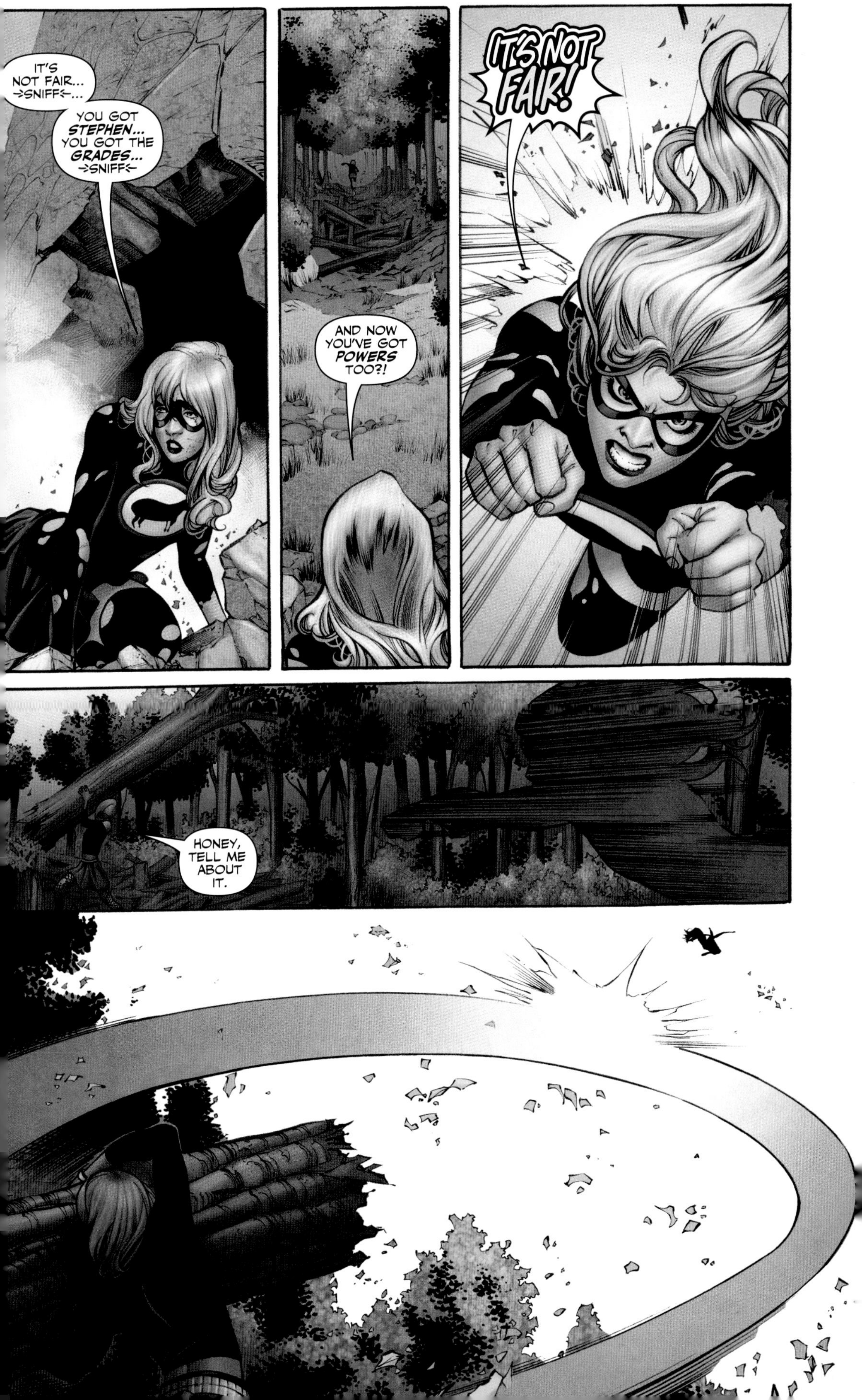
IT'S NOT FAIR... SNIFF...
YOU GOT STEPHEN... YOU GOT THE GRADES... SNIFF
AND NOW YOU'VE GOT POWERS TOO?!
IT'S NOT FAIR!
HONEY, TELL ME ABOUT IT.

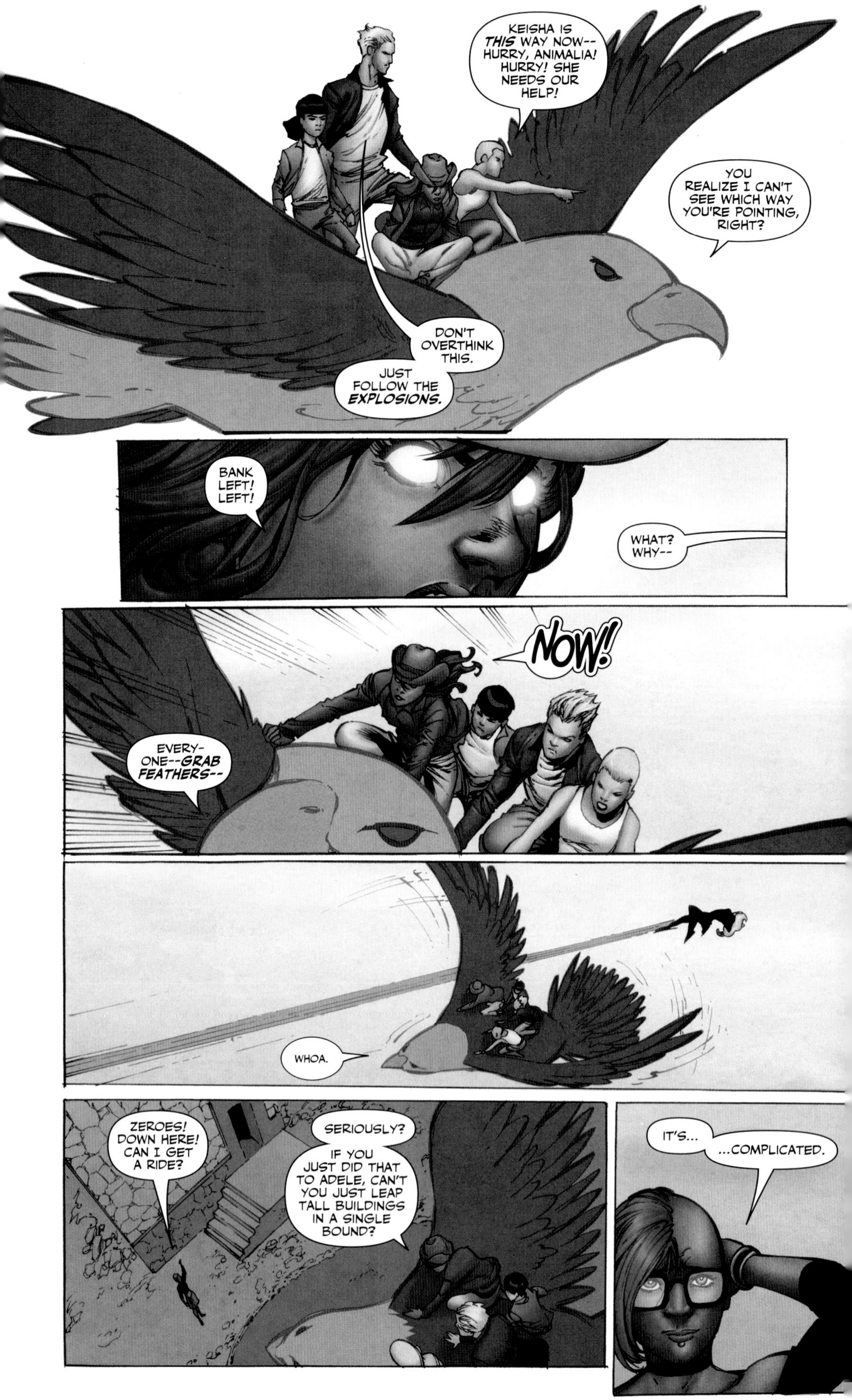
KEISHA IS *THIS* WAY NOW-- HURRY, ANIMALIA! HURRY! SHE NEEDS OUR HELP!
YOU REALIZE I CAN'T SEE WHICH WAY YOU'RE POINTING, RIGHT?
DON'T OVERTHINK THIS.
JUST FOLLOW THE *EXPLOSIONS.*
BANK LEFT! LEFT!
WHAT? WHY--
NOW!
EVERY-ONE--*GRAB FEATHERS--*
WHOA.
ZEROES! DOWN HERE! CAN I GET A RIDE?
SERIOUSLY?
IF YOU JUST DID THAT TO ADELE, CAN'T YOU JUST LEAP TALL BUILDINGS IN A SINGLE BOUND?
IT'S...
...COMPLICATED.

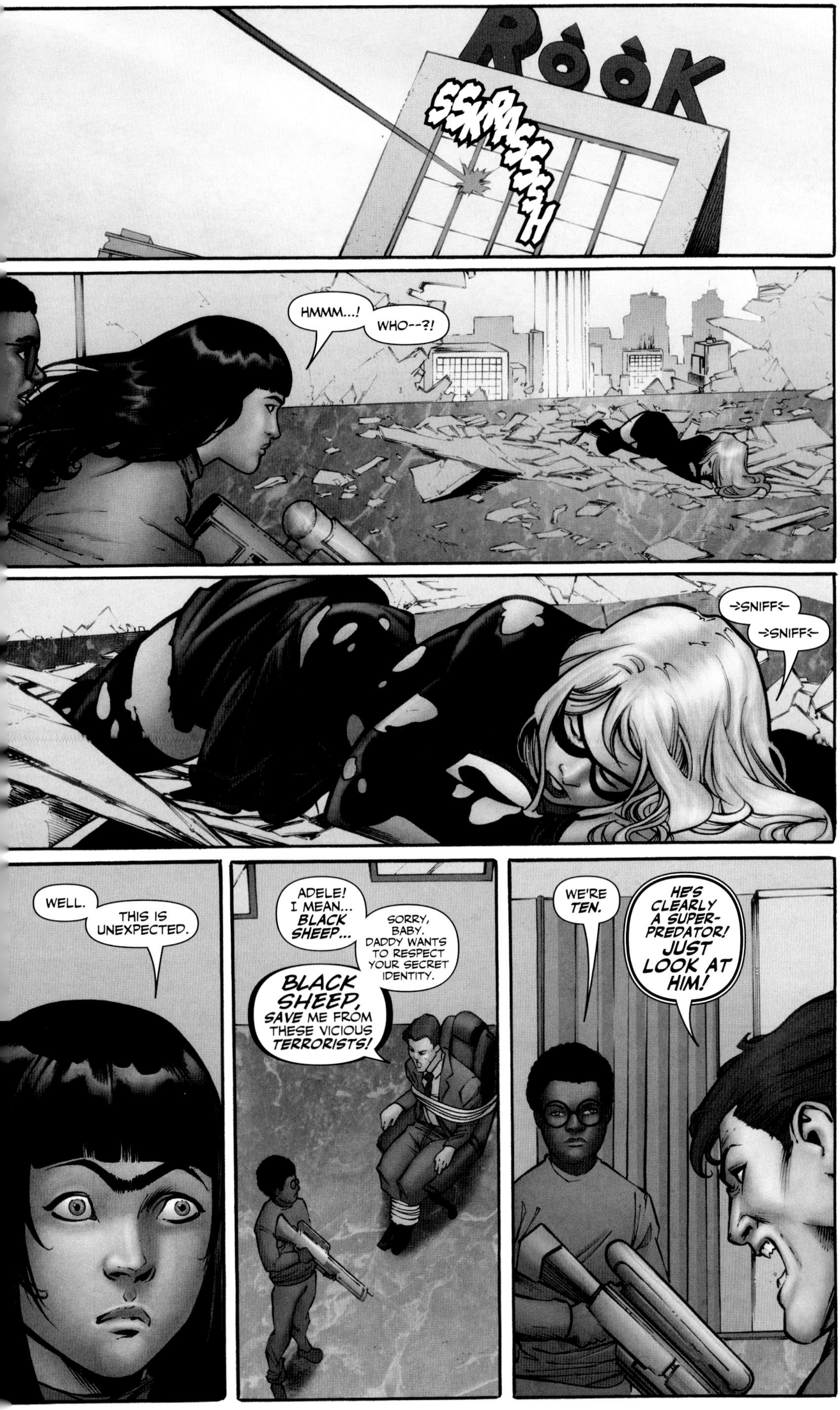
ROOK
SSKRASSSH
HMMM...!
WHO--?!
SNIFF
SNIFF
WELL.
THIS IS UNEXPECTED.
ADELE! I MEAN... BLACK SHEEP...
SORRY, BABY. DADDY WANTS TO RESPECT YOUR SECRET IDENTITY.
BLACK SHEEP, SAVE ME FROM THESE VICIOUS TERRORISTS!
WE'RE TEN.
HE'S CLEARLY A SUPER-PREDATOR! JUST LOOK AT HIM!

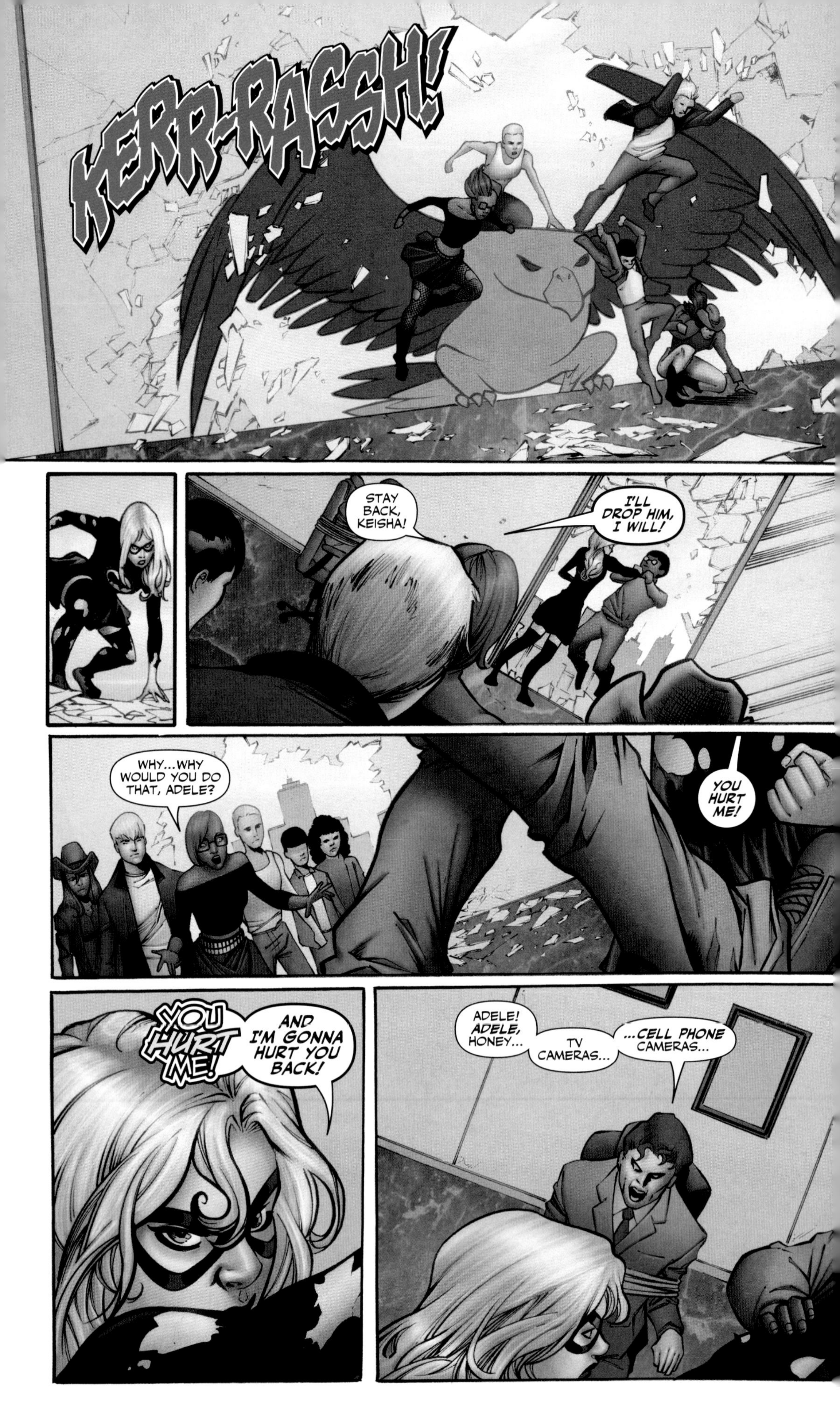
KERR-RASSH!
STAY BACK, KEISHA!
I'LL DROP HIM, I WILL!
WHY...WHY WOULD YOU DO THAT, ADELE?
YOU HURT ME!
YOU HURT ME!
AND I'M GONNA HURT YOU BACK!
ADELE! ADELE, HONEY...
TV CAMERAS...
...CELL PHONE CAMERAS...

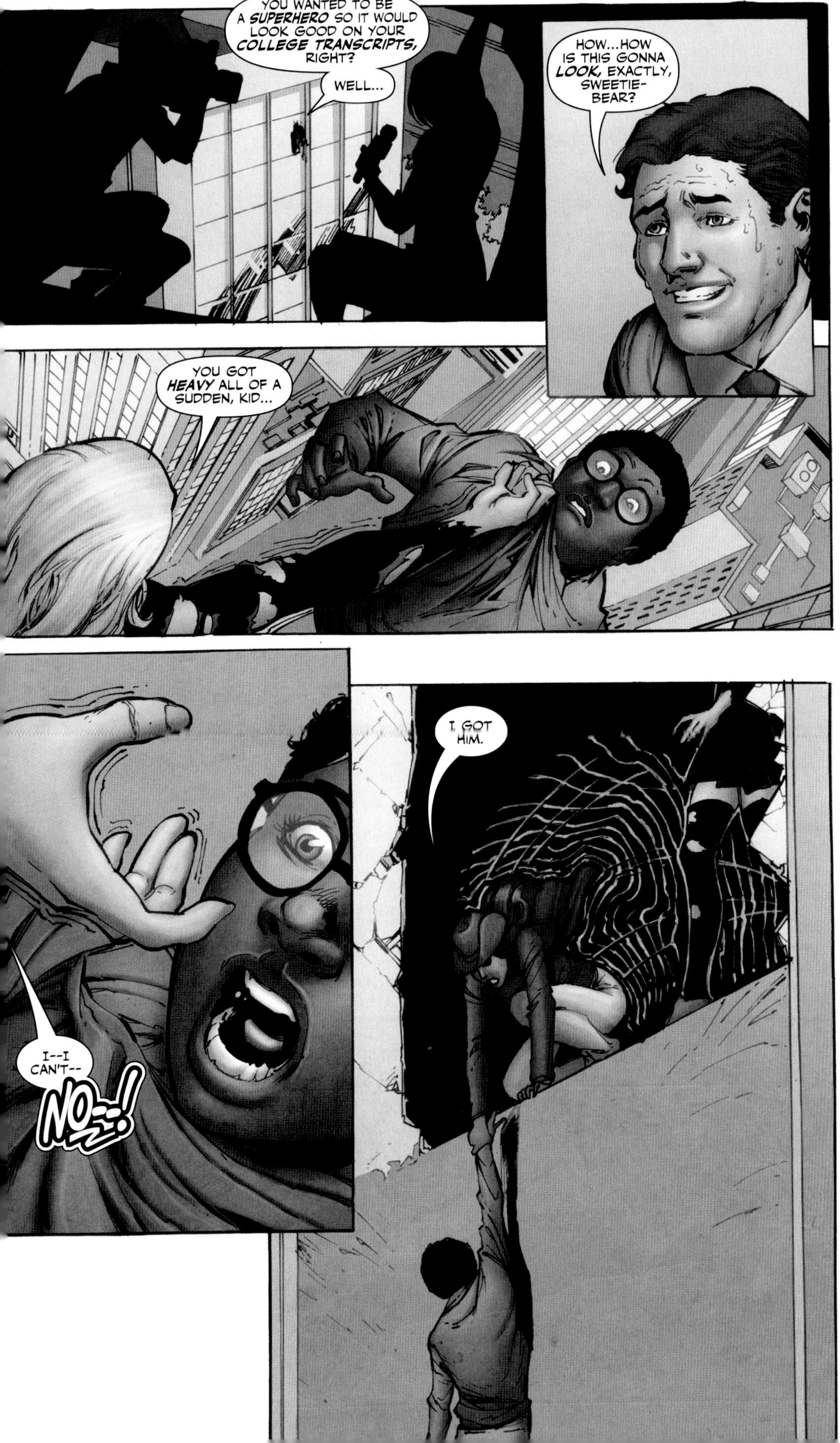
YOU WANTED TO BE A SUPERHERO SO IT WOULD LOOK GOOD ON YOUR COLLEGE TRANSCRIPTS, RIGHT?
WELL...
HOW...HOW IS THIS GONNA LOOK, EXACTLY, SWEETIE-BEAR?
YOU GOT HEAVY ALL OF A SUDDEN, KID...
I--I CAN'T--
NO--!
I GOT HIM.

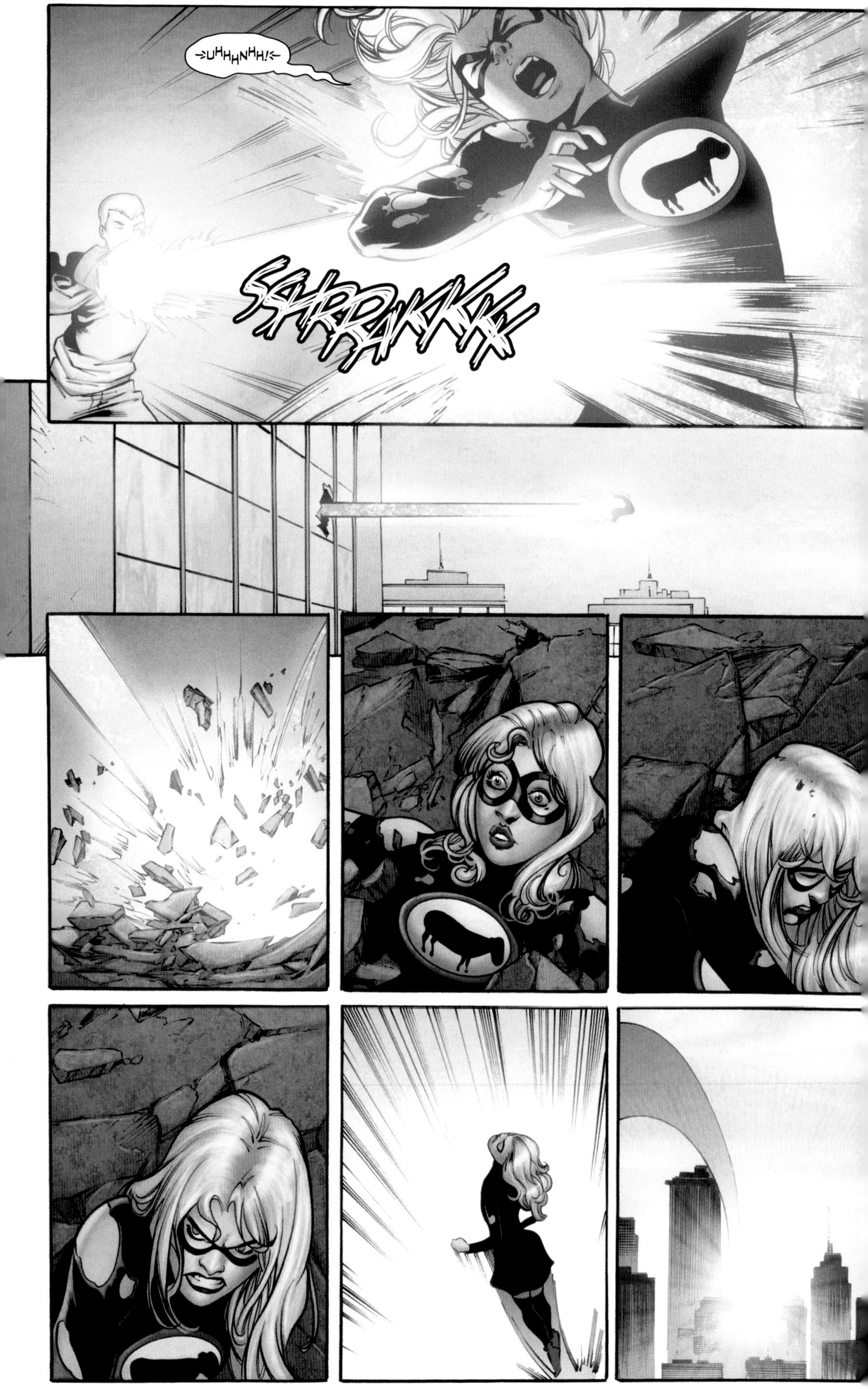
UHHHNHH!
SSHRRAKKKK

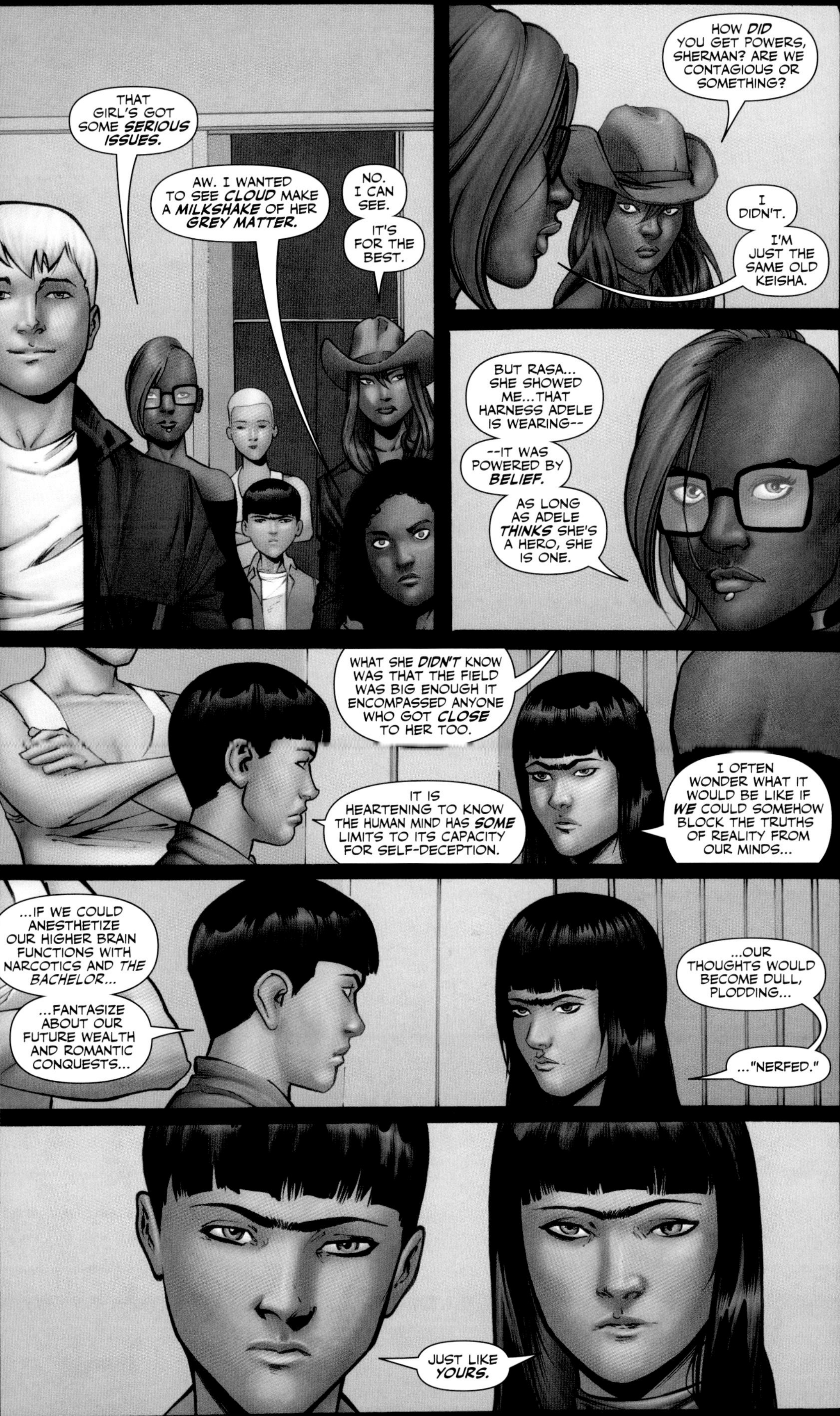
THAT GIRL'S GOT SOME *SERIOUS ISSUES.*
AW. I WANTED TO SEE *CLOUD* MAKE A *MILKSHAKE* OF HER *GREY MATTER.*
NO. I CAN SEE.
IT'S FOR THE BEST.
HOW *DID* YOU GET POWERS, SHERMAN? ARE WE CONTAGIOUS OR SOMETHING?
I DIDN'T.
I'M JUST THE SAME OLD KEISHA.
BUT RASA... SHE SHOWED ME...THAT HARNESS ADELE IS WEARING--
--IT WAS POWERED BY *BELIEF.*
AS LONG AS ADELE *THINKS* SHE'S A HERO, SHE IS ONE.
WHAT SHE *DIDN'T* KNOW WAS THAT THE FIELD WAS BIG ENOUGH IT ENCOMPASSED ANYONE WHO GOT *CLOSE* TO HER TOO.
IT IS HEARTENING TO KNOW THE HUMAN MIND HAS *SOME* LIMITS TO ITS CAPACITY FOR SELF-DECEPTION.
I OFTEN WONDER WHAT IT WOULD BE LIKE IF *WE* COULD SOMEHOW BLOCK THE TRUTHS OF REALITY FROM OUR MINDS...
...IF WE COULD ANESTHETIZE OUR HIGHER BRAIN FUNCTIONS WITH NARCOTICS AND *THE BACHELOR*...
...FANTASIZE ABOUT OUR FUTURE WEALTH AND ROMANTIC CONQUESTS...
...OUR THOUGHTS WOULD BECOME DULL, PLODDING...
..."NERFED."
JUST LIKE *YOURS.*

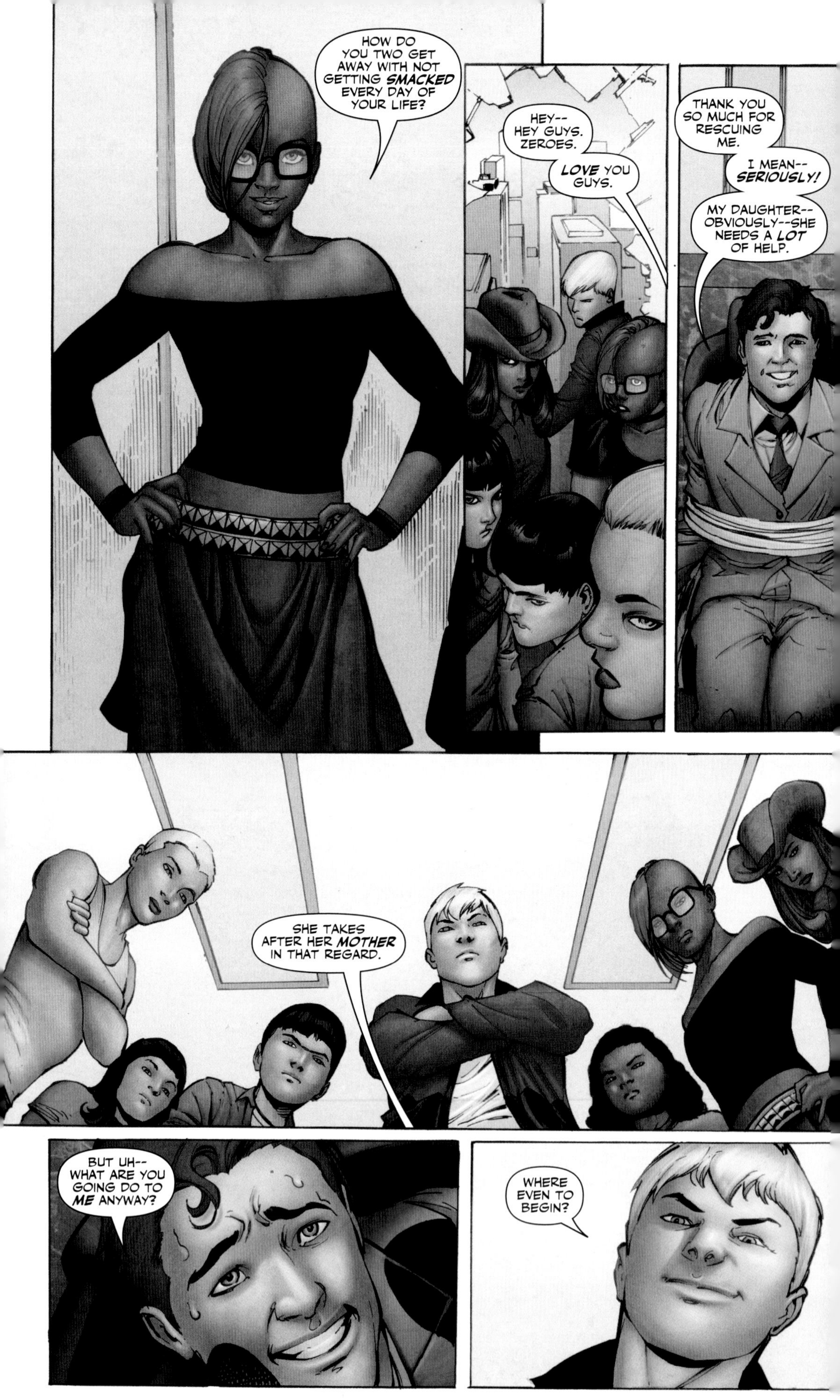
HOW DO YOU TWO GET AWAY WITH NOT GETTING SMACKED EVERY DAY OF YOUR LIFE?
HEY-- HEY GUYS. ZEROES.
LOVE YOU GUYS.
THANK YOU SO MUCH FOR RESCUING ME.
I MEAN-- SERIOUSLY!
MY DAUGHTER-- OBVIOUSLY--SHE NEEDS A LOT OF HELP.
SHE TAKES AFTER HER MOTHER IN THAT REGARD.
BUT UH-- WHAT ARE YOU GOING DO TO ME ANYWAY?
WHERE EVEN TO BEGIN?

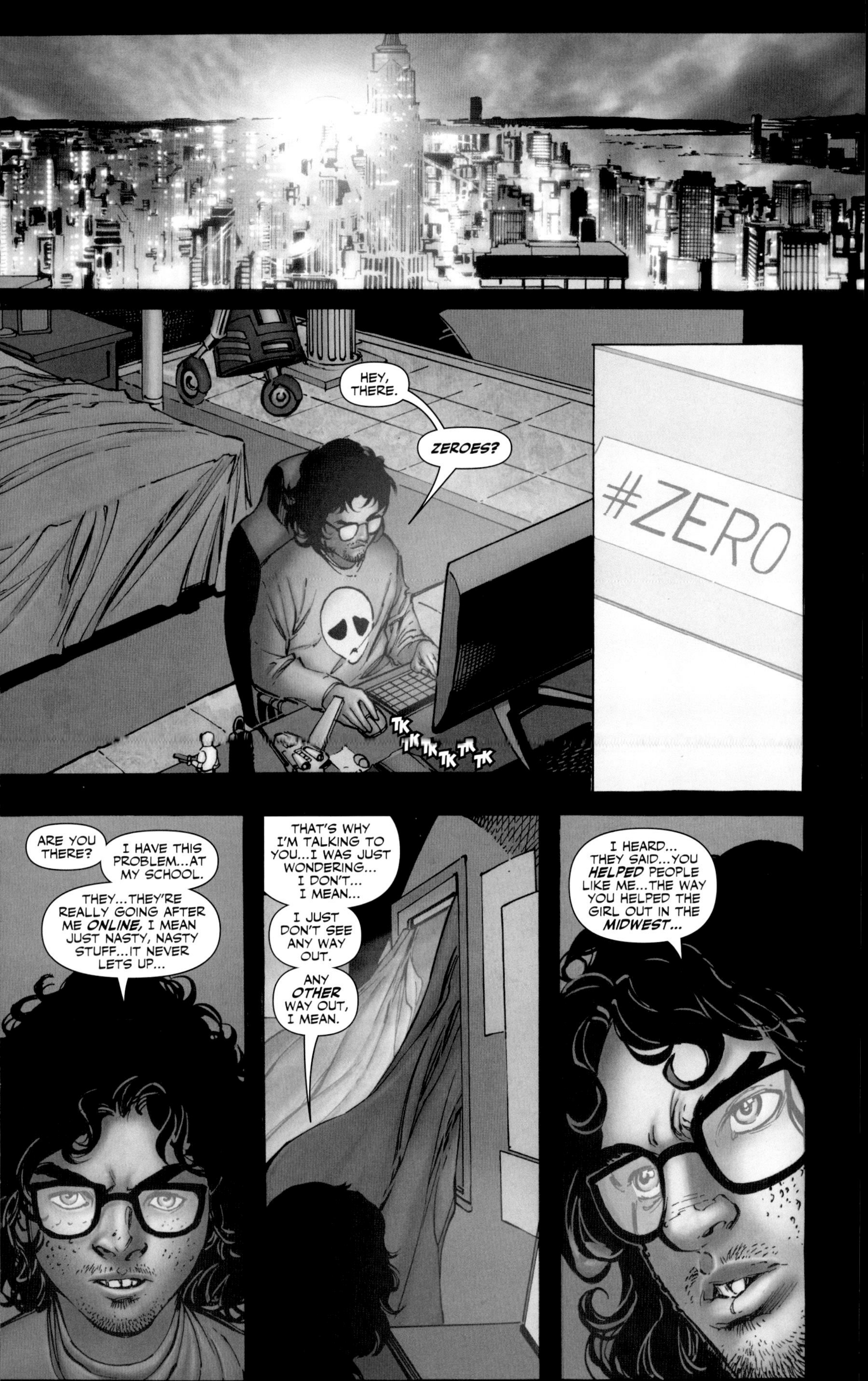
HEY, THERE.
ZEROES?
TK TK TK TK TK TK
#ZERO
ARE YOU THERE?
I HAVE THIS PROBLEM...AT MY SCHOOL.
THEY...THEY'RE REALLY GOING AFTER ME ONLINE, I MEAN JUST NASTY, NASTY STUFF...IT NEVER LETS UP...
THAT'S WHY I'M TALKING TO YOU...I WAS JUST WONDERING... I DON'T... I MEAN...
I JUST DON'T SEE ANY WAY OUT.
ANY OTHER WAY OUT, I MEAN.
I HEARD... THEY SAID...YOU HELPED PEOPLE LIKE ME...THE WAY YOU HELPED THE GIRL OUT IN THE MIDWEST...

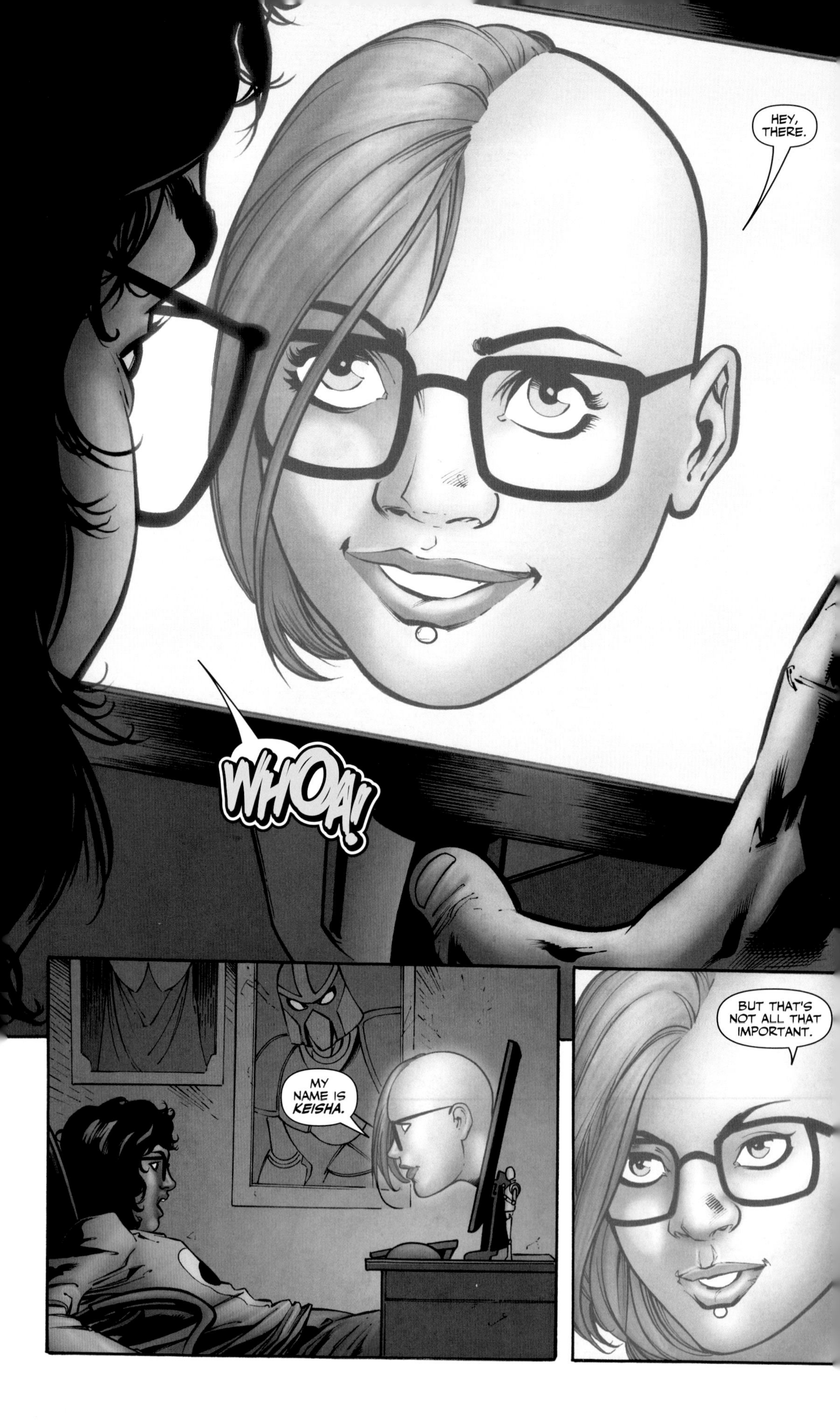
HEY, THERE.
WHOA!
MY NAME IS KEISHA.
BUT THAT'S NOT ALL THAT IMPORTANT.

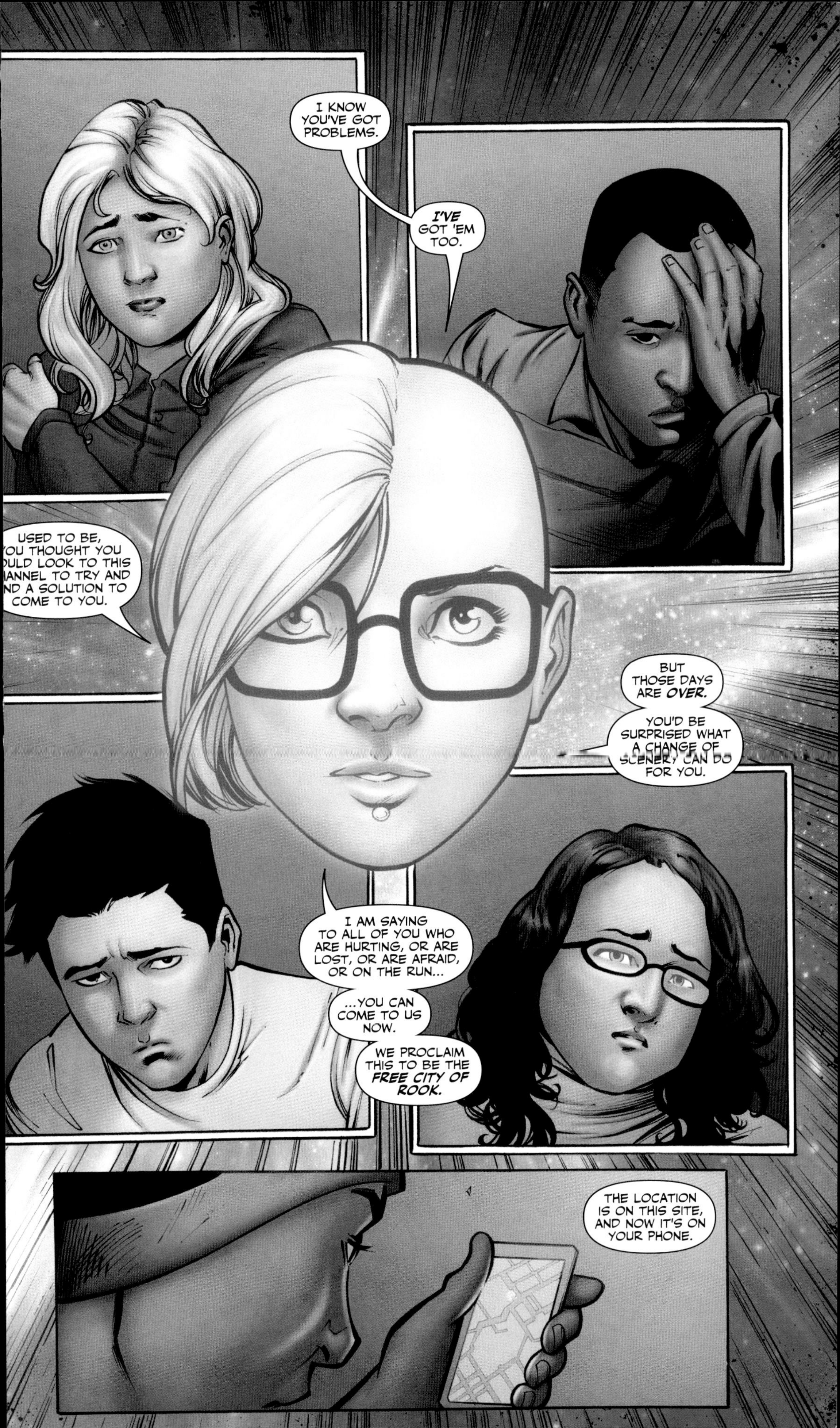

I KNOW YOU'VE GOT PROBLEMS.
I'VE GOT 'EM TOO.
USED TO BE, YOU THOUGHT YOU COULD LOOK TO THIS CHANNEL TO TRY AND FIND A SOLUTION TO COME TO YOU.
BUT THOSE DAYS ARE *OVER.*
YOU'D BE SURPRISED WHAT A CHANGE OF SCENERY CAN DO FOR YOU.
I AM SAYING TO ALL OF YOU WHO ARE HURTING, OR ARE LOST, OR ARE AFRAID, OR ON THE RUN...
...YOU CAN COME TO US NOW.
WE PROCLAIM THIS TO BE THE *FREE CITY OF ROOK.*
THE LOCATION IS ON THIS SITE, AND NOW IT'S ON YOUR PHONE.

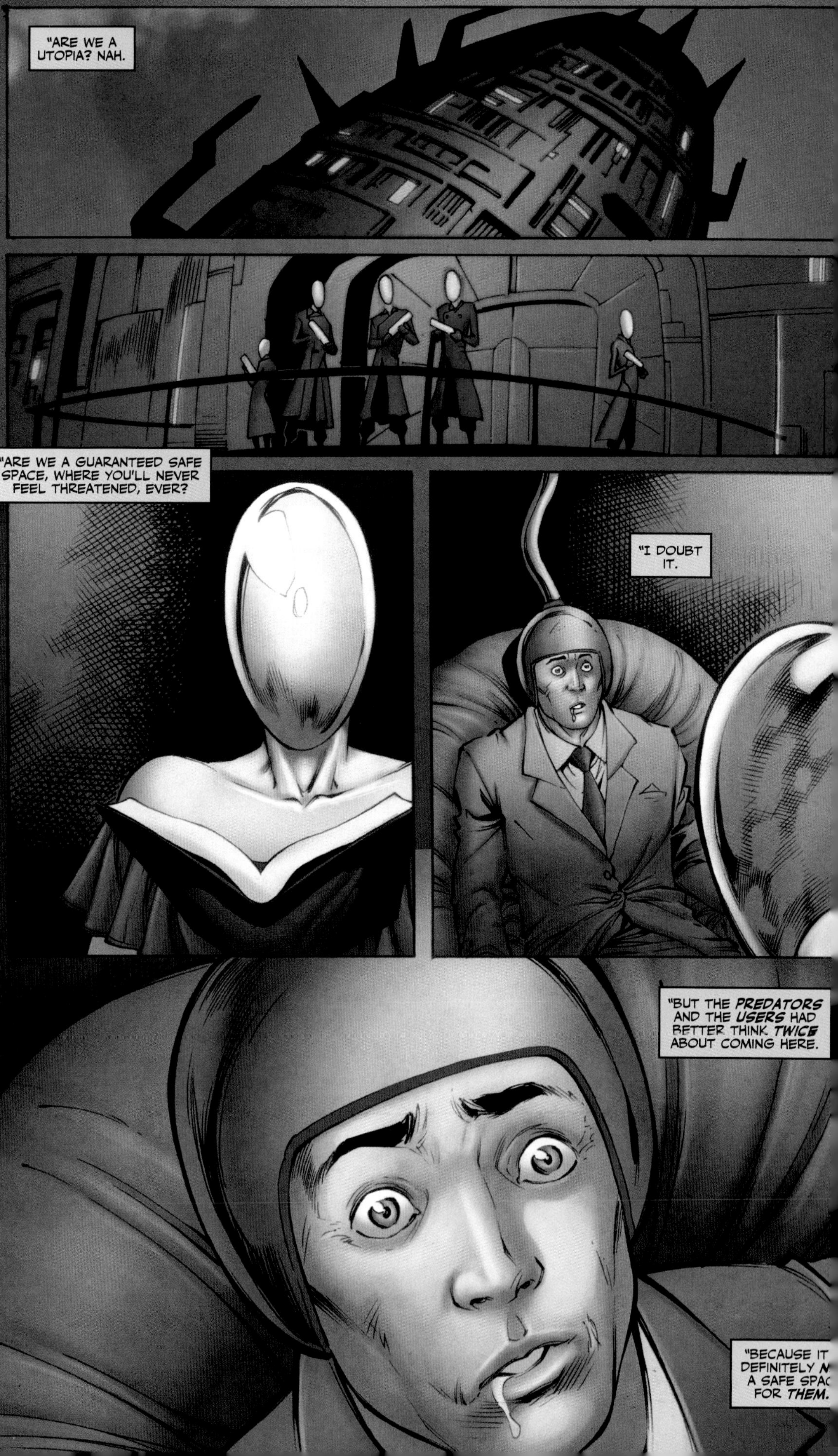
"ARE WE A UTOPIA? NAH.
"ARE WE A GUARANTEED SAFE SPACE, WHERE YOU'LL NEVER FEEL THREATENED, EVER?
"I DOUBT IT.
"BUT THE PREDATORS AND THE USERS HAD BETTER THINK TWICE ABOUT COMING HERE.
"BECAUSE IT DEFINITELY
A SAFE SPA
FOR THEM.

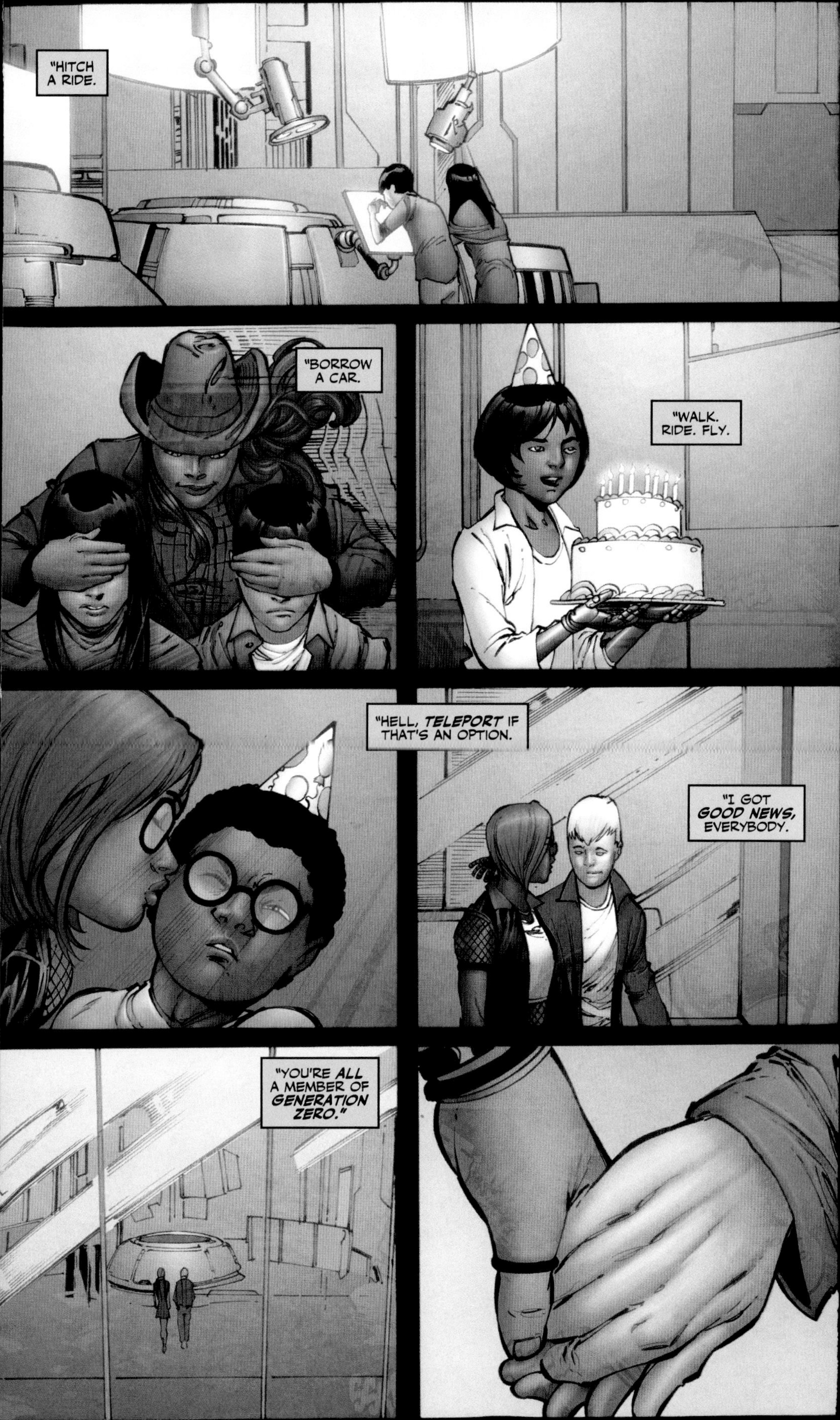
"HITCH A RIDE.
"BORROW A CAR.
"WALK. RIDE. FLY.
"HELL, *TELEPORT* IF THAT'S AN OPTION.
"I GOT *GOOD NEWS,* EVERYBODY.
"YOU'RE *ALL* A MEMBER OF *GENERATION ZERO.*"

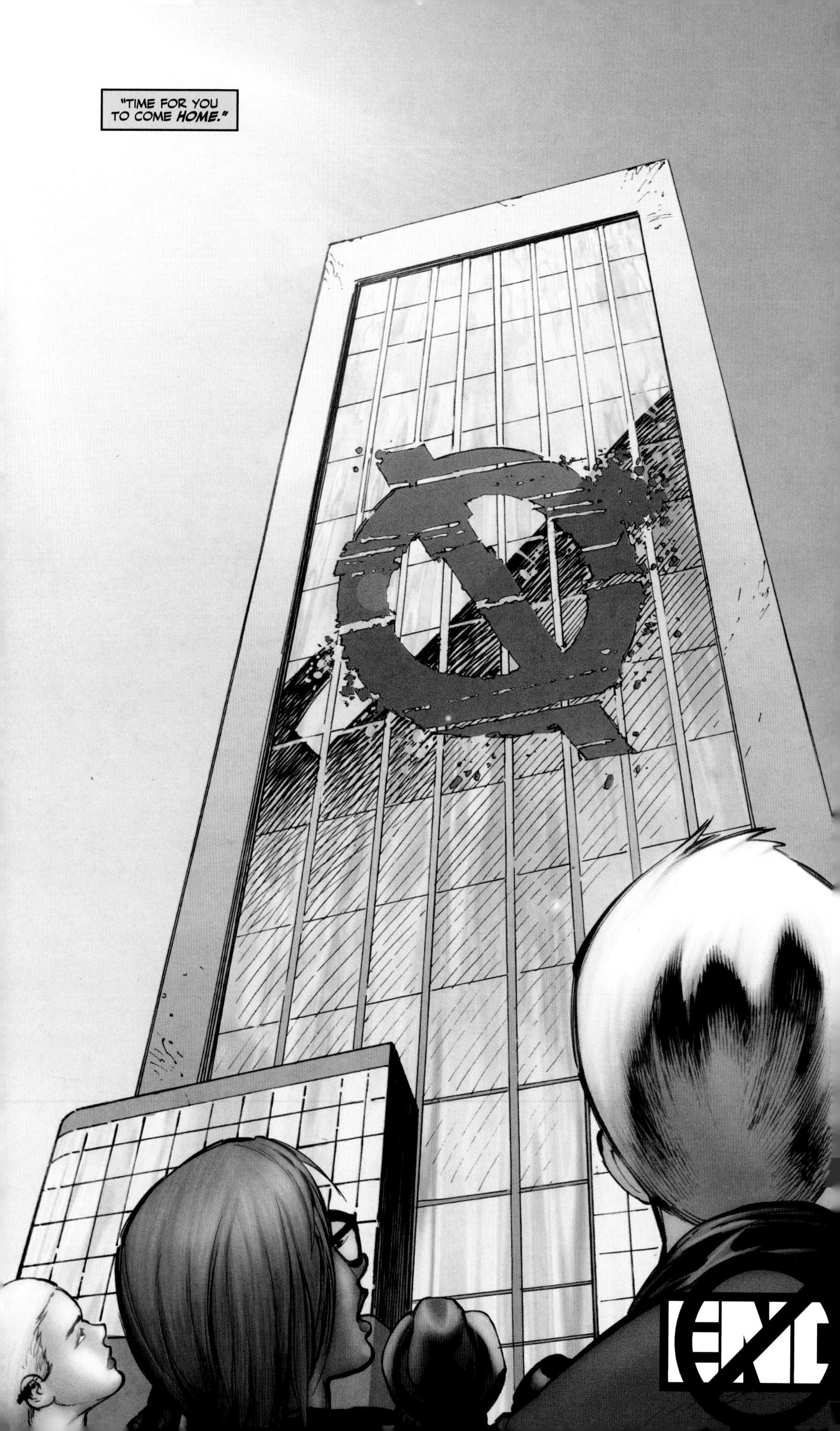
"TIME FOR YOU TO COME *HOME.*"
END

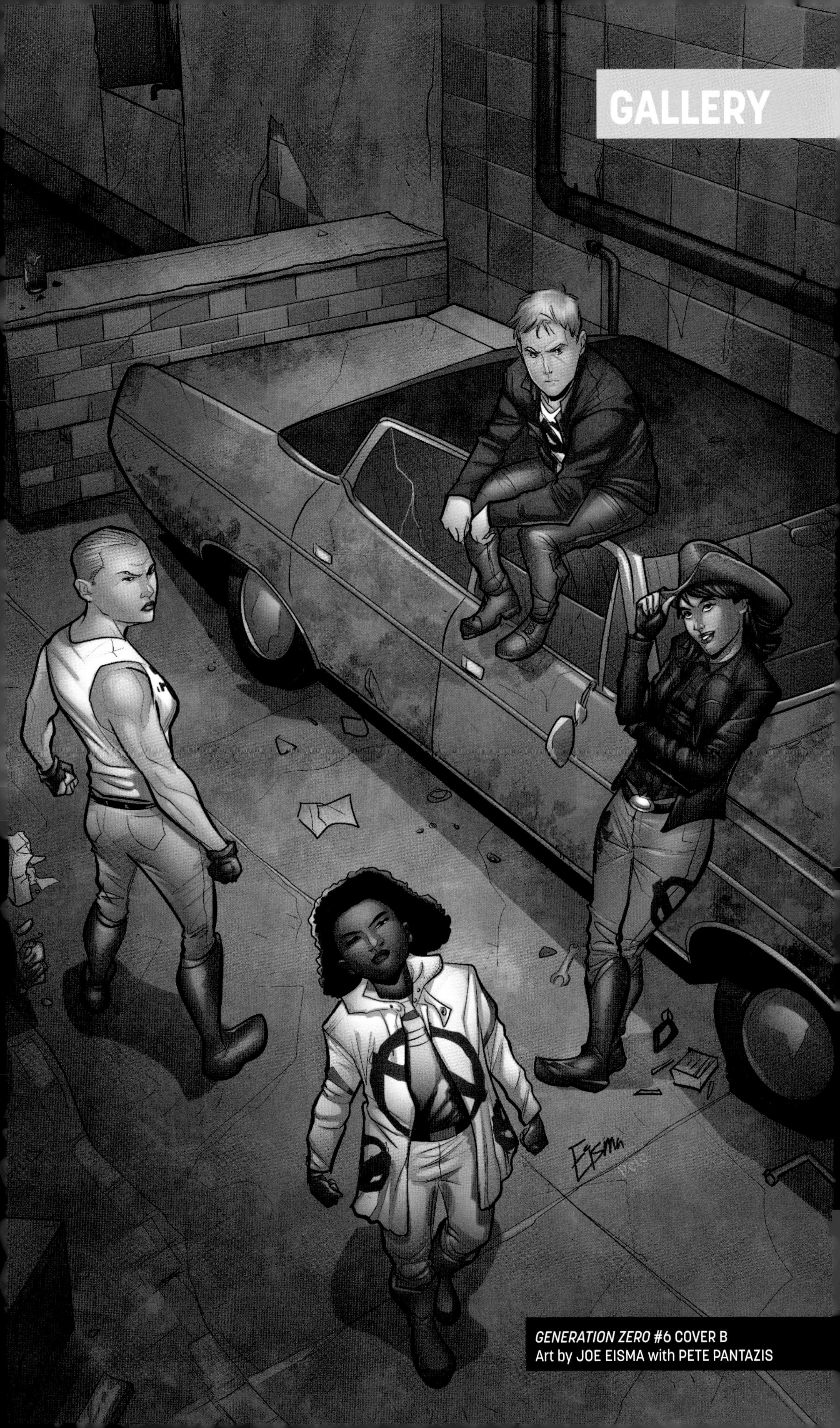
Eisma
Pete

GENERATION ZERO #6 COVER B
Art by JOE EISMA with PETE PANTAZIS

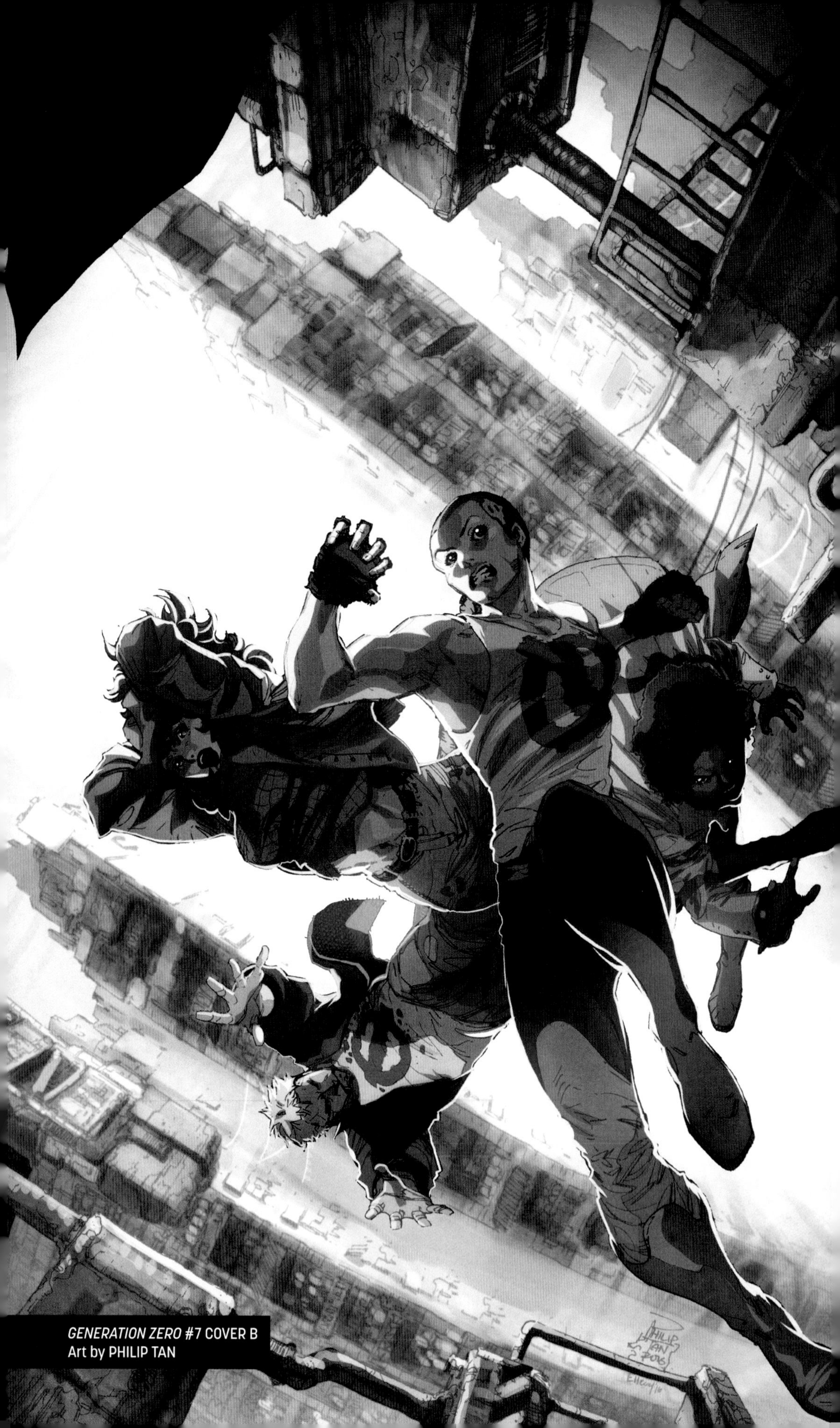

GENERATION ZERO #7 COVER B
Art by PHILIP TAN

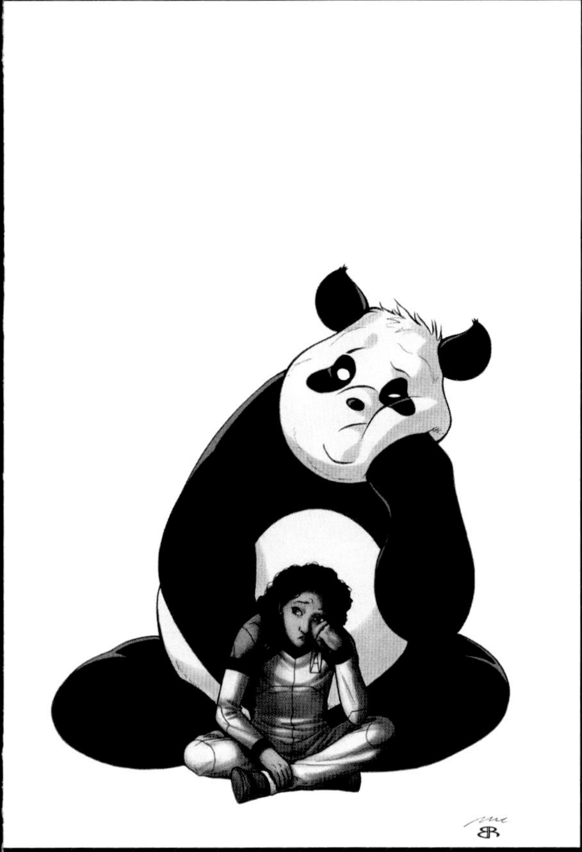

GENERATION ZERO #8 VARIANT COVER
Art by PERE PÉREZ with BRIAN REBER

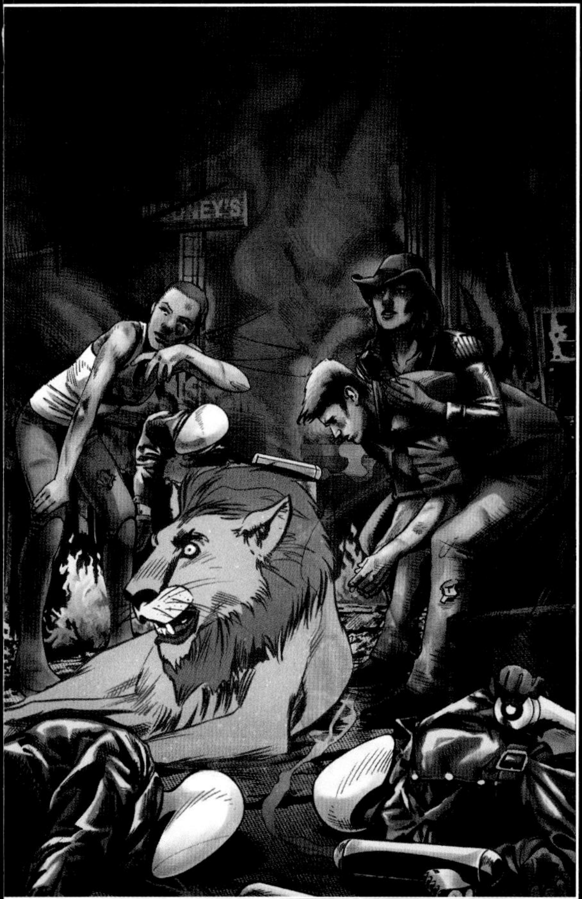

GENERATION ZERO #9 VARIANT COVER
Art by STEPHEN MOONEY

GENERATION ZERO #6, p. 2
Art by DIEGO BERNARD

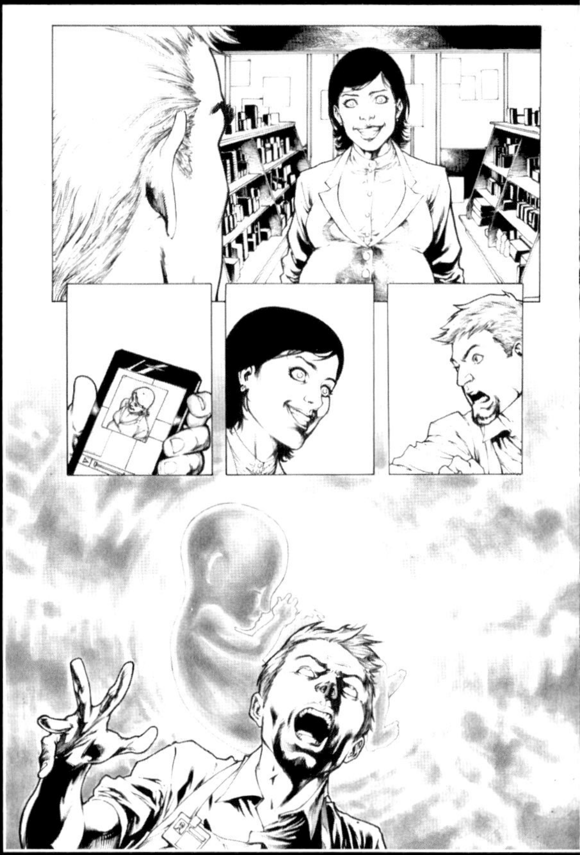

GENERATION ZERO #6, p. 3
Art by DIEGO BERNARD

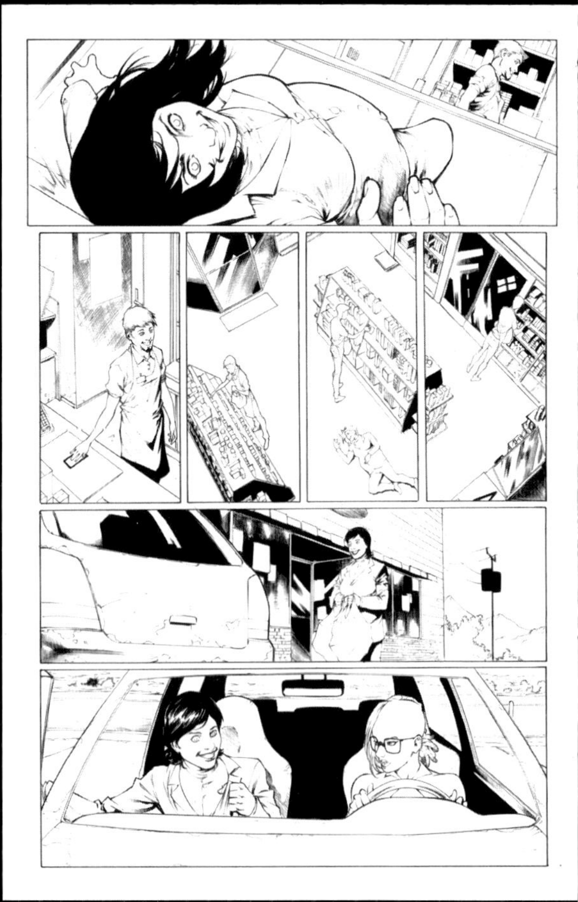

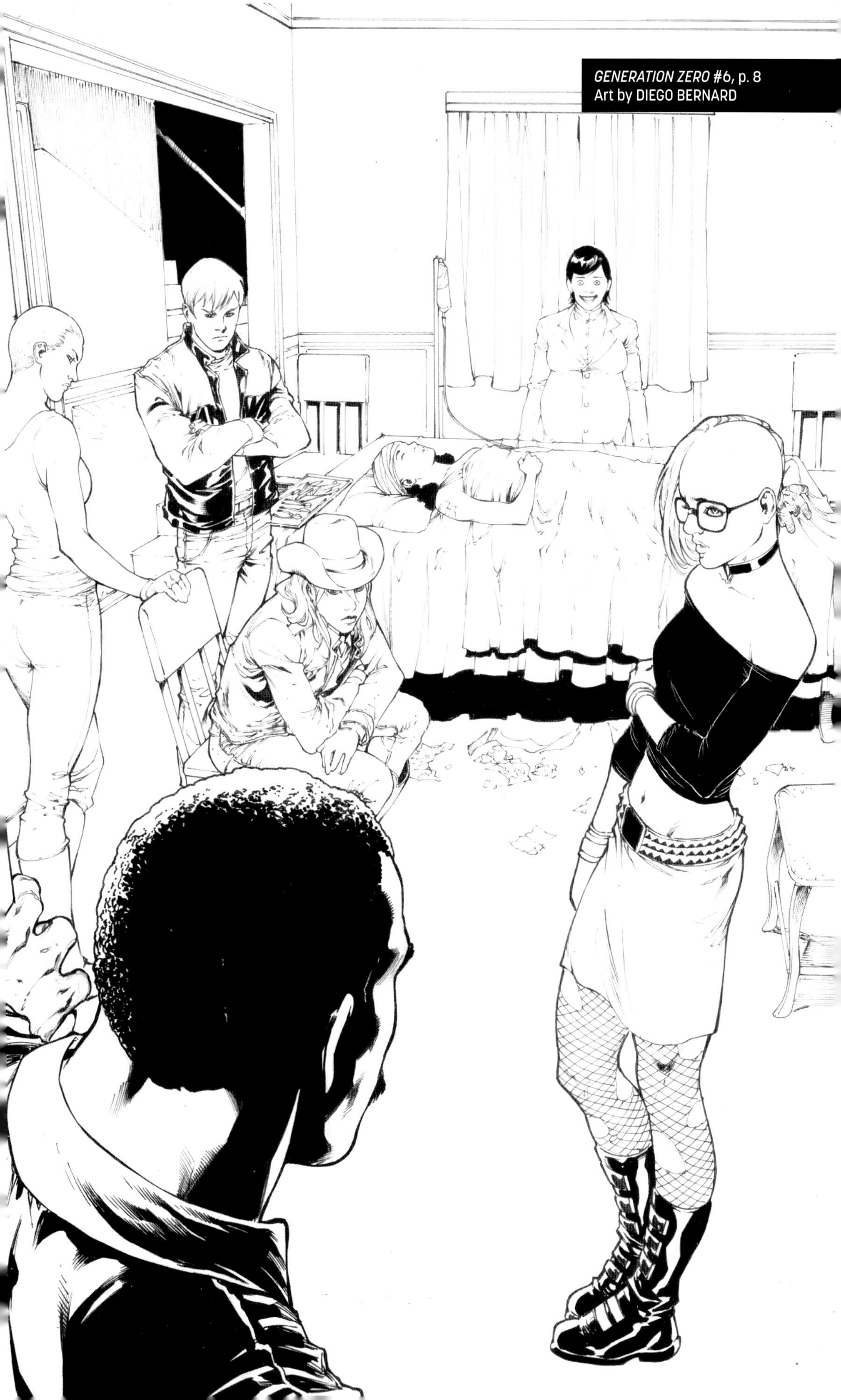

GENERATION ZERO #6, p. 8
Art by DIEGO BERNARD

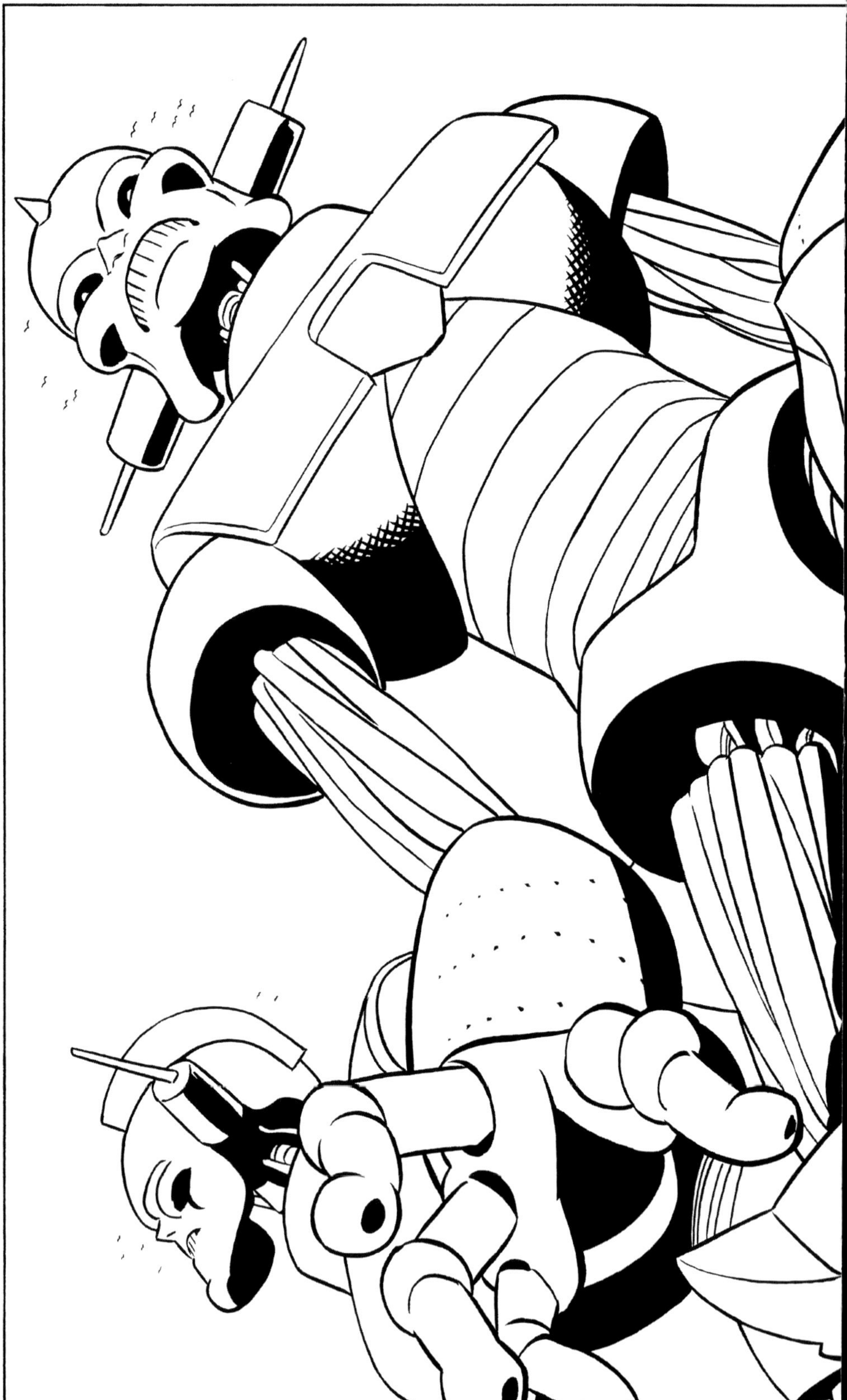

GENERATION ZERO #6, pages 18-19
Art by JAVIER PULIDO

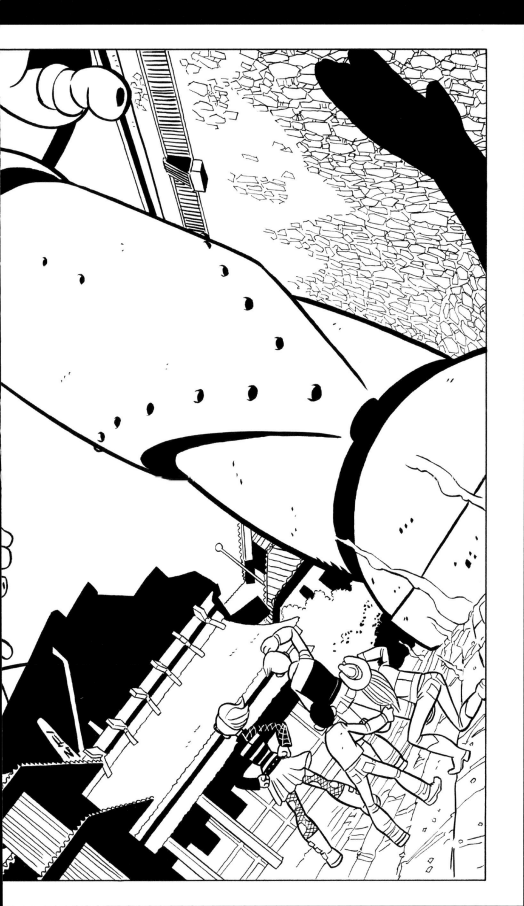

EXPLORE THE VALIANT UNIVERSE

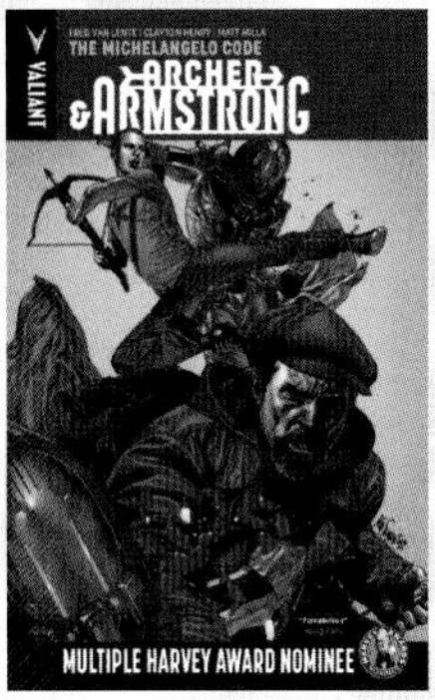
VALIANT
THE MICHELANGELO CODE
ARCHER & ARMSTRONG
MULTIPLE HARVEY AWARD NOMINEE

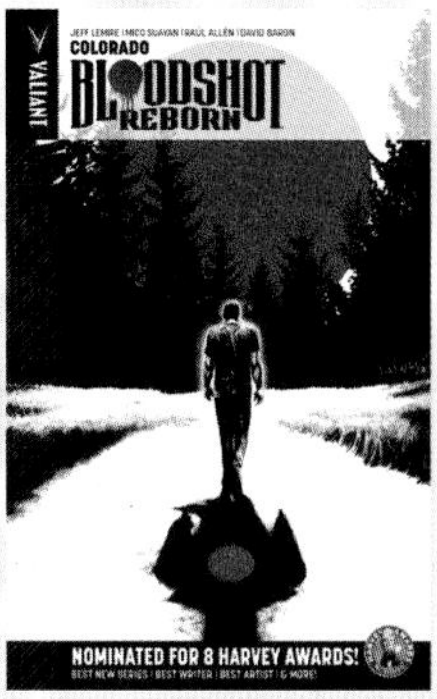
VALIANT
COLORADO
BLOODSHOT REBORN
NOMINATED FOR 8 HARVEY AWARDS!

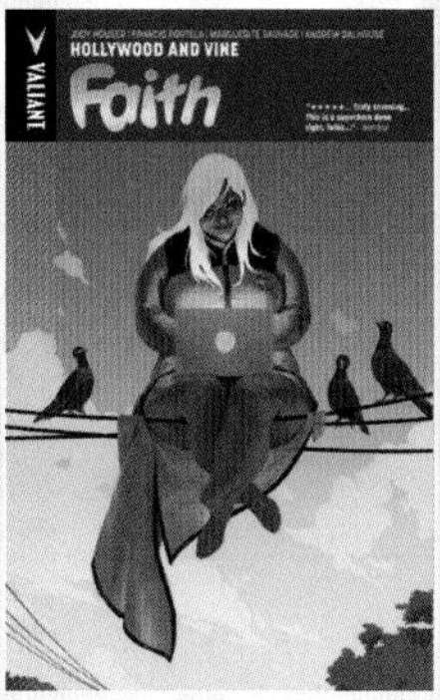
VALIANT
HOLLYWOOD AND VINE
Faith

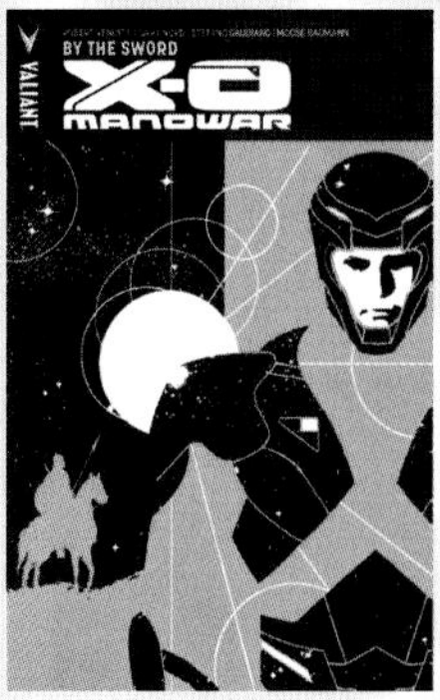
VALIANT
BY THE SWORD
X-O MANOWAR

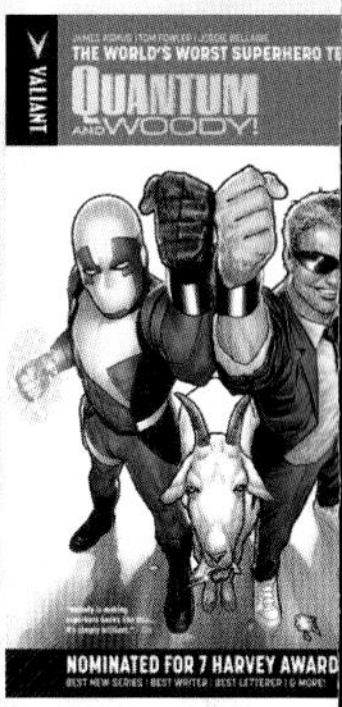
VALIANT
QUANTUM AND WOODY!
NOMINATED FOR 7 HARVEY AWARD

4001 A.D.

4001 A.D.
ISBN: 9781682151433

4001 A.D.: Beyond New Japan
ISBN: 9781682151464

Rai Vol 4: 4001 A.D.
ISBN: 9781682151471

A&A: THE ADVENTURES OF ARCHER AND ARMSTRONG

Volume 1: In the Bag
ISBN: 9781682151495

Volume 2: Romance and Road Trips
ISBN: 9781682151716

ARCHER & ARMSTRONG

Volume 1: The Michelangelo Code
ISBN: 9780979640988

Volume 2: Wrath of the Eternal Warrior
ISBN: 9781939346049

Volume 3: Far Faraway
ISBN: 9781939346148

Volume 4: Sect Civil War
ISBN: 9781939346254

Volume 5: Mission: Improbable
ISBN: 9781939346353

Volume 6: American Wasteland
ISBN: 9781939346421

Volume 7: The One Percent and Other Tales
ISBN: 9781939346537

ARMOR HUNTERS

Armor Hunters
ISBN: 9781939346452

Armor Hunters: Bloodshot
ISBN: 9781939346469

Armor Hunters: Harbinger
ISBN: 9781939346506

Unity Vol. 3: Armor Hunters
ISBN: 9781939346445

X-O Manowar Vol. 7: Armor Hunters
ISBN: 9781939346476

BLOODSHOT

Volume 1: Setting the World on Fire
ISBN: 9780979640964

Volume 2: The Rise and the Fall
ISBN: 9781939346032

Volume 3: Harbinger Wars
ISBN: 9781939346124

Volume 4: H.A.R.D. Corps
ISBN: 9781939346193

Volume 5: Get Some!
ISBN: 9781939346315

Volume 6: The Glitch and Other Tales
ISBN: 9781939346711

BLOODSHOT REBORN

Volume 1: Colorado
ISBN: 9781939346674

Volume 2: The Hunt
ISBN: 9781939346827

Volume 3: The Analog Man
ISBN: 9781682151334

Volume 4: Bloodshot Island
ISBN: 9781682151952

BLOODSHOT U.S.A.

ISBN: 9781682151952

BOOK OF DEATH

Book of Death
ISBN: 9781939346971

Book of Death: The Fall of the Valiant Universe
ISBN: 9781939346988

BRITANNIA

Volume 1
ISBN: 9781682151853

DEAD DROP

ISBN: 9781939346858

THE DEATH-DEFYING DOCTOR MIRAGE

Volume 1
ISBN: 9781939346490

Volume 2: Second Lives
ISBN: 9781682151297

THE DELINQUENTS

ISBN: 9781939346513

DIVINITY

Volume 1
ISBN: 9781939346766

Volume 2
ISBN: 9781682151518

Volume 3
ISBN: 9781682151914

Divinity III: Glorious Heroes of the Stalinver
ISBN: 9781682152072

ETERNAL WARRIOR

Volume 1: Sword of the Wild
ISBN: 9781939346209

Volume 2: Eternal Emperor
ISBN: 9781939346292

Volume 3: Days of Steel
ISBN: 9781939346742

WRATH OF THE ETERNAL WARI

Volume 1: Risen
ISBN: 9781682151235

Volume 2: Labyrinth
ISBN: 9781682151594

Volume 3: Deal With a Devil
ISBN: 9781682151976

FAITH

Faith Vol 1: Hollywood and Vine
ISBN: 9781682151402

Faith Vol 2: California Scheming
ISBN: 9781682151631

GENERATION ZERO

Volume 1: We Are the Future
ISBN: 9781682151754

HARBINGER

Volume 1: Omega Rising
ISBN: 9780979640957

Volume 2: Renegades
ISBN: 9781939346025

Volume 3: Harbinger Wars
ISBN: 9781939346117

Volume 4: Perfect Day
ISBN: 9781939346155

Volume 5: Death of a Renegade
ISBN: 9781939346339

Volume 6: Omegas
ISBN: 9781939346384

EXPLORE THE VALIANT UNIVERSE

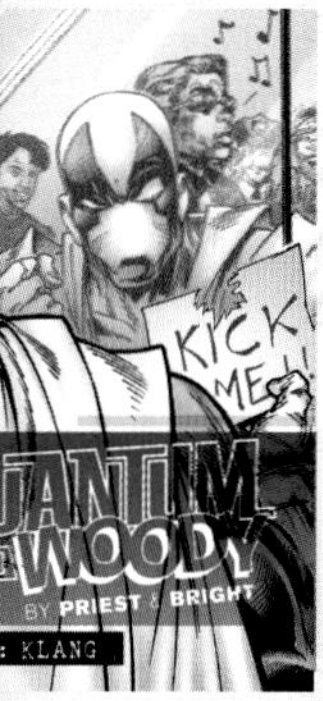
KICK ME
ANTUM
WOODY
BY PRIEST & BRIGHT
KLANG

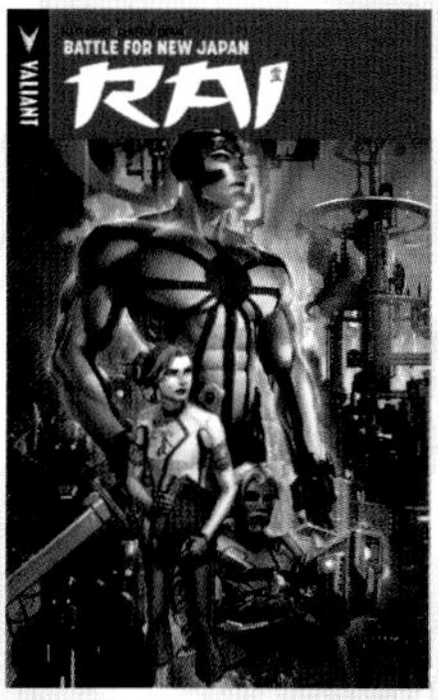
VALIANT
BATTLE FOR NEW JAPAN
RAI

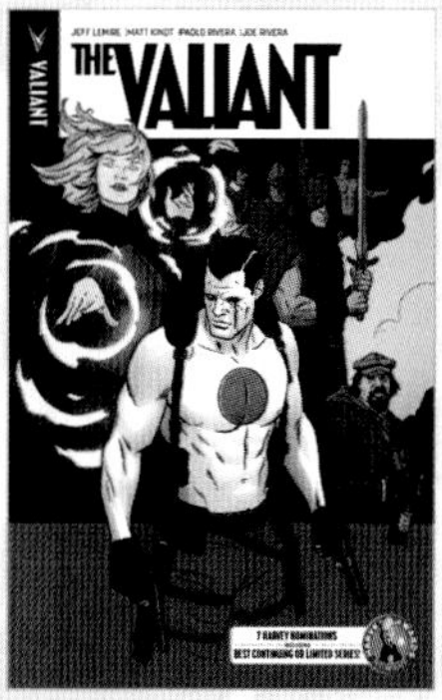
VALIANT
THE VALIANT

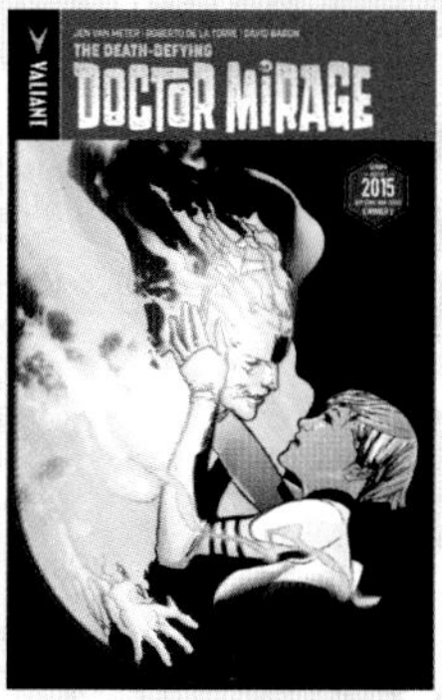
VALIANT
THE DEATH-DEFYING
DOCTOR MIRAGE
2015

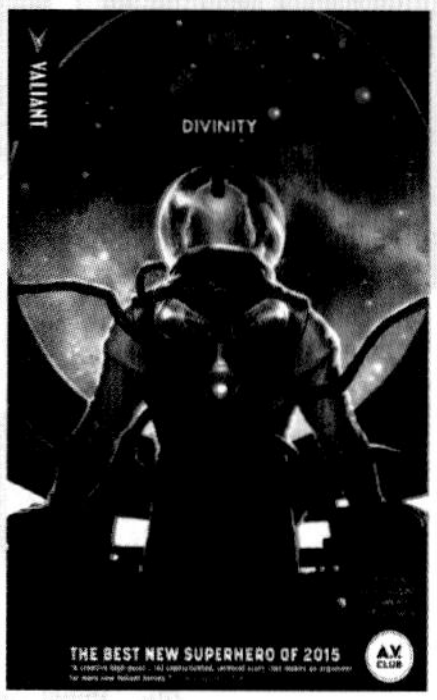
VALIANT
DIVINITY
THE BEST NEW SUPERHERO OF 2015
A.V. CLUB

BINGER RENEGADE

1: The Judgment of Solomon
781682151693

BINGER WARS

ger Wars
781939346094
hot Vol. 3: Harbinger Wars
781939346124
ger Vol. 3: Harbinger Wars
781939346117

ERIUM

1: Collecting Monsters
781939346759
2: Broken Angels
781939346896
3: The Vine Imperative
781682151112
4: Stormbreak
781682151372

AK

1: Weaponeer
781939346667
2: The Shadow Wars
781939346940
3: Operation: Deadside
781682151259
4: The Siege of King's Castle
781682151617
5: The Fist & The Steel
781682151792

TUM AND WOODY

1: The World's Worst Superhero Team
781939346186
2: In Security
781939346230
3: Crooked Pasts, Present Tense
781939346391
4: Quantum and Woody Must Die!
781939346629

TUM AND WOODY RIEST & BRIGHT

1: Klang
781939346780

Volume 2: Switch
ISBN: 9781939346803
Volume 3: And So...
ISBN: 9781939346865
Volume 4: Q2 - The Return
ISBN: 9781682151099

RAI

Volume 1: Welcome to New Japan
ISBN: 9781939346414
Volume 2: Battle for New Japan
ISBN: 9781939346612
Volume 3: The Orphan
ISBN: 9781939346841
Rai Vol 4: 4001 A.D.
ISBN: 9781682151471

SHADOWMAN

Volume 1: Birth Rites
ISBN: 9781939346001
Volume 2: Darque Reckoning
ISBN: 9781939346056
Volume 3: Deadside Blues
ISBN: 9781939346162
Volume 4: Fear, Blood, And Shadows
ISBN: 9781939346278
Volume 5: End Times
ISBN: 9781939346377

SHADOWMAN BY ENNIS & WOOD

ISBN: 9781682151358

IVAR, TIMEWALKER

Volume 1: Making History
ISBN: 9781939346636
Volume 2: Breaking History
ISBN: 9781939346834
Volume 3: Ending History
ISBN: 9781939346995

UNITY

Volume 1: To Kill a King
ISBN: 9781939346261
Volume 2: Trapped by Webnet
ISBN: 9781939346346
Volume 3: Armor Hunters
ISBN: 9781939346445
Volume 4: The United
ISBN: 9781939346544

Volume 5: Homefront
ISBN: 9781939346797
Volume 6: The War-Monger
ISBN: 9781939346902
Volume 7: Revenge of the Armor Hunters
ISBN: 9781682151136

THE VALIANT

ISBN: 9781939346605

VALIANT ZEROES AND ORIGINS

ISBN: 9781939346582

X-O MANOWAR

Volume 1: By the Sword
ISBN: 9780979640940
Volume 2: Enter Ninjak
ISBN: 9780979640995
Volume 3: Planet Death
ISBN: 9781939346087
Volume 4: Homecoming
ISBN: 9781939346179
Volume 5: At War With Unity
ISBN: 9781939346247
Volume 6: Prelude to Armor Hunters
ISBN: 9781939346407
Volume 7: Armor Hunters
ISBN: 9781939346476
Volume 8: Enter: Armorines
ISBN: 9781939346551
Volume 9: Dead Hand
ISBN: 9781939346650
Volume 10: Exodus
ISBN: 9781939346933
Volume 11: The Kill List
ISBN: 9781682151273
Volume 12: Long Live the King
ISBN: 9781682151655
Volume 13: Succession and Other Tales
ISBN: 9781682151754

X-O MANOWAR (2017)

Volume 1: Soldier
ISBN: 9781682152058

EXPLORE THE VALIANT UNIVERSE

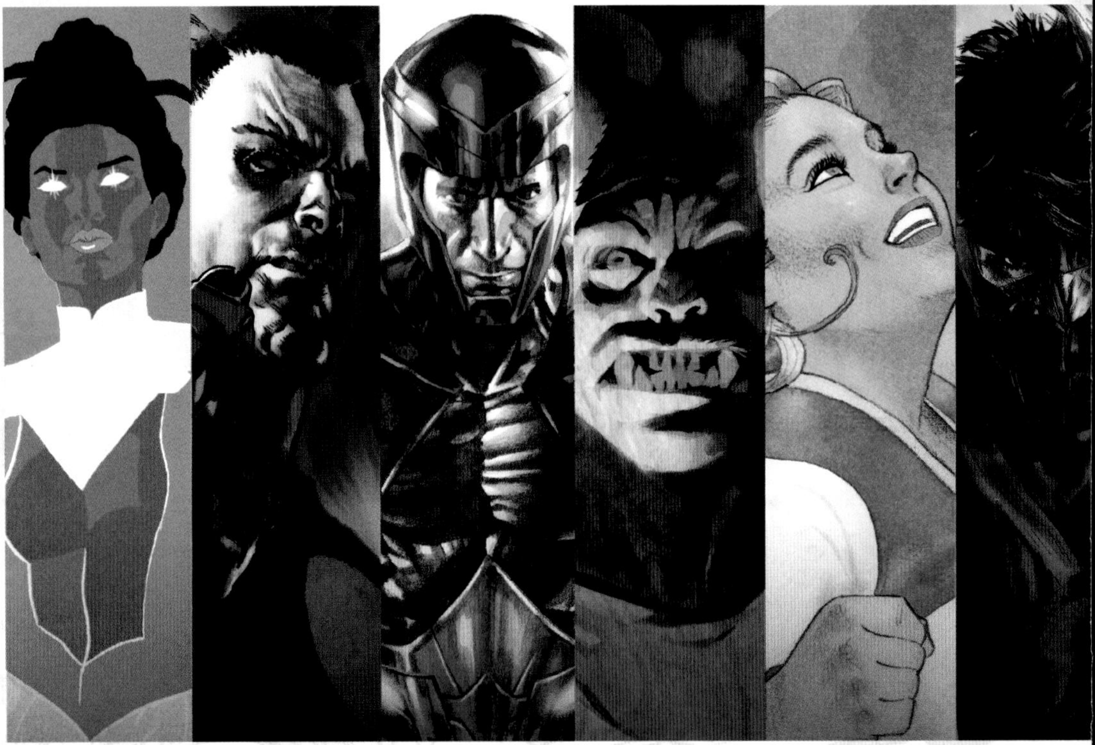

4001 A.D. DELUXE EDITION
ISBN: 978-1-68215-193-8

ARCHER & ARMSTRONG DELUXE EDITIONS
Book 1: ISBN: 978-1-939346-22-3
Book 2: ISBN: 978-1-939346-95-7

ARMOR HUNTERS DELUXE EDITION
ISBN: 978-1-939346-72-8

BLOODSHOT DELUXE EDITIONS
Book 1: ISBN: 978-1-939346-21-6
Book 2: ISBN: 978-1-939346-81-0

BLOODSHOT REBORN DELUXE EDITIONS
Book 1: ISBN: 978-1-68215-155-6
Book 2: ISBN: 978-1-68215-227-0

BOOK OF DEATH DELUXE EDITION
ISBN: 978-1-68215-115-0

THE DEATH-DEFYING DOCTOR MIRAGE DELUXE EDITION
ISBN: 978-1-68215-153-2

DIVINITY DELUXE EDITION
ISBN: 978-1-939346-92-6

FAITH: HOLLYWOOD & VINE DELUXE EDITION
ISBN: 978-1-68215-201-0

HARBINGER DELUXE EDITIONS
Book 1: ISBN: 978-1-939346-13-1
Book 2: ISBN: 978-1-939346-77-3

HARBINGER WARS DELUXE EDITION
ISBN: 978-1-939346-32-2

IVAR, TIMEWALKER DELUXE EDITION
Book 1: ISBN: 978-1-68215-119-8

NINJAK DELUXE EDITION
Book 1: ISBN: 978-1-68215-157-0

QUANTUM AND WOODY DELUXE EDITION
Book 1: ISBN: 978-1-939346-68-1

RAI DELUXE EDITION
Book 1: ISBN: 978-1-68215-117-4

SHADOWMAN DELUXE EDITION
Book 1: ISBN: 978-1-939346-43-8

UNITY DELUXE EDITION
Book 1: 978-1-939346-57-5

THE VALIANT DELUXE EDITION
ISBN: 978-1-939346-91-9

X-O MANOWAR DELUXE EDITIONS
Book 1: ISBN: 978-1-939346-10-0
Book 2: ISBN: 978-1-939346-52-0
Book 3 : ISBN: 978-1-68215-131-0
Book 4: ISBN: 978-1-68215-183-9
Book 5: ISBN: 978-1-68215-215-7

VALIANT CLASSIC

ARCHER & ARMSTRONG: THE COMPLETE CLASSIC OMNIBUS
ISBN: 978-1-939346-87-2

QUANTUM AND WOODY: THE COMPLETE CLASSIC OMNIBUS
ISBN: 978-1-939346-36-0

Q2: THE RETURN OF QUANTUM AND WOODY DELUXE EDITION
ISBN: 978-1-939346-56-8

VALIANT MASTERS: BLOODSHOT VOL. 1 - BLOOD OF THE MACHINE
ISBN: 978-0-9796409-3-3

VALIANT MASTERS: HARBINGER VOL. 1 - CHILDREN OF THE EIGHTH
ISBN: 978-1-939346-48-3

VALIANT MASTERS: H.A.R.D. CORPS VOL. 1 - SEARCH AND DESTROY
ISBN: 978-1-939346-28-5

VALIANT MASTERS: NINJAK VOL. 1 - BLACK WATER
ISBN: 978-0-9796409-7-1

VALIANT MASTERS: RAI VOL. 1 - FROM HONOR TO STRENGT
ISBN: 978-1-939346-07-0

VALIANT MASTERS: SHADOWMAN VOL. 1 - SPIRITS WITHIN
ISBN: 978-1-939346-01-8

X-O MANOWAR CLASSIC OMNIBUS
Vol. 1: ISBN: 978-1-939346-30-8

GENERATION ZERO | READING ORDER

ARBINGER
WARS

arbinger Wars
(OPTIONAL)

VALIANT
WE ARE THE FUTURE
GENERATION
ZERO
SCHOOL BUS
762
762
UNLAWFUL TO PASS
WHEN
RED LIGHTS FLASH

Generation Zero Vol. 1:
We Are the Future

VALIANT
HEROSCAPE
GENERATION
ZERO

Generation Zero Vol. 2:
Heroscape

VALIANT
MASSACRE
Harbinger
RENEGADE

Harbinger Renegade Vol. 2:
Massacre

Read the origins of Valiant's volatile team of teenaged walking warheads!

VALIANT
HARBINGER WARS
HARBINGER

Harbinger Vol. 3:
Harbinger Wars

VALIANT
HARBINGER WARS
BLOODSHOT

Bloodshot Vol. 3: Harbinger Wars

VALIANT
ARMOR HUNTERS:
HARBINGER

Armor Hunters:
Harbinger

VALIANT®

Harbinger® RENEGADE

VOLUME TWO: MASSACRE

"MASSACRE" BRINGS DEATH TO A MAJOR VALIANT HERO!

Toyo Harada's former protege - Alexander Solomon, a "psiot" with the ability to predict and analyze potential futures - has been waiting for this moment. With the Harbinger Renegades - Peter Stanchek, Faith, Kris Hathaway, and Torque - now reunited as a result of his covert manipulations, his ultimate gambit can now begin. But he's not the only one who has been watching. Major Charlie Palmer has just re-assigned a new division of the militarized psiot hunters codenamed H.A.R.D. Corps to active duty...and they're about to bring a torrent of blood and calamity roaring into the streets of a major American metropolis for an all-out firefight.

The Harbinger Renegades. Livewire. Alexander Solomon. Generation Zero. Toyo Harada. Secret Weapons. Imperium. None of them are safe...and, when the smoke clears, a pivotal Valiant hero will become the first sacrifice of the massive Harbinger War that is to come...

Harvey Award-nominated writer Rafer Roberts (*Plastic Farm*) and superstar artist Darick Robertson (*The Boys*, *Transmetropolitan*) begin THE ROAD TO HARBINGER WARS 2 - right here with a bang that will reverberate throughout the entire Valiant Universe...and claim the life of a major hero!

Collecting HARBINGER RENEGADE #5-8.

VALIANT
RAFER ROBERTS | DARICK ROBERTSON
MASSACRE
Harbinger
RENEGADE

TRADE PAPERBACK
ISBN: 978-1-68215-223-2